The Astrology
of
Awakening

Volume 1: Eclipse of the Ego

Eric Meyers, M.A.

The Astrology of Awakening
Volume 1: Eclipse of the Ego

Published by Astrology Sight Publishing
Swannanoa, North Carolina

ISBN Number: 978-0-9747766-6-8

Printed in the United States of America

For more info about Eric's astrology services, books, newsletter,
blog, and other media, please visit the website:

www.SoulVisionConsulting.com

email: eric@soulvisionconsulting.com

Cover images from NASA

Graphic design and interior figures in Chapters 8 and 10 by Bill
Streett. Other images from Wikimedia Commons.

Back cover photograph taken by Drew Meyers.

THE SOUL IS INTERESTED IN EVOLUTION WHILE THE PERSONALITY
   IS MORE INTERESTED IN IMMEDIATE NEEDS   38

EVERY SOUL IS ENROLLED IN A DIFFERENT CURRICULUM

WHEN WE ARE NOT IN CONSCIOUS CONNECTION WITH THE
   EVOLUTIONARY PURPOSE OF A PLANETARY ENERGY,
   IT TENDS TO MANIFEST DARKLY 49

CARL JUNG SAID, " WHO LOOKS OUTSIDE DREAMS; WHO LOOKS
   INSIDE AWAKES." 52

                    132, 168, (169) 185
QUOTES TO USE : 54,56,57, 72,73,83,87, 89 (97) (98) 99, 109

SPIRITUAL AWAKENING INVOLVES INCLUDING THE ENERGY BODY INTO
OUR IDENTITY... IT IS OUR SOUL CONNECTION WITH SPIRIT...
OUR DIVINE GPS 61

YOU DON'T HAVE A SOUL, YOU ARE A SOUL, YOU HAVE A BODY
                                                    C S LEWIS 68

Dedicated to all of my teachers,
    and to the future of astrology.

THE DEVELOPMENT OF CONSCIOUSNESS IS THE CENTRAL TASK
   OF OUR SPIRITUAL EVOLUTION 68

PERHAPS WHAT WE REALLY SEEK IS TO AWAKEN INTO SOUL
   REALIZATION 83

"UNTHINKING RESPECT FOR AUTHORITY IS THE GREATEST
   ENEMY OF TRUTH" ALBERT EINSTEIN 83

WE EXPAND AND AWAKEN INTO OUR TRUE SELF BY INTEGRATING
   AWARENESS INTO THE UNCONSCIOUS. 95

ECLIPSES ARE THE SEASON OF HIGH DRAMA IN DEVELOPING
   CONSCIOUSNESS AND FURTHERING OUR SOUL EVOLUTION 108

AS WE SPIRITUALLY DEVELOP AND BRING SOUL TO MANIFESTATION,
   EVERYTHING ABOUT US IS PART OF THE PROCESS   110

Also by the author:

Elements & Evolution:
The Spiritual Landscape of Astrology
(2010)

Uranus: The Constant of Change
(2008)

Between Past & Presence:
A Spiritual View of the Moon & Sun
(2006)

The Arrow's Ascent:
Astrology & The Quest for Meaning
(2004)

A human being is part of the whole, called by us 'Universe,' a part limited in time and space. He experiences himself, his thoughts and feelings as something separated from the rest - a kind of optical delusion of his consciousness. This delusion is a kind of prison for us, restricting us to our personal desires and to affection for a few persons nearest to us. Our task must be to free ourselves from this prison by widening our circle of compassion to embrace all living creatures and the whole nature in its beauty.   ~Albert Einstein

It's as though we have two selves or two natures or two wills with two contrary viewpoints...your lower self sees you at the center of the universe, and your higher self sees you as a cell in the body of humanity.   ~Peace Pilgrim

So it all comes down to a case of mistaken identity...thinking that we are something other than the One. Of course, the only thing that can convince you that you are other than the One is thinking.   ~Adyashanti

In astrology, the Sun symbolizes Spirit. The Sun is the source of life on Earth. All living organisms "lean" towards the Sun...Every soul is becoming the Sun. Every soul seeks to be life force itself.
                                    ~Raymond Merriman

Contents

Introduction

In recent years, the terms "awakening" and "spiritual awakening" have proliferated in spiritual circles and also in the broader public lexicon. There's a growing sense that we can all become clearer, more present, and more connected to ourselves and each other. Awakening involves the loosening of our identity as a separate self. Instead, we come to experience how we are intimately a part of life itself.

There has been considerable debate throughout recorded history as to whether awakening is a discreet, one-time event or a more gradual, ongoing process. The great Indian sage, Ramana Maharshi, addressed this issue by asking, "When the Sun rises, does the darkness go gradually or all at once?" His view that it's a gradual process is the one that makes sense to me. In this book I'll be discussing awakening as the universal *process* of becoming more conscious, which unfolds progressively over time.

Awakening is a topic that is relevant for all of us since we're all in the process of becoming more awake and present, whether we know it or not. The main purpose of this book is to place astrology within the context of this universal process. One of the strengths of astrology is the diversity of viewpoints, approaches, and even paradigms which inform our inquiry. This book aims to add to the great buffet table of ideas to consider. I want to spark discussion on the relationship between consciousness and astrology, and to take a fresh look at some of the underlying assumptions we bring to the field. I invite you to join me in dialogue on the important questions and issues being raised.

You may wonder if I'm qualified to address spiritual awakening at all. What I can tell you is that I'm strongly engaged in my own process of awakening—perhaps just as you are. I'm grateful to have access to wonderful teachers and teachings, and I see myself as a translator. Just as the psychological wave of astrology in the 20th Century brought many new perspectives into astrology, our current time frame is ripe for importing more progressive understandings of spiritual growth.

Since my awareness is limited, there will of course be blind spots in the book. I'm ok with that! I'm inspired to offer something new to the field without needing it to be fully formed and complete right out of the gate. I want to help renew and refresh astrology for the 21st Century and connect it to the larger shift in consciousness occurring across the planet. In the spirit of Uranus in Aries, we may boldly venture forth into new explorations.

My broad intention is the full inclusion of the transpersonal into astrology. In Chapter 1 we will explore the nature of ego and how awakening fits in with the present time. Chapter 2 discusses the transpersonal in more depth including Oneness and the awakening process. Chapters 3 and 4 discuss the Sun and Moon, which serve as the centerpiece to this new paradigm. Chapter 3 focuses on how they relate to the development of consciousness, while Chapter 4 addresses their role in bridging the physical with the nonphysical.

The Sun and Moon form the center of identity and consciousness. Chapters 5, 6, & 7 explore how all the major planets are used in service to this center. Depending on the development of consciousness, we gradually learn to use planetary energy in alignment with soul, not just for egoic reasons. After this examination of planets, we look at the evolution of consciousness in

Chapter 8, particularly how it relates to astrology. The next 3 chapters bring the issue of awakening into many facets of how we approach and use astrology. Chapter 9 addresses how the dominant paradigm of astrology varies from the awakened view, while Chapter 10 offers some suggestions of how to renew astrology in accordance with it. Finally, Chapter 11 invites further consideration on how astrology can promote the realization of Oneness. This book aims to get the conversation started. Many of the ideas will be further developed in subsequent books in *The Astrology of Awakening* series.

Chapter 1
The Ego & 2012

Astrology describes the way that energy flows through each of us and our world. It offers an objective map to chart this energy. It can serve as a profound invitation for people to question their assumptions about reality. This book invites the field of astrology itself to do such a review of its assumptions and paradigms. It strengthens any field to do an internal inventory in order to clarify and make adjustments to its fundamental philosophy.

This book puts forth many ideas of how astrology can further modernize. Purists may ask, "If it isn't broken, why try to fix it?" My view is not that astrology is broken, but rather that it's incomplete. There are two ways to approach this claim. The first would be to see astrology as unalterable truth, just as many religious people view the Bible. The second is to see astrology as similar to every other field of knowledge which grows over time, and this is the approach I'm advocating.

<u>Astrology reflects the human consciousness that is participating in its development.</u> As evolution unfolds and consciousness expands, it's not only appropriate, but necessary to put forth sensible adaptations that reflect this growth. The failure to modernize would increasingly make astrology irrelevant to the consciousness which surpasses it. It would be seen as a relic of days passed, and this is a view of it.

There is a growing divide between those on a path of spiritual awakening and those interested in astrology. I'm still surprised by the extent to which astrology is seen as quaint, irrelevant, or even a joke to many individuals who find greater spiritual nourishment in other teachings and paths. This dismissal seems in part a result of their ignorance of astrology's true capacities, but it's also due to the approaches and guiding assumptions of astrologers, and more broadly, the field itself.

Though there are certainly forms of astrology that are of great interest to those interested in spiritual evolution, the *dominant paradigm* that guides astrology is my focus here. A quick glance at the top-selling astrology books illustrates my point. With a few notable exceptions, these books are geared toward basic egoic questions and self-gain: How can I get ahead in life? What does my future hold in store? Will it be "good" or "bad?" What kind of person is right for me? These questions are understandable, but they place heavy demands on astrology. They assume that astrology is focused solely on *personal* information, that it reveals specifics, and that the universe rewards or punishes. This orientation limits astrology and keeps us orbiting around the ego. I want to support us in moving beyond it.

The Relative and the Transpersonal

In order to understand (and enjoy!) this book, it's important to see that there are two main levels of reality. The relative level of reality consists of separation consciousness. When we look through its lens, we see life as a multitude of separate things all moving through time and space. The transpersonal level, in contrast, is "beyond the personal," beyond the common orientation of the ego-self. (Please see the Glossary for more information on these terms and others.)

18

Part of the role of Saturn, an earth planet, is to provide structure to the physical world. Saturn circles the Sun within the larger orbit of the air planet Uranus, which is responsible for nonphysical organization. This arrangement portrays how the physical world is a subset of what is possible at the transpersonal level. However, the orientation within Saturn's level of reality (separation consciousness) is more immediate in our experience and therefore can marginalize the transpersonal altogether. The ancient mythological story of Saturn and Uranus frames our situation well. The Greeks wrote that Chronos (Saturn) castrated his father (Ouranos/Uranus)—the realm of the personal cut off access to the potency (and reality) of the transpersonal. The issue I'm focusing on is whether we will continue this severance or take measures to heal it.

The relative and transpersonal perspectives are vastly different from each other, though we can develop the ability to see life through both lenses and know when and how to employ them. Most are able to understand that there is only the present moment (transpersonal), yet there is the passage of time (relative). It may take some getting used to holding the paradox of these two perspectives, but it will be increasingly easier as we go. At the relative view, there are clearly defined boundaries and order. As separate individuals, we identify with a unique body, mind, and life history. The term "ego" is used to describe our identification in this realm.

At the interconnected transpersonal level, everything is understood as simply being energy. There are no personal interpretations about the energy and no attachment to what the energy does. From the transpersonal level, the separate self is seen as energy just like any other form in the manifest world. Personal identification, feelings and thoughts, everything that defines us as humans, exists at the relative level.

It's <u>difficult to discuss the transpersonal view</u> because it transcends language and logic (Mercury); <u>it's only understood through experience. It has to do with our soul connection to life</u> when we move beyond the familiar egoic boundaries. This may sound "airy fairy," but all of us have had tastes and glimpses of its timeless quality—in dreams or other "enhanced" states of consciousness, deep intimate exchanges, the absorption in a hobby or activity, out in nature, or in our hearts. Our mind quiets down enough to allow us to notice the background field of awareness that is always present. The temporary "losing" of the separate self somehow allows us to gain access to so much more.

Almost all of the time, our more immediate and familiar relative viewpoint is necessarily our preferred lens in perceiving and meeting life. We are autonomous individuals who must attend to the everyday. It's quite natural to see things in a dualistic way, as it's so incredibly obvious in our experience. However, the pitfall is deducing that the relative realm is all there is. There is formidable pressure to stay in the "real world," the Saturnian realm. The result is living in what has been termed the "soul cage," imprisoned in our separateness.

Although the relative perspective can and often does negate the transpersonal, *a proper use of the transpersonal would never negate the validity of the relative.* I'm advocating complementing the relative by incorporating the transpersonal, not somehow transcending the relative and seeing it as illusory. From on high, the transpersonal might see everyone as caught in illusion, but this isn't true for the person living in the Saturnian world! In the relative world, dualities are for real. Criminals are certainly "wrong" at the relative level, and Marilyn Monroe was a female. <u>The transpersonal *gives perspective to what occurs at the relative level*</u>. Ultimately we can learn to bridge these two worlds.

Why must we bother with integrating this other perspective into our lives and into our astrology? Incorporating the transpersonal not only honors the greater complexity of life, but it's also necessary for us to continue our collective evolution. When we sever our link to the transpersonal, we may become convinced that our separation defines our reality. From this position, the ego is in control and tries to make the best of it. Saturn is a contracting energy. If we do not move beyond it, we as a species will eventually contract into extinction. We see this outcome with companies that are unable to modernize—they eventually fail. Moving beyond the personal to the transpersonal is an evolutionary step which is *necessary for our survival.* ✳

The application of the transpersonal may seem controversial to conventional thinking. However, the outer planets represent 30% of the major planets in our system. Since they are transpersonal, we must use that lens in order to understand them appropriately. The transpersonal lens is at the beginning stages of being developed and promoted within the astrological context. As a result, the transpersonal facets in the system are sometimes looked at through the relative lens. I use the term "egoic takeover" to describe the situation where we interpret the transpersonal at the personal (relative) level. This mistake is most obvious with Sun sign simplifications, which is perhaps the most widespread and popular use of astrology. We will discuss how the Sun may actually have a central role in our spiritual growth—the awakening from ego.

We'll be exploring the ego and how it's functioned in history. It's obviously had a very important role in our evolution, which deserves to be honored. Some believe that the ego is antithetical to spiritual growth, but that is not the view I endorse. Like the body, mind, or emotions, the ego is a necessary part of being human. Transpersonal philosopher Ken Wilber said, "the ego is not an obstruction to Spirit, but a radiant

21

manifestation of Spirit." Ultimately, it enables us to bridge the nonphysical with the physical, to bring "heaven" to "earth."

It's been said, "You gotta be somebody before you're nobody," which is a clever way to suggest that securing a viable ego is part of the developmental program before it can be authentically transcended. Historically, we have been very good at seeing to our viability, but less adept at transcendence. Perhaps we are at the time in history when we more clearly see the workings of the ego, when our collective evolution brings the transpersonal fully into our awareness. Central to this shift is to understand our reliance on dualities, and so Mercury gets our attention next.

Mercury's Great Heist

As mentioned earlier, Saturn structures the manifest world in the realm of separation consciousness. Within Saturn's orbit is the planet Mercury, which is associated with intelligence and communication. It enables us to personally understand existence but, like everything else, Mercury is susceptible to being misused by egoic agendas. In mythology, Mercury (Hermes) is a trickster and a thief. The mind has great reasoning capacities, but we may not always use it with clarity or ethics. Since the mind is such a big part of our inner experience, we tend to identify with it and therefore trust it, even when its knowledge is off base. We can slip into believing that we know the absolute truth, blind to the possibility that there is more that we're not seeing.

The two signs connected with Mercury, Gemini and Virgo, are associated with the formative years of being a student, basic education, learning skills, research, and apprenticeship. They deal with maturation rather than the pinnacle of wisdom. Since left-brain accomplishment is highly valued in society, there

22

is little incentive or awareness to move beyond it, but astrology tells us otherwise. Many astrologers consider Uranus the "higher octave" of Mercury, suggesting that there is another intellectual level to grasp and implement. Much of the movement towards Uranus involves going beyond dualistic thinking and seeing things as inseparable parts of the whole.

Due to its proximity to the Sun, the planet Mercury has one side which is blazingly hot and another that is freezing—a swing of about a thousand degrees! This contrast echoes the polarities of dualistic thinking: hot/cold, good/bad, up/down, male/female, day/night, and every other possible pairing. Mercury tends to separate phenomena for analysis. This ability is incredibly useful in understanding life within the realm of separation, but not very helpful if we'd like to move beyond.

Since astrology developed when Saturn was understood as the farthest orbiting planet, it is no surprise that Mercury has been employed for our astrological understanding. Consequently, the astrology we've inherited is blatantly dualistic: benefics/malefics, good/bad aspects, exaltations/falls, etc. There are male/female designations for all of the various components too. If we hold astrology in an evolutionary framework that reflects our consciousness as it develops, this emphasis on duality is completely understandable. However, I believe that we're at a pivotal moment of *fully* including Uranus and the transpersonal realm.

Albert Einstein said, "The intuitive mind is a sacred gift and the rational mind is a faithful servant. We have created a society that honors the servant and has forgotten the gift." The goal to refresh and renew astrology includes Mercury serving as a faithful servant to Uranus rather than to the ego. This would be quite a change for this sneaky thief and trickster who committed the ultimate heist—stealing astrology from Uranus, who sits castrated, watching from afar. Now that this crime has been

23

spotted, what are we going to do about it? Are we going to be willing accomplices to Mercury's ruse? Or are we going to use the personal mind (Mercury) in association with the broader intelligence of reality (Uranus) to honor both the relative and the transpersonal perspectives?

The Egoic Mindset

In *The Power of Now*, Eckhart Tolle writes, "Emotions, being part of the dualistic mind, are subject to the laws of opposites. This simply means that you cannot have good without bad."[i] As we'll explore further in the chapters on the planets, Mercury and the Moon have a strong relationship. They're part of forming our basic orientation to life, which rests on our thoughts and emotions. Mercury assesses life with an eye on our survival and happiness—the two primary desires of the ego. Survival involves moving away from perceived negative experiences, while happiness involves the movement towards what is perceived as positive. The ego is continually evaluating experiences along these lines. If we didn't have this function our species would likely perish, so the ego has a hugely important role.

Most of us have lives filled with expectations, responsibilities, and endless demands. We need enough resources to feel stable and secure. The ego sees failure as unacceptable, so it's vigilant about its success, and it's often never quite satisfied. As soon as a pinnacle is reached, there is anxiety about maintaining it!

For many, this self-preoccupation settles down enough to accept the rules and ways of the everyday world. However, those in the grips of unquenchable ego needs tend to scream the loudest and therefore exert control in how society is shaped—its norms, accepted paradigms, channels of information and power.

The dominant values of a culture tend to support and perpetuate what is rewarded by that culture. And in a society where success and status is measured by material wealth, not social contribution, it is easy to see why the state of the world is what it is today. We are dealing with a value system disorder, completely de-natured; where the priority of personal and social health has become secondary to the detrimental notions of artificial wealth and limitless growth. And like a virus, this disorder now permeates every facet of government, news media, entertainment, and even academia. And built into its structure are mechanisms for protection from anything that might interfere. Disciples of the monetary market religion, the self-appointed guardians of the status quo, constantly seek out ways to avoid any form of thought which might interfere with their beliefs. The most common of which are projected dualities.[ii] –*Zeitgeist: Moving Forward*.

The ways in which astrology is approached and understood have been consistent with this value system disorder, which can be found throughout Western thought. I don't mean to point the finger at astrology, for it has simply been one of many canvases upon which the broader issue has been projected. The situation is far more widespread—the ego's domination has been apparent throughout history in practically every realm of life.

It's simply a matter of historical fact that the dominant intellectual culture of any particular society reflects the interests of the dominant group in that society. If you look across the board, the ideas that pervade psychology, sociology, history, and political science fundamentally reflect certain elite interests. And the academics who question that too much tend to get shunned to the side or to be seen as radicals.[iii] --Dr. Gábor Máté

Like every other field, astrology has been influenced by the ego's urgency for self-gain. However, it can also help us unravel the problem too. We know that Mercury relates to dualistic thinking, which turns out to not be the most mature use of our minds. We can retract projected dualities and learn to see things differently. For instance, we can understand that social strategizing and accumulating material wealth as part of Venus, but also that Venus has more conscious expressions. We will explore how everything in astrology has a range—from the darkness of unconscious ego, to the brightness of more awakened uses. Ultimately a more conscious use of astrology can be of great assistance in our collective movement beyond our current global situation.

The Patriarchal Value System

Society conditions us to do our best to get ahead—to "go for it" and succeed. The ego often uses assertiveness, self-promotion, and control to try to feel secure. These attributes do sound conventionally "masculine," which is a reflection of a Patriarchal Value System (PVS)—the value system that has dominated Western culture for thousands of years. We will be discussing the PVS throughout this book, so a thorough examination of it is included here at the start.

26

The PVS has set the tone of culture and society in line with the masculine need to conquer. Due to biological reality, women have largely assumed the role of being the principle nurturers. Maintaining peace and equilibrium is a preferable environment for raising children, so it has naturally benefitted women not to protest too strongly about the Patriarchal emphasis. However, the price of this acquiescence has been historical disempowerment. The 20th Century saw the rise of the Feminist Movement, which attempted to change this dynamic. The rise of women in all areas is an irreversible and much needed trend. The PVS is being increasingly challenged by both women and men. The goal, however, is not to switch to a Matriarchal Value System, but rather to move towards a more awakened paradigm which is beyond the historical battle of the sexes.

Only recently in history has there been overt conflict about the PVS. Traditionally, the two sexes created a workable arrangement of power (men) and nurturance (women), a polarization of the yang and yin. This division has been functional to some degree, but it hasn't promoted further spiritual growth. Ideally, every individual has access to the entire range of human experiences, rather than only identifying with one side of any dualistic split. So the traditional arrangement is now becoming less acceptable for anyone interested in achieving greater wholeness. We can refrain from assigning blame about the inequities in the past and see history—including all its painful elements—as steps in our collective evolution.

Although Patriarchy has taken many forms in many cultures, we can still have a *general* understanding of its basic assumptions and motivations. Unquestionably, the world is seen as a place to conquer, and the mindset is that men are most qualified to perform this task. Due to their natural orientation with hunting and the development of physical prowess, men are competitive, strongly engaged in the survival of the fittest. As a result, conflict and wars are a central motif in history, and the threat of violence is always lurking even in times of relative peace. An open heart or an appreciation of interdependence would temper the knee-jerk reaction to fight, but the PVS demands that the masculine not appear weak.

Out of touch with what is often called "feminine" wisdom, the masculine tends to become enthralled with absolute supremacy, even to the point of believing it can be God. Kings, dictators, and certain clergy members are just a few examples of men who have brazenly declared they are infallible. More commonly, in attempts to appear strong, the masculine swells with pride. We see this with the refusal to admit mistakes or to stop and ask for directions. A drive to dominate eclipses any possibility of humility.

A central Patriarchal value is to control resources, be it money, commodities, or natural resources such as land or oil. Men try to bolster and maintain power through this accumulation, which serves as an intimidating fortress of strength should others think of usurping power. With the mindset of "the more money the better," it's easy to see the trap of never being satisfied. Combine this with the competitive urge, and we have the table set for immense clashing over resources. The theater of military supremacy, which has been going on for millennia, is a striking illustration.

Men are expected to be focused on their career and the outer world, to work hard and achieve status. And the best way to be a good provider is to excel within the prevailing systems, to climb the established ladders of success. Endurance, attaining experience, and achieving status are championed values. There is pressure to strengthen the system, honor its history, and promote the possibility that any man who climbs the ladder with these values should have his eventual turn at the top.

The PVS expects women to be stable nurturers in the family system and yield to men's decisions and positions of power. Though women often have authority when it comes to the children, men consider themselves to be the chief decision-makers in a more general sense. The PVS asserts that men are clear-headed and logical (left-brain), and women are caring, sentimental, and intuitive (right-brain). By extension, men are held as being smart, while women are prone to irrationality. Note that the term "hysteria" used to be linked to disturbances in the womb, a notion now roundly rejected. Even in the present day we hear concerns that women, who might be dealing with premenstrual syndrome, shouldn't be in charge of nuclear weapons. I'll spill the beans and say that I've heard chatter all my life among men (behind women's backs) that belittles women's intelligence. Sometimes it's subtle or unconscious, but the flavor is the same.

As men tend to identify with the left-brain, the PVS promotes reason, practicality, results, and precision. The valued mindset is skeptical and insists on tangible and definitive proof before changing positions. The sensory, physical world has the least ambiguity to it, so working effectively in this realm is championed. Figuring out how to do things well is what serves society, not pie-in-the-sky abstractions.

Aside from child-rearing, women's other main role is to be sexually alluring. Due to the mindset that women hold the energy of attraction, men become intimidated, sometimes fearful, of the sexuality of other men. For some, this discomfort has led to homophobia, but more broadly there's a masculine over-idealization of feminine beauty. Women have also been seen as something to conquer—and men who excel are often admired and respected. This mindset has not only led to the proliferation of pornography, it even blames women for men's abusiveness—the mentality that "she was asking for it."

Receptive and docile women are seen as attractive, and the proverbial "trophy wife" is highly valued. The PVS demands that women accept their subservient role. It welcomes their seductive flair and mystery, but makes no space for them to be competitive with men.

The PVS instills many norms for society. Men govern systems of laws, and should someone break these laws, there are rightful punishments. It serves everyone to maintain social civility, so being respectful of others, and especially authority, is valued. The cultural norm is that men propose marriage and women are expected to take their name. Culture and the arts are welcome, but they should be tasteful and reflect the values of society. Commerce is especially important—the buying and selling of goods benefits everyone, so the PVS promotes materialism and consumption. Status equates to having the finer things: expensive wine, trendy name brand products, luxury accommodations, season tickets, etc.

The PVS wants to maintain tradition, values home and hearth, reveres patriotic and nationalistic sentiments. Creating communities and having like-minded and agreeable people as neighbors strengthens the fabric of society. In fact, the PVS likes to expand community through sports leagues, church activities, and other ways of bringing people together. Family values are championed, such as getting married, being heterosexual, and having children. These values aren't necessarily "old fashioned." They're what support a stable society.

A Farewell to Kings?

Noam Chomsky says, "The most effective way to restrict democracy is to transfer decision making from the public arena to unaccountable institutions: kings and princes, priestly castes, military juntas, party dictatorships, or modern corporations."

The ego thrives in all of these areas. We will explore the ego in modern contexts, but an exploration of royalty is our starting point.

The ego believes that the world can be its kingdom. Although there have been benevolent and admirable kings, more often than not they portray the unbalanced ego's tyrannical mindset. We find an exaggerated version of the PVS, which helps to understand the more subtle form which permeates modern life. Also, in earlier times, the court astrologer played an instrumental role as an advisor to the king. Therefore, there is also relevance here in our understanding of the consciousness which shaped the development of astrology.

Kings (and dictators) are interested in maximizing and hoarding wealth and power. As the reigning alpha male, the king occupies the most favored and glorious position. And from this perch, the ego can have delusions of grandeur. This grandiosity is seen in the "divine right of kings," the political and religious doctrine that asserts that a monarch rules directly from the will of God. A king does not have to comply with the will of his people, his advisors, or any other earthly authority. His control is absolute; he's considered a human embodiment of the divine. Questioning or opposing the king's complete authority is sacrilegious and usually comes with severe punishment, even execution.

It's noteworthy that this "divine right" has been pervasive across the planet; in many countries and cultures both Eastern and Western. It can be traced back to the first "god king" Gilgamesh, who ruled over 2,000 years before the Common Era. The proliferation of monarchies across the globe is strong evidence of how intrinsic this need is for connecting humans to divinity. Ruling monarchs full of egoic greed are, of course, a far cry from true awakened beings.

The King ceremoniously claims his "divine right" in the emblematic act of coronation. In astronomy, a corona is literally the outer atmosphere of a star such as our Sun, which gives it a halo effect. The king's crown is designed to resemble a corona and is the quintessential accoutrement of the monarch. Crowns are usually gold, suggesting the color and regality of the Sun. They often have spikes or protuberances that resemble solar flares. Crowns are placed on the head, the most defining body part of the egoic self.

It is fascinating that the Sun's corona is most easily noticed during a *solar eclipse*, when the Moon covers the disc of the Sun. As we'll be discussing in great detail, the Moon will be associated with *the separate self*, our basic humanness, while the Sun is equated with our source energy, our soul connection with Spirit. The coronation is an illustration of how humans attempt to take over the role of God. At a solar eclipse, the radiance of Spirit (Sun) is obscured by the ego (Moon). This is the egoic takeover, the separate self claiming ownership of energy instead of having the humility to know that we only *borrow* it from our source.

The Sun is the center of the Solar System, and everything revolves around it. It's the power source in the system and is far larger than everything else combined. Conventional astrology, driven by the PVS, equates the astrological Sun with ego and "the masculine," a vivid portrayal of the egoic takeover. The Moon, which *reflects the light of the Sun*, is generally considered to be feminine. This framework is mirrored by the custom of women assuming the surname of their husbands and noted in the saying, "She's having *his* baby."An alternative is to see the Sun in terms of awakening from ego, the self-realization that we are Spirit. This movement parallels the shift from Saturn to Uranus (the so-called "Great Awakener") as the organizational energy of astrology.

32

In the Saturnian realm, hierarchies reign. There are distinctions of class, race, gender, religious affiliation, and ethnicity. Everyone is judged to be at a certain place in the pecking order. Though the ascension to power can in theory be conducted with morality and grace, oftentimes the process is ruthless and corrupt. The political, financial, and military power grabbers are famous for using propaganda, demonizing, or outright violence to control others, preying on people's basic fears and insecurities. All of this is driven by the *unresolved* ego, the most destructive and tyrannical force ever to be unleashed on the planet.

In the heyday of kings, there was a feudal system that carefully organized who has what degree of power and influence. We can find a similar organization with caste systems, the various ranks in military, government, and the corporate business world. We advance through various grades in school, and attain different certifications and acknowledgements upon reaching certain levels in sports or other activities. There is nothing wrong with incremental growth that can be measured in such a way. The issue is that these various systems tend to promote certain interests or abilities, conformity to systems, and are run by unquestioned authority. Since Patriarchal tendencies have been dominant, the person at the top of the totem pole is usually a male.

There have been matriarchies and many female leaders throughout history. However, I don't think anyone would disagree that men have overwhelmingly controlled the strings of power in Western civilization for thousands of years. (Feminists have noted that history has the words *his story* in it.) Monarchs and dictators have been overwhelmingly male, as have Presidents, Prime Ministers, CEOs, and other leaders. Many look to the United States as the epitome of democracy, freedom and opportunity, but the current tally for U.S. Presidents is 44 male, 0 female.

As mentioned before, the court astrologer played the important role of advisor. Instead of using astrology for spiritual maturation, the king was interested in getting information: what's going to happen, when it will happen, and will it be favorable for the empire. This attitude holds astrology as a tool for prediction, focusing on content instead of process, and is blatantly egoic in scope. The incorporation of the transpersonal involves *partnering* with the universe instead of attempting to dominate, which inevitably requires that we have humility. When we break through Saturn and get to the outer planets, we may embrace the freedom (Uranus) to consciously dream (Neptune) and realize our spiritual empowerment (Pluto). Undoubtedly, the order and hierarchies that the ego has worked so hard to establish will feel threatened, so spiritual growth is actually discouraged by the PVS.

The divine right of kings substantially lost its hold in the 18th Century. This was not only the time of the American and French Revolutions, but the discovery of Uranus, which levels hierarchies in order to embrace true equality. Uranus makes no distinctions or judgments on the value of any one individual, and we can bring this perspective to how we approach astrology. Instead of forming judgments about the various facets of the astrological system, everything can be fully embraced for its spiritual value.

Stardom

We see the egoic takeover vividly portrayed with kings, but this issue is played out more generally in the notion of attaining stardom, another version of it as the Sun is a star. The

Sun is boundless creative potential, but the ego wants to claim stardom for very personal reasons.

In any field, there are "rising stars" and "luminaries." Recently, the term "rock star" is being used more broadly to suggest a person with dynamic accomplishment and appeal. There is even a designation for "superstars" who are set above your everyday stars. Those who attain star status usually get preferential treatment: the table at the fine restaurant, gifts, access to coveted events, awards and recognition, sometimes sexual favors or entourages—all the trappings of fame. In one way or another, elevating oneself to star status is the universal dream—there are versions of it in most groups, cultures, societies, and countries. The truly awakened Sun has no more need for self-promotion than a flower or any other part of nature.

It is Sprit that is everlasting, but the star motivated by ego wants to achieve immortality. We have Halls of Fame, museums, and other ways to elevate certain persons to "legendary" status. Literally having a star on the Hollywood Walk of Fame captures it perfectly. Indeed, the entertainment industry showcases the royal egoic takeover quite clearly. Elvis was the "King of Rock," Michael Jackson the "King of Pop," Aretha Franklin is the "Queen of Soul," and Kitty Wells was the "Queen of Country Music."

Other divine or royal nicknames include God, Godfather, Godmother, Prince, Princess, Pope, or Empress. This promotion is not limited to music. Clark Gable was known as "The King of Hollywood;" baseball player Félix Hernández is known as "The King;" basketball player Lebron James is called "King James." You can find it in just about any field. The promoted value is to become the best in a chosen field, "Number 1." This too is indicative of the egoic takeover—"I'm #1," instead of the humility that we exist in Oneness. (When I was writing this section I hilariously saw a guy with a t-shirt which read, "I'm the King of Fucking Everything!")

As a reflection of Patriarchy, you might have heard the saying, "Who's your daddy?" when a man's domination becomes evident. Many men make no secret that they'd prefer to have sons (similar to suns), and there is a custom of naming boys after their fathers—being made in the image of the more powerful paternal figure. The word "father" has associations with "the divine father," God. In fact, the most common pronoun used for God is "He," another reflection of the egoic takeover. In addition to "King," one of the most frequently used honorific nicknames is "Father." Robert Oppenheimer was the "Father of the atomic bomb," and Galileo was dubbed the "Father of modern science." This claiming of divine attributes is also found with many types of inventors or innovators who are dubbed, "The creator of" certain products or advancements—the automobile or computer for example.

We have many ways to systematically categorize who is "the best." There are careful rankings to establish the #1 golfer in the world, the wealthiest CEO, the most successful restaurant chain. We award the top movie at the Oscars, tournaments tell us who the top athletes are, and many follow these ranking systems faithfully. When children do well on a test, they may receive a gold star to signify the accomplishment. The flags of many countries feature star symbology, which shows the nationalistic level to this issue.

In almost every possible field, the PVS challenges us to dominate, to reach #1 on the charts, to be the employee-of-the-month with a picture on the wall. If not, then our ability to make a living might be compromised. We are at a time when more people are starting to question whether we should live on the planet like this.

A Time of Crisis

Ram Dass said, "If I'm an ego, I am judging everything as it relates to my own survival...Souls love. That's what souls do. Egos don't, but souls do." This is the basic crux of the issue—are we going to steer from the ego or from the soul? Perhaps this is the theme of 2012, the fabled year of potential climax on this planet. As of this writing (early 2012), the purported end date of the Mayan Calendar "long count" is directly ahead. We are in the midst of the Uranus-Pluto square (discussed next). There is a palpable, growing sense of collective wonder. The crisis may not be in only dealing with outer circumstances. With the right attitude and intention, humans are equipped to handle just about anything. The job is more personal. We need to locate, heal, and move beyond the true culprit responsible for the state of this planet.

The ego has infiltrated everything that we know and all of who we think we are. As mentioned earlier, survival is important—the ego has a most necessary job. The issue is *over-identification* with ego and bolstering the self disproportionally to what is necessary. Most people are simply unaware that there is something that lies beyond it. Transpersonal terrain is largely uncharted. It's elusive to begin with and easy to dismiss. Many have the assumption that existential issues will be appropriately dealt with if they should happen to appear upon death. There is an assumption that this world and a potential next world are miles apart, so let's deal with reality as we immediately perceive it. The reality may be that our preservation depends on bridging these worlds.

Astrology developed under the mindset of separation consciousness and became anchored to its assumptions. At the relative level, we may not see any issue. Astrology works and can be in service to egoic needs. However, like anything that is ego-based, conventional forms of astrology are less focused on transpersonal matters—the existential issues and questions pertinent to spiritual growth. <u>The soul is interested in evolution, while the personality is more interested in immediate needs</u>. The question is whether the soul can be *fully* included in astrology?

We are at a crossroads of consciousness. In one direction we can see almost certain peril. We will gobble up the Earth's resources and continue fighting each other in bloody wars. Of course, this is what has been occurring for millennia—the stakes are just higher now. Or, we can correct our navigation and realize that we are intrinsically a part of nature and inexorably interconnected with all other people. <u>Anything detrimental we do to the planet or others, we are actually doing to ourself! The only way we're going to survive is to counter-intuitively relax the egoic survival mechanism and learn to operate from the soul.</u>

This imperative doesn't mean that we need to suffocate individuality. We can celebrate our autonomy and bask in our uniqueness. Every individual is irreplaceable and necessary. Aries (the will of the separate self) is just as important as Pisces (where we dissolve into Oneness). We can forge a balance between the personal and the transpersonal, instead of the current imbalance, which is no longer working. If we move forward from the position of love, rather than being driven by the anxiety of survival, we can live with greater inter-dependence. We can increase our awareness of existing within an intelligent and benevolent universe, which invites greater intimacy and connection with it and with ourselves.

The Uranus/Pluto Square

Uranus in Aries and Pluto in Capricorn are currently involved in a decade-long square off with 2012—2015 being the peak years. This planetary combination involves the liberation of what has been pushed into the unconscious—collective uprising, modernization, further awakening about the human condition and our place in the cosmos, and dealing with issues of physical, economic, social, and political destruction or realignment. All of these issues were highlighted during the Uranus-Pluto conjunction in the 1960s. The current square is picking up on these themes and bringing them to the next level.

The waxing square is a time of confrontation and hard work, facing crisis, and finding necessary solutions. <u>Pluto suggests the death of stagnant modes of operating</u>, while <u>Uranus points to the development of new ways of being</u>. The square has the flavor of urgency—our lives may depend upon it. Astrologically, the pieces are in place for a most dramatic time period with the largest of stakes.

Aries and Capricorn can both be competitive. Capricorn wants to preserve and centralize power. While Pluto transits this sign, it will expose detrimental excesses of this nature in order to catalyze reform, to transform any institutions that limit or derail progress. Uranus in Aries invites the courage to forge a more conscious direction through communal empowerment instead of plutocratic control from a privileged few. Awakening from Patriarchy and ego precisely fits this combination, which is currently being played out in scores of ways. Considering that cherished businesses, legacies, paradigms, and the familiar social organization are at stake, there is bound to be marked resistance to reform from those who have benefitted most. We might see this as conservative versus progressive, but "past" is clashing with "future" in a more general sense.

At the time of this writing (early 2012), the Uranus-Pluto square is building in intensity and is vividly playing out. In 2011 we saw the struggle to overthrow dictators in the Middle East region in the "Arab Spring," and the worldwide phenomenon of the "Occupy" movement, which began with "Occupy Wall

Street." In both of these examples we see the petitioning to overthrow a dominating power structure in order to have greater fairness—large scale efforts to dismantle the power-grabbing of ego. Tyrants and those who benefit handsomely in the financial sector both maximize self-gain through institutional advantage. The impact of their privilege (the 1%) undercuts opportunity for all (the 99%)—indicative of how the *dark* Saturn limits evolution for its own aims (dominance, money, status).

We can identify 6 pillars of Patriarchy (as seen in the Western world, with an emphasis on the U.S.): 1) Sex: Male; 2) Race: White; 3) Class: Wealthy; 4) Age: Older; 5) Religion: Christian; 6): Sexual Orientation: Heterosexual. During Uranus-Pluto times, those not in the dominant categories rise up to challenge the PVS to break free of its control. This is true in general and especially now with Uranus squaring Pluto in tradition-oriented Capricorn.

1) Patriarchy is defined by being male-centric. Right on schedule, the phrase "War on Women" has resurfaced. There is much discussion on reproductive rights and contraception. State legislatures have passed a series of restrictive measures on abortion and birth control. Of note is a measure in Virginia which forces a highly invasive procedure on women who want an abortion, making them view the fetus on a screen positioned inches from their faces. This, and similar measures, are being discussed at the national level as part of the 2012 Presidential campaign. As the Uranus-Pluto square was applying in 2008, Hillary Clinton launched the most successful campaign by a woman seeking the Presidency. Her bid picked up on the Feminist Movement, which was occurring at the conjunction in the 1960s. Women are the largest voting bloc in the country, and they are assertively claiming that power.

2) In 2008 Barack Obama was elected President, which ended the string of only white Presidents. Now, there is much

talk of "taking the country back," and subtle (and sometimes not so subtle) racial themes are noted in the opposition to this President, particularly from the Tea Party movement. The number of hate groups has dramatically increased. Immigration is also a passionate and controversial issue which is being debated. The rise of Hispanics in the United States is further eroding the possibility of maintaining a white power structure. Sociologists tell us that by 2050 more people will be speaking Spanish than English in the U.S. The country which used to enslave minorities is now learning to adapt to sharing power. At the time of this writing, there is a major outcry against the unnecessary shooting of an African-American youth (Trayvon Martin) which has put race in the national dialogue once more.

3) The pillar of wealth is where there is the most urgency for change. There has never been this much polarization between the "haves" and the "have-nots." The Occupy movement focuses on the inequities of class. Likely Republican nominee Mitt Romney is highlighting income disparity issues with his candidacy. The admission that he, a multi-millionaire, pays a lower tax rate than most Americans has raised eyebrows. He has also committed a string of "gaffes" that underscore his elitism. Issues of tax policy, predatory lenders, corporate bonuses, and business regulation are in the news. As the U.S. recovers from recession, the wealthiest are benefitting most, while they were the least impacted by the economic downturn.

4) At the Uranus-Pluto conjunction in the 1960s, the youth led the countercultural movement. Again, we find them leading the Occupy Movement. Another phenomenon has been *The Hunger Games*, a movie about teenagers, which has attained enormous popularity. It portrays how young people must deal with growing up in a value system reminiscent of the PVS. It has themes of survival, a culture enthralled by competition and violence, and the need to satisfy this culture and participate in

41

the "game." There is an emphasis on being "liked," attaining corporate sponsorships, all the while being manipulated and exploited. The dominant culture is portrayed as fake, preoccupied with appearances, overly stylized. Also coming out during the Uranus-Pluto square was *Avatar*, which illustrated the clash between domination consciousness, and a more collaborative and universal approach based on our energetic interconnectedness. Similarly, it was young people in Avatar who led the rebellion.

5) The dominant power structure puts forth the idea that the U.S. is a "Christian Nation," despite millions who do not identify with this. The separation of church and state is being debated through many current issues. The 9/11 attacks ignited suspicion of Islam, and religious liberty continues to be a topic of public debate. Interestingly, conservatives are claiming that the Obama Administration (an alleged "war on religion") is encroaching on religious freedom by advocating the availability, and insurance coverage, of contraception. Every winter there is a very public celebration of Christmas which pervades mainstream culture and society. Those who speak out against this are sometimes accused of waging a "war on Christmas." The corporatization (Pluto in Capricorn) of this and other holidays and celebrations is becoming more obvious, and less satisfying, for many people.

6) Gay marriage and civil unions continue to gain prominence in the national dialogue. Many measures that expand the rights of same-sex pairings are being passed. There is also impassioned and vocal opposition to such measures including rallies and demonstrations. It has become evident that young people overwhelmingly support the rights of those with alternative sexual orientations, and society is adapting to this reality.

Many turn to astrology as a way to deviate from the mainstream paradigm in pursuit of broader truth. However, the astrology we've inherited comes well before Uranus was discovered. In many ways, both subtle and obvious, Saturn has also controlled astrology, which is to be expected since evolution unfolds over time. We can now see more clearly that astrology is largely geared toward serving the ego's need for self-gain (indicative of the 1%), and actually restricts a vision of more universal principles (championed by the 99%). We'll explore the dominant view of the Sun, as well as many other examples of the egoic takeover and the PVS in conventional astrology. We are at the threshold of a new era—an astrology that centers around Spirit.

Chapter 2
Oneness & Spiritual Awakening

The great wisdom traditions tell us we are born from love, though we tend to quickly lose that connection and go on autopilot much of the time. Though the universe has love as part of its essential nature, we become shut off from it. And life can be full of suffering.

We all get physically sick and our bodies sometimes ache. There are abundant opportunities to feel let down by others or be frustrated with ourself. And the world at large—now there's a circus! We are confronted with all sorts of painful, alarming situations—abuse of all kinds, starvation, poverty, war, corporate depravity. On any given day we might get into a car accident or learn that someone we love has died.

We all get banged up by life, so it's legitimate and necessary to take care of ourselves. We have developed many coping strategies so we can roll out of bed each morning and face the world. And however useful and understandable, we may overuse and over-identify with these same strategies. The contraction in our defense mechanisms is the major concern of this book. We become cut off from love, from trusting life, from being with all that is. Pain is part of being human, but compounding pain into suffering is completely optional.

A passage in *A Course in Miracles* states, "Your task is not to seek for love, but merely to seek and find all the barriers within yourself that you have built against it."[iv] This book is full of interesting ideas, but at its heart, it is a cosmic love story of epic scope. Perhaps the only One there really is.

Oneness

The idea and experience of Oneness has played a major role in our collective consciousness. Science tells us that we reside in a *unified field of energy* called the universe. Every major religion, spiritual path, and wisdom tradition has some version of Oneness as its centerpiece. It is broadly understood that the universe divides (relative), while also remaining interconnected (transpersonal).

There are many terms associated with Oneness: God, Spirit, Allah, Shunyata, Brahman, The One, The Tao, The Self, The Absolute, etc. And many paths support its realization: Advaita Vedanta is a Nondual tradition from India. Sikhism is a religion explicitly promoting the Nondual view. Zen can be thought of as practices to experience the Nondual state. Buddhism has the concept of No-Self (or "anatman" in Sanskrit), which points toward the ephemeral nature of individual identity. Mahayana Buddhism is the branch that most directly discusses the experience of duality and encourages compassion for those caught in this perspective.

Nondual themes are also found in Native American spirituality. Within Christianity, the Gnostic tradition is the most recognized Nondual branch. *A Course of Miracles* is written from the perspective of Nonduality and is not a part of conventional Christianity, though it's composed of teachings that are allegedly from Jesus. The Chasidic branch of Judaism is focused on direct mystical and Nondual experience, and the Kaballah is the collection of wisdom teachings that informs its practice.

The Nondual philosophy of Plotinus has had great influence in the Western world. Friedrich Wilhelm Joseph Schelling created the first evolutionary Nondual philosophy in the West, while Sri Aurobindo did the same in the East. There is great consensus about Oneness, but because of the spiritual implications, it tends to be downplayed in secular education and obscured by mainstream western religion. We live at a time when this idea is becoming less framed in terms of certain paradigms or perspectives and more universally integrated. Exciting times, indeed!

Spiritual Awakening

Spiritual awakening is *the transcendence of ego as the primary orientation and identification.* The process expands towards the direct experience of Oneness. Nowadays, many people are engaging in workshops, contemplative classes, and other spiritually-focused pursuits to facilitate this opening. However, attaining spiritual "credentials" does not necessarily foster awakening. In fact, the ego can easily find a new foothold in a "better, more spiritual" identity.

As we awaken, we begin to bridge separation consciousness with life beyond it. As mentioned earlier, I hold awakening as an ongoing *process*, while the term "enlightenment" points to an end point of this process when spiritual awakening becomes fully realized as *a pervasive and abiding experience.*

In some branches of Buddhism, enlightenment indicates the condition of freedom from suffering and ignorance. The soul is released from the cycles of samsāra, the perpetual series of incarnations. The Japanese used the word "kensho" to describe the state when one realizes Nonduality. In Hinduism, the term "moksha" concerns the freedom from worldly passions. Christian ideas of salvation and transcendence have some similarity to Eastern notions of enlightenment, though there is more emphasis on theology instead of states of consciousness.

47

In some forms of New Age Christianity, enlightenment may be achieved directly from the "Sacred Rays." The Jewish Kaballah offers guidance and practices towards enlightenment. The same is found with Sufism, the mystical branch of Islam. It appears that transcendence of ego is universally understood as a part of spiritual development.

There is a story that goes something like this: A young spiritual seeker runs into a master who is carrying a great load on his shoulders. He asks him, "What does it mean to be enlightened?" The master takes the load off his back and puts it on the ground, then broadly smiles from the sense of liberation. The seeker asks, "What happens next?" The master picks up the load, puts it on his shoulders, and walks away.

As this story illustrates, once we become more awake, we still have to attend to life within the everyday world. Astrologically, we can understand this dynamic in terms of the relationship between Saturn and Uranus.

♄

The Saturnian Gate

Saturn is like a wall or gate that creates a boundary between the relative and the transpersonal domains, similar to our skin at the personal level. In order to pass through the gate, Saturn requires us to completely *accept reality*. We must accept our mortality, everything that has occurred in the past, our personal limitations, unmet needs, our deepest fears and vulnerabilities. Any place where we're caught in or resisting the personal story will prevent us from moving through the gate.

Resisting reality keeps us in an adversarial relationship with it. A common way reality is resisted is by looking at it negatively, as if we are its victims. "Life isn't fair!" In astrology, this takes the form of classifying Saturn as a "malefic." In using this term, we create distance from Saturn and block our ability to see that it actually exists to support our evolution. When we are not in conscious connection with the evolutionary purpose of a planetary energy, it tends to manifest darkly. The unconscious Saturn is preoccupied with control and domination. It set up the PVS as a way to control the uncontrollable—nature itself—which operates by its own rhythms, cycles, and intelligence.

Life does appear random at times, and this can be threatening to the ego. When we move beyond Saturn, we reach the intelligent organization of Uranus. Associated with air, Uranus creates invisible connective pathways analogous to the neural circuitry of our brains. Although we are enveloped within its intricacy, we don't readily see it. Astrology has served the function of pointing it out to many of us. We can trust the coherency of this connective matrix and know that we are a part of its unfolding. Since we are a strand in the tapestry, we can cooperate with the larger design. Then, we can participate with the necessary spiritual lessons that the universe is bringing us. The challenge is reconciling the ego, whose agenda of self-preservation may subvert this opening to the broader matrix.

As Uranus resides beyond Saturn, we must accept reality in order to access the transpersonal. Saturn also serves as a gate in the other direction—from the transpersonal to the relative world. It grounds evolutionary possibilities into form. Evolution is emergent in the creativity of the eternal present. However, the transpersonal is in relationship with the relative world, so we can see evolution as unfolding in linear time. Imagine evolutionary possibilities as an unending line extending infinitely into the future (Uranus). In order to function in the everyday world (Saturn), we must contract possibilities and deal with matters directly at hand. We implement and refine certain advances and create a workable civilization. This process of "earthing" necessarily shuts out possibilities that are ahead. Saturn is like a

49

vise grip applied to the evolutionary line. It's sturdy, holds things in place, and makes life functional.

The issue is that application of the Saturn vise can become rigid. When we become comfortable, familiar, and dependent on certain ways of operating, it's destabilizing to want to move the vise further down the evolutionary line. Certain paradigms or institutions may not want to change, usually because they benefit by maintaining the status quo. If we do not open to further evolutionary possibilities, pressure builds towards some type of cataclysm. Integrating outer planet energies into the status quo is a delicate balance. With too much Saturn, we strangle infinity. Without enough Saturn, we get chaos.

The current Uranus activity, particularly the square with Pluto, indicates the urgency to move the vise grip further down. At this point in history, we have made many impressive advances in our collective evolution, yet we may only be at the *beginning* of a very long process. Consider that Uranus was discovered about 230 years ago, a small fraction of world history. Hopefully we'll be on this planet for thousands of years to come, so there will be many opportunities to seize the evolutionary possibilities that lie ahead.

Uranus is often called "The Great Awakener." It involves the removal of social conditioning in order to awaken into one's authentic spiritual truth, We can learn to identify as a soul that is having a human experience and see life through the transpersonal lens.

The Transpersonal Lens

The great Persian mystical poet Rumi wrote, "Everyone sees the unseen in proportion to the clarity of their heart." Clarity is discovered when we remove our egoic distortions by cultivating awareness. We are then able to recognize the spiritual lessons being presented in our experiences. The rational mind sees occurrences, takes in data, and forms judgments. In viewing through the transpersonal lens, we intuitively understand why life is unfolding as it is. Astrology can also be helpful in revealing what these lessons are. It's an elaborate system that describes the nature of the energies that surround us at any time—energies that can be viewed through both the relative and transpersonal lenses.

The Sun illuminates all experiences and makes life possible. When we are able to practice being present and aware, we have greater access to what is actually happening in the solar field. At subtle levels there are resonances, synchronicities, messages—phenomena which connect with our consciousness in nonphysical ways. Admittedly, most of what occurs in this realm is not part of consensus reality or even acknowledged as being real. However, an indescribable "knowing"—the seeds of creativity and inspiration—have been discussed by countless artists, sages, yogis, and "intuitives."

Inspiration and intuition are worked with in the manifest world—timeless creativity is brought into time. The soul is the part of us which connects in nonphysical ways with this solar field, while the ego resides in the relative world. The soul and ego are involved in a co-creative relationship despite the ego's frequent negation of the transpersonal realm. We can see a similarity in dreams—how we simultaneously design and experience them ourselves. We are the character in the action (relative), while at the transpersonal level we are the director. This arrangement is actually no different from what we experience in waking life. Author and teacher Don Jose Ruiz puts it this way:

People live in their own world, in their own movie, in their own story. They invest all their faith into that story and that story is truth for them. But it's a relative truth, because it's not truth for you. Now you can see that all their opinions about you really just concern the characters in their movie, not in yours.[v]

By definition, separation consciousness is rooted in the belief that the external world is separate. The ego believes that it's dealing with things that are unrelated to it. It resides "in here" and everything else is "out there." In keeping consciousness solely at this level, we cannot see our role in co-creating all of our experiences. When we accept the transpersonal reality, we learn to see the self reflected in everything and find ways to connect with it consciously. We become more aware of what is actually happening because we've located the projector. Carl Jung said, "Who looks outside, dreams; who looks inside awakes." Awakening stems from the inside—the more awareness we have of our unconscious, the more we're able to see its designs everywhere.

The quality of our consciousness radiates into the world, and we meet the self in countless guises. Our energy is like a "dreambody," a combination of the nonphysical with the physical, the transpersonal with the relative, soul with body. If we're willing to accept this view—or at least experiment with it—we can partner with the universe on behalf of our spiritual growth. The more common reaction is to reject it and continue to endlessly strategize for experiences that the ego finds preferable. In short, this is the paradigm shift. By seeing through the transpersonal lens, we take responsibility for our role in co-creating life, and life itself turns out to appear quite differently from what we previously thought it to be.

Implications of the Transpersonal View

The transpersonal view liberates us from taking respon-sibility for how others are navigating their own ego dreams. When we're still caught in a personal, egoic view, we can easily fall into the pattern of trying to fix, save, or please other people. We might see the self-other dynamic as something to get better at in order to have positive experiences or to avoid conflict. With this external focus, we might lose ourselves in the preferences that other people have for us. They will receive and interpret life according to their ego dream, but we can offer love and support and model what we know to be in alignment with our own integrity. Still, they may misinterpret our actions, and that is actually none of our business — unless we make it so.

Our job is to strive to live our most conscious self. Other people always get exactly what they need from us, *no matter what we do*. We don't have to take responsibility for how others receive us, and we never have to take the actions of others personally. If we are not acting consciously, then it serves our growth to recognize and own that. We can take responsibility, but ultimately it's not for others' benefit. They are connecting with themselves *through* us, so they will approach and interpret us influenced by their ego dreams no matter what we do. Our growth is not dependent on other people waking up.

An implication of this view is that the world doesn't hurt us — *we hurt ourselves through the world.* Every person resides in the center of their own subjectivity no matter how challenging that can be to accept. Rainer Maria Rilke says:

> We have no cause to be mistrustful of our World, for it is not against us. If it has terrors, they are our terrors; if it has abysses, those abysses belong to us, if dangers are there we must strive to love them.[vi]

When we truly love ourselves, we will not experience harmful energy from the outside. The world is an enormous reflection of our psyche. Our job is to attend to the source of the projections, not the mirrors. Anais Nin says, "We see things not as they are. We see things as we are."

We are all interconnected like billions of mirrors endlessly reflecting and often stimulating each other's growth. Whenever a situation provokes physical discomfort or heightened emotion—a "charge"—we can take that as a signal to get curious and pay attention. School is in session! It's as if we have energetic *hooks* that match up with others who are working with the same issues. These hooks are there to ensure that we get tangled up enough to get the lessons we need. Becoming aware of our hooks improves our ability to manage the lessons.

It is our natal charts, of course, which give us an objective map of our curriculum. We can see our attachments, patterns, and wounding, as well as the intentions for healing and further growth. While this kind of transparency is exciting and valuable to many people, others are quite uncomfortable with it. These folks are likely skeptical of astrology and perhaps the idea of Spirit. Skepticism of any type of larger intelligence is often rooted in the ego's desire for control and what it imagines to be freedom. A path of awakening typically brings increasing awareness and appreciation for the larger reality that we are each connected to and enveloped within.

A wonderfully liberating feature of the transpersonal level is that nothing "bad" could possibly happen! Negative interpretation only occurs in the small, separate mind. Eckhart Tolle asks, "Have you ever seen an unhappy flower or a stressed oak tree?"[vii] If we're able to identify primarily as energy (transpersonal level), rather than only as a separate ego, then we can exist in harmony with nature. The transpersonal level knows that the universe does things *for* us, not *to* us. Everything is a benevolent lesson—it's our mental stories that tell us otherwise. Stress, frustration or any type of so-called "negative" emotion is just an indication of what needs attention, just invitations to expand our awareness. The main feature here is trust. Trusting what the present moment brings, over and over--welcoming the master teacher in all of its guises.

Along with acceptance of our own experience, relaxing into trust generates compassion for others. We can see this Earthly journey like a passage through a school. We wouldn't be harsh with a first-grader for not yet knowing what he'll learn in second grade. He needs to learn first grade first. We are all emerging from unconsciousness, and we all have fumbled in the dark. It turns out that this is the natural course of evolution and its all ok.

Getting Comfortable with Paradox

The personal and transpersonal perspectives are not only vastly different from each other, they are often delightfully paradoxical. We're all familiar with the personal perspectives. Spiritual awakening brings more understanding and experience of the transpersonal views. Let's see how reality shifts and then discuss how to live in both worlds. Check out these paradoxes:

When we figure out who we are, it turns out to be nobody. At the transpersonal level, we're just energy, a part of Spirit—the personal falls away. Self-development eventually leads to self-transcendence.

Mind thinks us. We are accustomed to the individual mind thinking about larger frameworks, such as God or nature. The transpersonal perspective sees the individual mind like a nerve-ending of the larger, spiritual brain. The Universal Mind *thought up* each of us.

55

We awaken to the dream. From the relative view, we think of waking out of sleep and into everyday living. Upon spiritual awakening, we see that life is actually the projection of the ego dream.

Liberation is found through surrender. In the familiar realms, liberation is found through strength, freedom, and autonomy. At the transpersonal level, liberation into Spirit is found through surrendering the personal ego. Without this surrender, another paradox emerges: (*Egoic*) *freedom is bondage.* We are stuck within the Saturnian realm.

Once nothing matters anymore, everything is precious. When we relax egoic preferences, there is gratitude for what is. We may become more sensitive to the subtleties and nuances of life and appreciate the preciousness in everything.

Saying "I don't know" shows the most knowledge. Within the Saturnian world, we demand certainty and clarity. At the transpersonal level, knowledge is not so clear-cut, so the ability to say "I don't know" shows a willingness not to constrict the infinite, to remain open to its reach. The rational mind may say that the opposite of a truth is a lie, but the Uranian view is that the opposite of a truth is another truth—an observation made by many talented thinkers.

You can't think outside the box because the box is thinking. Orbiting within Saturn, Mercury reduces the transpersonal to language and rationality. As it's written in the Tao te Ching, "The Tao that can be told is not the eternal Tao." Mercury functions within the box of reason (Saturn).

Nature tames people. The egoic view is that we can master nature and create civilization. The broader view turns it around: Nature is connecting to itself *through* us. When we cooperate with this evolutionary unfolding, we may consciously contribute. As we spiritually develop, our unconscious and immature parts become tamed.

Failing is growing, losing is winning. <u>The ego wants to succeed, whereas the soul wants to grow.</u> Situations the ego may construe as failures or losses may in fact introduce rich and necessary spiritual lessons. The most trying situations are actually *gifts,* no matter how much the ego rolls its eyes at such a notion.

Accidents are on purpose. Randomness is a product of the skeptical mind that cannot fathom a larger design. The transpersonal view is that all energy is interconnected. Therefore, accidents or coincidences are actually synchronicities—how the universe connects to itself in order to stimulate awakening.

The imperfections of the world are perfect. Evolution is proceeding in its own way, in its own time. We all have imperfections, and these are perfect for us to address. We may lament that the world is filled with many social, political, or even spiritual ills or imperfections, but these *perfectly* catalyze growth. Spirit doesn't have to be corrected by us. Instead, when we correct ourselves by removing egoic distortions, we can experience Spirit's perfection.

Our view of the world is really our view of the self. Infinite mirrors in unending guises reflect back who we are so that we can awaken to the authentic self—which, turns out to be, the universe itself. From the personal standpoint it may sound narcissistic to think that the entire world is who we are; that everything "out there" is really inside. The transpersonal view yields another paradox: *Not accepting that the world is the self is narcissism* because it indicates entrapment in the personal story.

I don't care what happens to you because I love you. From the transpersonal view, *all* experiences are necessary no matter what value judgments we assign. The deeper spiritual love we may have towards each others' growth is unwavering and unconditional. Instead of coddling or investing in so-called "positive" outcomes for another, we can love them as they

57

struggle—to not wish for any alteration of these necessary and rich experiences, however painful to the personality.

The objective is to see through objectivity. The quest for objectivity has driven much of science and the Western mindset. It would provide the ego with great security and certainty if the world could be objectively understood. Then, we could figure out everything and learn to master our environment. It turns out that all perspectives of reality are relative to the observer. In fact, science tells us that "the observer impacts the object of observation," which basically means that there is no way to remove our subjective filter. Though we go around in our lives with a high degree of certainty that what we experience can be shared by others, this too is just an illusion.

Our notions of death are dying. Another tenet from science is the conservation of energy. This informs us that energy can never be created or destroyed, it just recycles and transforms. Nothing ever dies, including us. Certainly, there is a transition upon death, and it's quite difficult to know what might be on the other side. However, our shamans, sages, mystics, and other wise men and women throughout history are in agreement that there are indeed metaphysical levels of reality. From the transpersonal perspective, there is no death.

Questioning the Spiritual Quest. The central conundrum of the spiritual quest is that it's more about the quest than the outcome. The ego might be driven to attain enlightenment, but it turns out to be an incredible disappointment because the ego becomes transcended, reduced in importance. Spiritual teacher Jed McKenna says that, "Self cannot achieve no-self." Because this paradox is not generally understood, enlightenment is often packaged as something that the ego can attain. This has created a prosperous spiritual industry, but it has also hindered the awakening process. About this folly, he remarks, "No one gets the grail, but if you understand the fundamental conflict, you'll see that no one really wanted it anyway."

And this is really the central question: Do we *really* want to awake out of ego? Many would answer affirmatively, but this response may not fully consider the implications. If this desire is genuine, we must have the courage to connect awakened consciousness with our guiding paradigms and our institutions, including astrology. This is the spiritual work of the 21st Century—either we take measures to reign in the tyranny of the ego, or we unwittingly contribute to the perpetuation of it. We must assertively put forth the awakened view, no matter how inconvenient its truth is for traditional paradigms.

Two Bodies

In the realm of separateness, we tend to identify with our physical bodies. The skin provides a discernible boundary between the self and the outside world. Here's an exercise to see how strong this boundary can be: spit into a clean glass, then drink it. Most people find this idea to be disgusting, but it's the exact same saliva that was inside the mouth just a second ago. When the saliva moves beyond the apparent boundary of self, it's *no longer perceived as being a part of the self* and therefore looked at suspiciously. Is it a threat to my survival? Is it going to make me happy? If there's any question, then it's best to leave it alone.

It serves our survival to investigate what we put into our bodies. We can certainly honor this instinct, and we might also see that we can extend beyond the parameters of our physical body in ways that are not egoic. Since *all* energy is interconnected, we are connected to our environment; how can we not be?

The energy that extends outwards from the body is often called an aura. We'll call it the "energy body" because it involves light, as well as heat (or presence). The energy body is depicted in art in many cultures throughout history. We're all familiar with the halo, which portrays the idea that our energy is connected to a spiritual source beyond us. However, more general illustrations of our radiance or luminescence are a frequent motif in much spiritually-inspired imagery. We now can capture the energy body with the technology of Kirlian Photography.

Through intention, invocation, or some types of spiritual practice, we may increase our awareness of the energy body. We might also attempt to expand our energy body and make more intentional contact with our surroundings in any situation. Many of us have had experiences in nature where we feel connected to our environment. There is usually a sense of expansion beyond ego, often a general feeling of lightness and contentment with life. Many spiritual teachers inform us that there is no end to the energy body—we can be in contact with everything! Deepak Chopra says,

> Usually, I look at a tree and I don't see it as my lungs. I look at the rivers, the waters, and I don't see them as my circulation. I look at the atmosphere, I don't see it as my breath. But in fact, it is: The tree is my lungs; the earth is my body; the waters are my circulation. It's not environment; it's your extended body. It's you.[viii]

The contracting quality of the ego might feel threatened by a perceived loss of control and sabotage the process. It may hunker down in discursive thoughts, emotional charges, or a strong identification with being a physical body. Many people simply have no awareness or idea that we can extend in such a way. Therefore, the mainstream view is the usual way of separateness, and the energy body is marginalized or even ridiculed as something flaky. Nevertheless, it's always there awaiting our participation.

Spiritual awakening involves including the energy body into our identity. We come to understand that we radiate out and connect with the external world, which turns out to be the projection of our own consciousness. The energy body is our soul connection with Spirit, and we'll be relating it astrologically to the Sun. The physical body is paired with the Moon. Candles are frequently used in spiritual ceremonies, art, and literature. They are symbolic of an individual being connected to a broader source of light. The wax is analogous to the Moon, while the flame is the Sun. We note how the flame illuminates the surrounding area just as our consciousness projects into the world. A candle's flame connects in with the unified energetic field (Oneness), which contains all experience.

Shamanic astrologer Benjamin Bernstein says that we can connect our awareness to a sort of "Divine GPS." We can attune to the energy body and learn to live by being informed by source energy, and use the ego in its service. This may sound fancy at first, but another way to think of it is simply living intuitively. Benjamin has developed a series of invocations designed to connect with the energy body. I've included them in the Extras.

P.
304

As most current paradigms (including the dominant understandings which govern astrology) do not acknowledge or promote the energy body, it is not something generally discussed or developed. However, we are indeed in a time of paradigm shift. In the following chapter, we will bring the notion of two bodies directly to the center of the astrological system. This idea forms the crux of the astrology of awakening.

Chapter 3
The Moon & Sun: From Darkness to Light

In this chapter, I'll dive more directly into astrology, starting with an exploration of the Sun and Moon. It's natural and accurate to see these two celestial bodies as holding prime significance due to their astronomical relevance to us here on Earth. The Sun is in the middle of the Solar System with all the planets revolving around it. It sustains life for us while also connecting this system to membership in the broader galaxy. The Moon is the Earth's satellite, the closest physical body to us as we speed through space. The Sun and Moon also appear as the largest objects in the sky and have served as the core planets in astrology for many centuries.

The Familiar Paradigm

The conventional way the luminaries are viewed is from the relative perspective. From our vantage point on Earth, the Sun and Moon take turns traversing the sky above. It's as if we were in the center of the universe with these two spheres our consistent, familiar companions. It's natural to project that most familiar of relationships—the one with our parents—onto them. Moon is seen as Mom, Sun as Dad. She is there for our tender moments, nursing us with a soft glow. He commands us to rise to a challenge, to meet the world with strength and radiance. And since the Sun and Moon appear the same size from Earth, we tend to see them as equals. The luminaries are conventionally categorized in the following ways:

Sun	Moon
Father	Mother
Masculine	Feminine
Active (Yang)	Receptive (Yin)
Day	Night
Light	Dark
Will	Instinct
Rational	Emotional
Hot	Cold
Ego	Id

The familiar, relative paradigm is based on seeing the luminaries as a complementary pair: light and dark, male and female. The unification of these opposites creates wholeness. Light and dark partnered produces the full experience of the day/night cycle. Male and female join to produce offspring. At the relative level—and despite Patriarchy's indoctrination—one side of a polarity is never *better*, or more important, than the other.

Is there another way we might view the Sun and Moon? Of course there is—from the transpersonal level where the soul, not the ego, is the main orientation. The familiar paradigm is that of separation consciousness. It only takes the switching of the first two letters to see that geocentric is egocentric. Incarnating on Earth is an agreement to venture into separation, and everything about our relative position here speaks to learning from this position. We know now, of course, that the Earth is really orbiting the Sun, but in the grand scheme of evolution this is a very recent understanding. For most of history, the collective consciousness has developed under the geocentric assumption, and the astrology we've inherited is consistent with it.

With the awareness of the heliocentric reality in this Solar System in the 16th Century, the collective was forced into a massive paradigm shift, a complete reevaluation of our life on this planet. Of particular interest was the tremendous opposition to the notion. Copernicus knew how revolutionary the finding was, how difficult it would be for some to accept. He didn't initially go public with the information due to the likely consequences of his assertion. Decades after Copernicus, Galileo was famously put under house arrest for advocating such "heresy." Official church doctrine not only influenced philosophy and belief systems, it controlled (Saturn) them. The typical response to the Uranian figures who point out another perspective is to vanquish, punish, and make an example of them to show the result of such deviation.

Intellectual conformity is not so demanded nowadays. However, worldviews from yesteryear which have shaped history still echo through tradition and institutions, woven through culture, lifestyles, and education. They have powerfully shaped the collective consciousness for hundreds and even thousands of years. This gives them tremendous momentum, which requires us to mount an effort to resist the undertow to the past if we're interested in living in the present-day consciousness or clearing a path in support of further evolution.

A Transpersonal View

At the transpersonal level, the Sun and Moon take on a new set of roles. The Moon becomes the representative of separation consciousness—it conveys the energy that has been *absorbed*, the emotional memory bank, and what unconscious

65

tendencies have been cultivated to survive. We are receptive to life—this is *lunar*, not exclusively feminine. The Sun signifies our soul connection with Spirit. We are learning to engage more radiantly in life by increasing our vitality and awareness. This is *solar*, far broader than the masculine.

We are loosening our attachments and egoic identity (Moon) in order to expand and awaken (Sun). This is not to suggest in any way that we need to become less feminine (Moon) and more masculine (Sun)! This would be applying the relative view to the transpersonal (the egoic takeover), a mistake I strongly urge the reader not to make. This error would make the new paradigm repugnantly sexist. What the transpersonal actually asserts is that gender (dualistic) is not relevant at the soul level. As we awaken, our identity and perspective changes dramatically. *All polarities are from the relative position of separation consciousness* when we are identified only in ego (Moon). With the transcendence of the ego, the perspective from the Sun (soul) is of Oneness.

The relative perspective is from the position of Earth and is immediate to our senses. We notice how the Moon gives forth light, and we call it "moonlight." Astrologically, the Moon is categorized as a "luminary." The transpersonal view does not have a privileged vantage point. Instead of seeing the Moon as a luminary, we notice how it *reflects the light of the Sun*. Instead of perceiving them as equal in size, we can see that the Sun actually occupies roughly as much space as 64 million Moons. The parallel meaning is that Spirit (Sun) exists on a wholly different scale than the ego (Moon).

The Moon *depends* on the Sun to hold it (and the Earth) in place through gravity, but *the Sun doesn't need the Moon*—it would shine whether or not the Earth has a satellite. The parallel is that Spirit does not need individuals for its existence, but we are enveloped in the Sun's sustenance. Sri Ramana Maharshi says, "the body cannot exist without the Self (his term for Spirit), whereas the Self can exist without the body."[ix] Just as the Moon reflects the light of the Sun, the separate self is a reflection of Spirit's magnificence.

The Moon relates to consolidated experience from the past, while the Sun suggests the awakening into the present. The Moon is our "small" self, invested in survival and the meeting of our basic human egoic needs, most of which are unconscious. The Sun is our "big" self, the awakening from the dream of separation, and the limitations of ego (Moon).

As for the Sun, it is conventionally seen as the separate self, the ego, as it serves as the central manager of our life. This "egoic takeover" of the Sun is resolved when we let go of ego as our primary identity. This shift of identity *gradually* liberates the Sun, allowing it to shine independent of the filter of the contracted ego-self. As the attachment to the past recedes, we become increasingly centered in the present moment.

Though classified as a "planet" in astrology, we know that the Sun is actually a *star*, a designation which connects it to the wider cosmos. Stars join together in clusters, systems, and galaxies. The Moon, like everything else within our Solar System, does not have that reach. With the Sun, our "big" self is unbound by time or space. As we awaken, we come to realize that our energy is on loan from Spirit, and we consciously act in accordance with this reality. Eckhart Tolle says that awakening is "a state of connectedness with something immeasurable and indestructible, something that, almost paradoxically, is essentially you and yet is much greater than you."[x]

Saturn organizes consensus reality in the relative world. It owes its existence in the system to the Sun, which holds it in place. Separation consciousness and the relative world are completely dependent on the broader spiritual source. Therefore, the relative view is secondary to the transpersonal. Instead of seeing

67

ourselves as humans capable of having spiritual experiences, we can identify as souls having human experiences. C.S. Lewis said, "You don't have a soul. You are a soul. You have a body."

Seeing the Sun in this spiritual way provides perspective on the lunar cycle. At the New Moon, they are together—individual consciousness (Moon) is merged with Spirit (Sun). The Moon moves away to gather experience and then eventually returns, just as individuals separate, incarnate, and then return to the Oneness of Spirit. In contrast, it's difficult to see how the lunar cycle pertains to the relationship between the masculine and feminine.

The Spectrum of Light

This development of consciousness is the central task of our spiritual evolution. We start out unconsciously and gradually awaken into broader creative possibilities. We can see this process outlined by a broad spectrum of development from darkness to light. In the relative world, the universe has distinctions and contrasts, which sets the stage for us to navigate as we see fit.

Dark/Unconscious————————————Bright/Conscious

Our consciousness is oriented somewhere along this spectrum, and we each develop at our own pace. This growth involves spurts, plateaus, and setbacks, and everyone's path is unique. Child poet Mattie Stepanek wrote poems of tremendous depth and spiritual insight at the age of 4, while Charles Manson is still a raving *lunatic* in his advanced age. We like to believe that all people are equal, and *this is true at an absolute level.* However, there are various levels of evolution and consciousness at the relative level.

The astrology we've inherited does not include this incredibly important variable. There is a focus on the perceived merits of various chart factors rather than the quality of consciousness of the chart owner. We can think of a natal chart as a car and the chart owner as the driver. Most astrological discussion and literature focuses on the components of the car—the aspects, the judgments of planetary placements in signs and houses, the condition of the so-called "benefics" and "malefics." Someone might claim, "I have a *strong* Mars!"

The reason for this emphasis is that notions of both psychological and spiritual development come many centuries later than the advent of astrology. Without the integration of the critical idea that consciousness evolves, we give our power away to the chart's layout. Ken Wilber calls the leveling of the depth of consciousness "flatland." He says that living on the "descended grid," there is no upward mobility toward greater spiritual heights—in fact, even having such a notion is seen as irrational. Synchronously, since we discovered that the world is not flat, we have progressively understood that life has many levels of depth. We can embrace this universal notion and finally bring it fully into astrology.

Instead of focusing on the car, we may shift to looking at the driver. No matter how impressive a Lamborghini is, a toddler is not going to drive it very well, while a professional driver is likely to handle the most common sedan with impressive skill and style. *Anything* in life can be lit up by awakened consciousness or remain shrouded in the darkness of unconsciousness. Therefore, there are no "good" or "bad" charts or factors which compose charts. We can take responsibility for how we drive, which goes along with taking full responsibility for our unconsciousness, the Moon.

Lunar Facts

In the typical use of astrology, the Moon is considered one of the "planets," just like Jupiter or Mercury. We notice how it travels around our charts every month, seeing it as another body that exists *away* from our Earthly home. What if the Moon is not separate from us? What if the Moon is actually our home? In *The Sun at the Center*, Philip Sedgwick writes,

> Science no longer maintains the view that the Moon is a satellite of the Earth, a captive vehicle subservient to the greater orbit of the larger body. Now the perception creates a pair of planets with a gravitational barycenter producing a nucleus of interaction of bilateral harmony.[xi]

This perspective means that the Earth and Moon form a *unit*, and we can then approach the rest of the system from this reference point. Sedgwick writes, "The Moon and the Earth are a part of one, not apart from one another." Upon the integration of this fundamental reality into our astrology, the Moon is no longer a planet existing "out there." Instead, it's the foundation of unconsciousness which initially surrounds us (just like the Moon orbits the Earth) prior to awakening. The evolutionary view is that we incarnate on Earth and renew the deep basin of unconscious patterns (Moon) as part of our soul journey.

There is further evidence of the Moon being associated with the earlier stages of development. Scientists speculate that the Moon was formed by the collision of another celestial body with the Earth. As the Moon gradually formed and became a satellite to Earth, the gravitational pull on the tides enabled life to begin. The tides create the necessary movement to stir the processes for life to be catalyzed in the water.

The Moon is moving away from the Earth at around 3cm per year. It used to be much closer to us, like a great mother in the sky. It was very strong, pulling the tides in a far more dramatic way. This proximity stirred life to grow, but there was also greater instability. This is consistent with early childhood, which is often marked by a similar heightened urgency and volatility. The Moon's gradual distancing from the Earth is analogous to life being less controlled by separation consciousness. As the Moon continues to move away from Earth, it will eventually be too small to totally obscure the Sun—there will no longer be solar eclipses. This might signal that farther down the road in our collective evolution, the egoic takeover may not be as relevant. However, at this time, the Moon is the perfect size to obscure the Sun, and the egoic takeover is the defining issue of our era.

The Moon has billions of gallons of frozen water at its polar regions. This iciness parallels the constricting egoic attachments that can freeze our growth. The Sun's heat is the perfect means of unfreezing water.

Attachment Patterns

Traditionally associated with the infant/mother relationship, the Moon does point to our initial foundation of nurturing. However, from the evolutionary view, we choose a specific familial environment which reflects our soul's history with such issues. This is how we become aware of the themes and resonances that have been buried in the unconscious. As the Moon extends back to the roots of personal evolution, it is far broader than just the mother.

The Moon is receptive; we *absorb* life. It's the repository of all the anger, joy, fear, love, or sadness we have accumulated. We are what we energetically "eat." And just as with food, we need to digest and then excrete the waste products of energy we take in. <u>Whatever we do not process and release becomes hardened and attached to us as our Moon</u>.

When we eat a pleasant, nutritious meal, we usually digest and release it without any trouble. It's finished, and we tend not to retain a memory of it. Do you remember what you had for dinner last Tuesday evening? Let's extend this idea out. Do you remember any of the events of October 15, 2005? For some, they might—perhaps it was a wedding day, a personal catastrophe, or anything else with an emotional charge. Most of us can't recall anything at all from this day. How about September 11, 2001? On that day, there were a lot of troubling emotions, and the ego vividly clings to the experience because *it has a need for a better story* than what occurred. This clinging keeps us tethered to the past, instead of being open to the limitless possibilities in the present.

The Moon holds on to experiences because deep down it wants love. When we don't feel loved, the egoic survival function is activated to see to this need. We stay preoccupied with this need and essentially at war with life until it is satisfied—all of this is driven by the unhealed Moon operating unconsciously. In order to heal the past, we must become conscious of it. We can review all the experiences that are unresolved and provide ourselves with the love we didn't get at the time. This is just as effective as if we initially got the love because *everything happens in the present*—the Sun is an enormous gift in this way. It connects us to everything throughout the entire universe. However, light can appear threatening to those used to the dark.

Part of the healing process is to touch in with the unresolved emotions that have become hardened inside us. Eckhart Tolle says, "So you need to become fully conscious of your emotions and be able to feel them before you can feel that which lies beyond them."[xii] The energy of awareness (Sun) that we bring in frees these attachments and allows them to move through us. <u>Energy in motion is emotion. This is how the Sun partners with the Moon for our growth.</u>

<u>Being willing to feel</u> <u>our repressed emotion dissolves the solidified lunar material</u>. Most people feel lighter and relieved after a good cry or a safe venting of anger. We could also move energy through breath work, exercise, or any means to free what's been pent up. By taking this initiative, our greatest pains become the foundation of our power. Completing the past opens us to the dynamism and possibilities of the present. We move along the spectrum from darkness to light and become better able to serve as catalysts for our own and others' spiritual growth. Though the Moon begins as a regressive pull to the past, with successful resolution, it transitions to being a *powerful vessel of light*. The conscious Moon is the "legs," or vessel, to carry out evolution—empowered, clear, and effective. It becomes a healed heart center, connected with Spirit, and radiating love.

Exposing painful feeling may also trigger the familiar self-protective measures once again. This is why some people spend so much time "being with their feelings" without ever moving beyond them. They are digging deeper into them, renewing and strengthening the ego's stories about them. The alternative is to meet the past from the soul (Sun), which is in the present. The hardened energy becomes liberated when we cease to identify with it. By accessing the stored material in the unconscious, we can either renew or break through our patterns—it's contingent on whether we are steering from the personality/ego, or from the soul.

Since the well of our accumulated experience is mostly unconscious, many people pretend that they are "fine." They choose to ignore issues with the justification that the passing of time, on its own, heals all wounds. Western society tends not to promote introspection and sees emotional work as needed only by those suffering some form of pathology. Spending time with the internal landscape is often seen as "weird" or cause for concern. The mainstream culture is emotionally immature, so much so that even discussing emotion tends to make people uncomfortable.

If we don't take it upon ourselves to voluntarily explore our past, life will inevitably bring it to us. Our unconscious material radiates outward into life and returns to us as the many faces of our teachers. All of it comes to our awareness for us to learn from, love, and integrate. In the absence of this perspective, evaluations of what's "good" and "bad" continue on and on, deepening our defense mechanisms. Tolle says,

> If you don't bring the light of your consciousness into the pain, you will be forced to relive it again and again. The pain-body may seem to you like a dangerous monster that you cannot bear to look at, but I assure you that it is an insubstantial phantom that cannot prevail against the power of your presence.[xiii]

The idea is to notice how a situation triggers painful emotions and then follow the thread. We are often too caught up in the immediate drama to understand that the feelings aroused reflect more complexity than just what's unfolding in the current moment. This is especially true when the intensity of an emotional response is out of proportion to the situation.

With the development of consciousness, we may learn to see trying events as opportunities for spiritual growth. For example, a pet may be killed by a car. This is no doubt tragic, and it's appropriate to grieve. The failure to do so will only cause further pain. What if *prior* tragic events were never fully

74

grieved? Then, we draw grief-laden events to us until we're through grieving the initial one(s).

Most astrology does not come from an evolutionary view, and therefore undercuts the reach of the Moon and simplifies it. Instead of tracing the Moon back to prior experiences, all of the unfinished work and regressive tendencies become assigned to the mother. This reflects the incredible emotional burden Patriarchy has given to women. An alternative is to consider that our egoic attachments have much to do with our spiritual evolution—a very long history of development.

The Development of Ego

From the standpoint of soul evolution, the Moon signifies how the ego (in whatever evolutionary state) learned to cope and navigate in this uncertain and threatening world. The Moon is a window into our historical process of adaptation.

Astrology presents 12 distinct archetypes—the signs of the Zodiac—each of which has many facets. The Moon approaches these archetypes in terms of how it might devise a strategy for survival. Since the ego is utterly preoccupied with itself, I've given the Moon a first-person voice in each of the signs below. The survival strategy is articulated first and then the underlying fear.

Aries: "I need to get ahead to survive. If I'm #1, then that clinches the deal. If necessary, I can be demanding and aggressive. I may not show you this, but inside I have a fiery will. If it looks like I may fail, I will become a force to be reckoned with. When the world thwarts my efforts, I get frustrated and angry— that way people will know I mean business. I approach others competitively since they may be a threat."

"Oh my God, I may not be as strong as I think. Maybe I'm not fooling anyone with this stance. I might get pushed around. What happens if I lose or die? It's probably best not to think of this."

Taurus: "I will fortify myself to ensure my survival. Through attaining money, possessions, or material comfort, I feel secure. I need the assurance of the earth to feel safe. When it looks like things are threatening, I'll make sure I have my share. My mood becomes determined (stubborn, fixed), and I refuse to compromise. This is how I survive. Others may not be trustworthy; I know I can rely on myself."

"I'll never have enough! It's pointless. I'm worthless. Everything will eventually crash down around me, so defeat is inevitable. I may as well be comfortable while I can."

Gemini: "I categorize everything in dualistic ways so that I know what is good for me and what isn't. Being clever allows me to get ahead of others. The world prizes intelligence, so I'll excel there. When threatened, I'll rely on my mind—emotions just get in the way."

"What if I'm not as smart as I think I am? Maybe I'm naïve, a child. If they ever find out, I'm toast. I'd better get my story ready to defend myself."

Cancer: "I survive by being protected. If there's danger out there, I'll stay inside where it's safe. The best offense is having a strong defense. I rely on family, and the "tried and true" ways of home life. Fostering loving bonds ensures my survival. It's important to pass my genes down, and care for my offspring. I survive by bonding with others."

"If people actually knew how weak, vulnerable, and needy I am, I would be squashed! Sometimes I feel like a bottomless pit that can never be filled. There's no way I'm going to let people in on this."

Leo: "Approval and popularity helps me succeed in life. If I am likable, my odds of survival go up. I'll develop a talent or colorful personality so that rewards will be bestowed on me and people will make sure I'm taken care of. If the world threatens me, I will roar and show you how mighty I am! If I'm larger than life, I am in control."

KATHY
BILL

"Holy crap, there's a chance they're going to see through my charade. I may not be so good at being likeable. They're going to see my insecurity and hurt me. Ok, stay positive. It's all going to be ok...right?"

<u>Virgo:</u> "I will take on challenges and get really good at something. My skills will be in demand, which ensures my survival. Others probably don't have the perseverance that I do. My skepticism of others, and the world, allows me to spot danger. When I prepare for the worst, I will be ready for anything. I will rely on earthy, practical know-how to win the support of others."

LENDA

"I'm a worthless piece of crap. I don't deserve anything and should just stop complaining. I'm not nearly as good as I pretend to be. Perhaps I should get back to work and try harder. Life sucks, so I better try to make the best of it."

<u>Libra:</u> "I will defer to others, allow them to make decisions, and support them. In this way, I will make many friends and allies who are critical for survival. When I'm tactful, charming, and socially adept, who can resist me? Keeping emotions light and superficial prevents problems from escalating."

JON

"At any point they might turn on me and eat me for dinner. I should put on the best looking smile imaginable. Though I will probably be rejected, the best thing to do is not to make it worse. Sometimes I have no idea who I am."

<u>Scorpio:</u> "I will become irresistible to you—that's how I'll survive! My depth and magnetism will enchant and hypnotize you. You'll let me into your heart, and I'll have access to all that you have. My undercurrents of intensity will subtly threaten you so you will submit to my needs. I understand how vulnerable

we all are, so I will use this to my advantage. Everyone manipulates to get what they need, so why shouldn't I?"

"I'm so hurt and pissed off. Why don't people *really* love me? Why do I get blamed for everything bad that happens? I'm steaming on the inside. Maybe I am unlovable. Maybe I deserve all of this. I'm miserable, and maybe I can get you to join me in this."

Sagittarius: "Everything I do will be justified. My beliefs give me permission to do as I please. I have an answer for everything and wisdom beyond my years. The world needs me! Let me convince you of my position. If everyone would listen, we'll be just fine. Please don't waste my time with triviality or sentiment."

"Oh no, there's a chance I'm wrong. Ok, even so, I'll never admit it. I'm not a hypocrite, am I? Ok, maybe I am, but I will keep it to myself. It's probably best to lead with more bluster to hide this."

Capricorn: "With my hand on the helm, I am in charge of my fate. I will garner your respect. That's my strategy for survival. I am willing to do whatever it takes to be the tough one. My endurance will eventually tire you out, making me the victor. Who can defeat me when it's my empire? If you feel intimidated by me, whose fault is that? I'm entitled to what I've built. Emotion is for children."

"Who am I kidding? Inside I'm a child, riddled with self-doubt. I may never succeed. They may not listen to me. It all may be for naught. I'd better keep this to myself, under lock and key, forever. "

Aquarius: "I survive by being invisible in my anonymity. Why draw attention in this dangerous world? I will pretend that I just don't care, though underneath I will develop my uniqueness. Someday soon it'll be my day. I'll be more advanced than anyone; therefore I'll be more than able to care for myself. Think I'm cold and robotic? It's just that I'm different from all of you. "

"I don't accept the things that have happened to me. I refuse to get in touch with it. There's a stranger inside of me, and I have no idea what to do about it. Maybe there's something very wrong with me."

Pisces: "If I love you, you won't hurt me, would you? I will surrender my needs, all my personal concerns in order to maintain tranquility. I am willing to be a martyr, just please let me be. I will not be a problem to anyone, that's how I'll survive. If I get you to feel your emotions, you will develop empathy and compassion, and we'll all get along just fine."

"I'm lonely, disappointed, disillusioned with life. I really don't know what I truly need. Life is confusing sometimes. I need a vacation. I have no idea what to do."

The 12 archetypes also extend beyond the personal. We can look at each in the darkness of unconsciousness and see that they all have the seeds of potential destruction.

Aries: With war and violence, there is mutual assured destruction. Today, it just takes the pressing of a button. The ego perceives the external world as a threat. Instead of seeing oneself in the sacred mirror of the other, the ego tries to smash the mirror. It's like the "Westerns" when both guys in a shootout fall to the ground — we're all dead. Aries the Ram doesn't know how to apply the brakes and eventually hits a wall.

Taurus: One possibility is that we become so embroiled in the game of security that the planet no longer can support us. The bull eats all the grass in the pasture. Selfishness motivates many crimes — most any scheme or venture has some kind of commodity involved. With Taurus, the process of destruction plays out over time. Eventually, our underlying self-doubts

79

become a massive wall of separation with the world. Disconnected from others, we implode.

Gemini: The lens of duality can shred all useful evaluation, leaving a naïve willingness to try *anything*. Why is one way better than another? The "anything goes" mentality eventually runs the ship aground. The Twins are like endless talking heads, pundits eternally locked in spin mode. Nothing productive or visionary comes from this pointless chatter. If we're not prepared for the winter, we die.

Cancer: The claws and hard shell of the Crab are the giveaway. Cancer can overdo self-defense. "I'll twist your arms off if you get anywhere near me." In the grips of survival, there is no collaboration or outreach of any kind. The ego turns within and develops a bitter story of a world gone bad. The protective shell is the only safe place. Isolation leads to not only a lack of empathy for others, but continual suspicion. This blindness in the self gradually creates a disconnected and mistrustful world plagued by debilitating problems. Sound familiar?

Leo: Like the other fire signs, the Lion's path toward annihilation involves dominance. The ego becomes enormous and completely obscures anything else in life. Similar to Cancer, there is blindness in the self, though here its projected outward. This narcissism roars over any collective endeavor necessary to ensure mutual benefit and progress. We perish in a fire of grandiosity. The Lion is not always so noble.

Virgo: The Virgin has virtue but, like all the other signs, also a fatal flaw. Here, the ego develops forms of neurosis or impairments that become convenient excuses for not growing. The ego dream is filled with limitation and pessimism, which leads to impotence and failure. Virgo may also enable the unconscious agendas of its superiors like the "sheep" who go along with a dictator. Virgo may do the dirty work for the "devil," done out of obligation and "acting responsibly."

Libra: The travesty here also involves relationships. Instead of hierarchical directives as seen with Virgo, Libra is more co-creative with destruction. We fall in love with the other and lose the ability to challenge each other or address conflict. Everything is "fine" at all times, and problems are never solved. As the ship goes down, there's a plastic smile on everyone's face. Superficiality and disempowerment do not secure our survival, no matter how lovely the presentation.

Scorpio: The ego is very uncomfortable with the deep immersion in the shadow. This arena holds everything we want to avoid. Remaining hidden or secretive keeps us living unconsciously, which eventually leads to annihilation. We may go to great lengths to make sure that particular material never becomes revealed. Then, we enter underhanded patterns including lying and cheating. The Scorpion has a deadly stinger that it is more than willing to use when threatened. The failure to bring light into the shadow will eventually create eternal darkness on this planet.

Sagittarius: The Archer fires arrows of verbal or physical attack. Weaponry flies through the air: nuclear missiles, planes flying into skyscrapers. Ends-justifying-the-means thinking has been responsible for widespread death and suffering to legions of people. Our planet has a long history of religious or philosophical wars—the Sagittarian shadow has been deadly.

Capricorn: The Goat is interested in the preservation of tradition and compliance with the status quo. The failure to modernize prevents a more evolved consciousness from inhabiting society. If we don't reform transportation systems, revise textbooks, or encourage innovation, we will be unable to address the natural growth and changes that inevitably unfold. When taken too far, the limits that Capricorn prizes lead to excessive control and contraction. The end result is extinction.

Aquarius: Ideally the Water Bearer brings us progress and reform. Its futuristic focus dazzles us with thrilling technological advances. This sign's dark side brings us annihilation through artificiality, the obliteration of humanness. Think of the dystopian society featured in *Brave New World* or similar works—worlds devoid of necessary intimacy. If life becomes completely dependent upon various gadgets, devices, and robots, the toll on our innately vulnerable humanity may be catastrophic.

Pisces: In order for consciousness to evolve, separate selves must do their individual work. We must be strong and willing to play a decisive role. The shadow of Pisces is the obliteration of this individualistic necessity. When we are not potent, we are prone to being swept away by external events. Even more insidious, the dark Pisces may not even care, "Have another drink, and let's watch the world crumble." Ineffectuality, ego-obliteration, and endless "poor me" complaining is not going to enlighten the world.

Every one of us has the Moon in one of these signs. We all could potentially contribute to our collective demise without cultivating awareness. It's important to note that the Moon sign is only one factor to explore. Every astrological factor related to the Moon (planets and houses involved) is part of its "profile." The full exploration of this topic is beyond the scope of this book. However, *The Astrology of Awakening 2: Chart Application*, my next book, will address it.

There is some irony in the ego's desperation to survive, the extension of which would be immortality. As we find in fiction and folklore about immortal characters, what initially appears as freedom eventually turns into a burden. After years of invincibility, they tend to reach exhaustion and pray for release.

It appears that the evolutionary task is to learn how to survive, then to *willingly* die. As the stories teach us, we really do not want to live forever! Those unwilling to let go become imprisoned in the manifest world, incarnating endlessly, continually repeating patterns.

The great irony may be that we *are* actually immortal! The soul is everlasting energy, continually connected with Spirit. Instead of egoic immortality, perhaps what we really seek is to awaken into soul realization.

Eternal Energy of Now

The Sun radiates its light and heat unconditionally, for everyone and everything to use. It sustains the planets through its enormous gravitational force and occupies the central position in our *Solar System* which is aptly named for it. The Sun is far larger than everything else in the Solar System combined. Energy is necessary for everything, and the Sun is our enormous source of it. We can't look directly at the Sun for more than a couple seconds—its blinding illumination demands that we show deference. The Sun puts out more energy in one second than the entire history of human civilization has collectively used. Do these characteristics sound like the ego or "the masculine," or do they rather sound more like Spirit?

The astrology we've inherited comes from a time when the Sun and Moon *appeared* to be equal partners. We weren't aware of the Sun's centrality in our system, that 64 million Moons fit into the Sun, or that the Moon reflects the light of the Sun. We must now have the courage to ask whether the conventional view on the Sun is consistent with our present understandings of reality. Albert Einstein says, "Unthinking respect for authority is the greatest enemy of truth." For those willing to consider the notion that the Sun pertains to spiritual realization, there is very rich support.

The Sun's two primary characteristics are light and heat, both of which have spiritual implications. Thich Nhat Hanh said, "Each thought, each action in the sunlight of awareness becomes sacred." The Sun's light is associated with awareness, which illuminates the dark and provides clarity. Understanding is achieved when something "comes to light," and the proverbial light bulb above the head glows brighter. Cultivating awareness brings us *awakening* or *enlightenment*—both of which have solar connotations.

Many spiritual teachers discuss awareness as a constant, the context or field of existence in which all content occurs. This context correlates with the pervasiveness of solar energy in this system, while the Moon is tied to the content. The Sun's light, like awareness, maintains a constant speed of about 186,000 miles per second. Light connects us with the unity that exists around us.

Sri Ramana Maharshi said, "The brain functions by light borrowed from another source." It might appear to us in separation consciousness that the awareness we experience is our own, but the spiritual view is vastly different. Maharshi continues, "the light within, that is, the Self, gives light to the ego, the intellect, the memory and the mind without itself being subject to processes of growth and decay."[xiv] (Note again that his term for "Spirit" is "the Self.")

Heat equates to *presence* and *vitality*, the sustaining energy of life. Science describes the law of the *conservation of energy*. The totality of energy in the universe is neither growing nor diminishing. This is similar to the "eternal flame," a concept used throughout religions and spiritual paths, as well as found in countless poems and works of art. Heat allows life to thrive and sustains it.

Dane Rudhyar writes, "If the Moon represents the 'past,' the Sun stands for the 'present'—simply because it provides the power to exist as a living organism here and now."[xv] When we become absorbed in the present moment there is often a quality of freedom and lightness. Being present may sound simple, but we tend to be chronically distracted by discursive thoughts, feelings, or sensations. Many forms of spiritual practice are designed to maintain awareness of the present, which is often called "mindfulness."

Most people do not realize how lost they are in the subjectivity of the separate self because it's so familiar. By practicing being present, we may learn to shift our awareness to being less self-consumed. However, the undertow of the unconscious can be quite strong, largely due to the urgency of unresolved needs. Eckhart Tolle provides some perspective on this:

> For most people, presence is experienced either never at all or only accidentally and briefly on rare occasions without being recognized for what it is. Most humans alternate not between consciousness and unconsciousness but only between different levels of unconsciousness.[xvi]

Cultivating mindfulness is a great frontier for those interested in spiritual growth. It allows us to develop the ability to see through the transpersonal lens and become more aware of how our souls are eternally connected to Oneness. From the relative view, the Sun is seen as yang. It radiates energy out, and is associated with the fire sign Leo. It's seen through the dualistic lens of Mercury.

The transpersonal lens (Uranus) changes the perspective by adding its characteristic paradox and complexity. In order to see the Sun in terms of unity consciousness, we understand that all dualities function *within* its scope. The iconic yin/yang symbol captures how this is possible.

On this symbol, the Sun correlates to the outer circle. Similar to the astrological symbol for the Sun (below), the circle is a symbol of wholeness. And within the astrological symbol for the Sun there is a dot, which is indicative of an individual within the broader wholeness—simultaneously *in* the circle, and *as* the circle.

From the position of separation consciousness in the circle, it's very difficult to perceive and experience the entire circle, for that is what we are awakening into. Imagine the dot (in the Sun symbol) moved above to the yin/yang symbol. The dot is *within* the dance of duality. This reflects our *immediate* experience in the relative world. Hence, we make the pairing that the Sun is playing the yang role to the Moon's yin. Ralph

Waldo Emerson said, "A field cannot be seen from within the field." From the position of separation consciousness, we cannot fathom the breadth of the Sun because we perceive it as an object, not as the field itself.

Our Soul Connection with Spirit

From the unified source of energetic Oneness, individual souls venture into physical form to learn lessons and live out a particular life mission. As mentioned earlier, Spirit is akin to an enormous blaze of fire, and each soul is like a candle. In the realm of separation, we are learning to consciously reconnect our candles with the broader, singular flame of Spirit.

By cultivating awareness (light) and presence (heat), we connect with Spirit's creative inspiration. Methods of cultivation include meditation, yoga, vision quests, and many others. Spirit is everywhere and everything, so we may connect with it through a wide range of activities. With the right attunement, anything can be meaningful for our soul growth.

We can strengthen and intensify our luminosity. Imagine the brightness of a light bulb increasing in wattage: from 10 to 100 to 1000, all the way to 10,000 and beyond. We all have access to soul realization by turning up our wattage, which is accomplished by *removing* our egoic barriers that compromise our radiance. When we get ourselves out of the way, we allow Spirit to flow through our energy. Releasing the egoic takeover greatly enhances our awakening.

The transpersonal view of the Sun is that it's paradoxically and simultaneously you and not you. It's the interface of the soul (Sun) with body (Moon); and also soul (individual flame) connects with the larger flame (Oneness of energy). Therefore, we can look at the Sun as being relevant to the

87

personal (each of us has a soul), while we can more broadly see it as representing Spirit too.

Throughout history the egoic takeover has been the standard way of being human on this planet. Now, we are collectively realizing that our energy actually belongs to our energetic source (Spirit). However, we do get to borrow it for 80+ years or so. Most of us are somewhere in the middle of the awakening process—we identify as ego, yet we intuit that there is life beyond it. We are learning to trust that when we shift our identification solely from ego, we'll remain intact. Tolle says, "When consciousness frees itself from its identification with physical and mental forms, it becomes what we may call pure or enlightened consciousness, or presence."[xvii] This movement must be made consciously, perhaps an act of faith.

If we do surrender to Spirit, there may be no end to the potential illumination of our Suns. The Sun is a star that connects to other stars in the universe. When we perform our personal work of awakening (in this Solar System), perhaps that grants us access to connect elsewhere. In this endless universe, there is likely to be many frontiers to explore. This is exciting to contemplate, but such notions lie beyond the immediate work. Enrollment in this particular "school" is evidence that we must focus here and develop soul realization.

As we spiritually mature, how do we manage the ego? And here's the great spiritual question: how do we *not* identify as a separate self? We all have a name, don't we? Ultimately, we work to loosen our attachments, resolve karma and come from love and compassion. Perhaps we can learn to see life as a great exchange of energy and be "in this world, but not of it." We can accept the role of bridging worlds and simultaneously identify with both. We can hold the knowledge that our physicality is temporary, while our energy is eternal. Ramana Maharshi says, "The "I" casts off the illusion of "I" and yet remains as "I." Such

88

is the paradox of Self-realization." Jed McKenna describes it another way:

> Yes, I have an ego and it looks similar to the one I dropped, as you say, to achieve nirvana. But then I came back all enlightened and everything, and I needed something to wear. I look around, and there's my discarded ego lying in a pile on the floor so I slip into it, and here I am.[xviii]

Pathways to Soul Realization

Just as we saw 12 pathways that the ego may take in its strategies to survive and gain satisfaction, there are 12 different pathways toward awakening into soul realization. However, keep in mind that the situation becomes far more complex when reviewing the entire profile of any person's Sun (sign, aspects to other planets, and house placement). Ultimately, the sign is but one piece of information. Through integrating other chart factors, more than one pathway is relevant for any particular person. Again, a thorough explanation, as well as chart application, is planned for my follow-up volume. For now, here is an introduction to the 12 signs as the basic pathways for soul realization. Notice how different it is to hold them in this framework as opposed to the way popular astrology focuses on the level of egoic personality.

At the soul level, astrology conveys *evolutionary lessons.* At the personality level, fire is assertive and daring, while at the spiritual level it offers the opportunity to develop courage and trust in our free will. These two levels are often conflated in astrological literature. The way to make a clear distinction is to consider psychological style vs. the spiritual lessons being addressed.

89

♈︎   Aries is learning to *align personal will and behavior with soul intent*. Aries is developing the courage to forge ahead in a focused and effective way, which requires the willingness to assert what the soul knows as its truth. Prior soul experiences may have lacked this warrior spirit, and now growth is furthered by displays of strength and boldness.

♉︎   The self-orientation of Taurus concerns *the attainment of self-worth and comfort in the body*. A solid connection to inner resources brings endurance and reliability. This can be expressed outwardly through a hands-on resourcefulness or tangible expressions of beauty. Ideally, prior soul experiences are smoothed out and Taurus learns to relax in the Self.

♊︎   Gemini is learning to *develop the intellect and communicate knowledge*. The awakening process has to do with seizing possibilities and being fascinated by life. First we address our own curriculum, which opens the possibility of teaching others. Prior soul experiences may not have been as open and free. The task is to become enthralled by learning and to use one's foundation as a springboard for further expansion.

♋︎   Cancer's lesson concerns the *development of self-love and* greater *sensitivity about our basic humanness*. Through introspection or investing in family, Cancer learns about bonding. Having learned well, Cancer becomes adept at assisting others out of their unconsciousness. There may be a lack of self-acceptance in the spiritual history, so Cancer awakens through self love. What's been previously absorbed can now be channeled into great wisdom and a heartfelt contribution.

♌︎   Leo is learning to *be radiantly present, noble, and self-aware*. This sign has the responsibility of displaying the creativity and jubilance of Spirit. Those awakening to this promise serve as vessels without egoic distortion. Those working on developing Leo may have soul histories where they didn't or couldn't express themselves. Now they have the necessary charisma and attractiveness to make others take notice. They can give animation to the human drama, which is largely informed by their own soul foundation.

Virgo seeks to *master a craft that assists with personal development*, which often requires focus and dedication. Virgo is smoothing out rough edges to reach greater completion and then be able to offer assistance to others. Whatever trying events that compose the soul foundation are perfect teachings for how Virgo now effectively serves the world.

Libra involves the lesson of *forming equitable relationships based on civility and mutual benefit*. The intention for awakening is to become social and engaged with the world. Prior soul experiences may have included injustice in some way. Through resolution, connection with the world is now available in ways that foster togetherness and peace.

Scorpio is learning to *intimately bond and emotionally share with others* in the name of developing fierceness and courage. The Scorpion is willing to be impacted by the world, as well as serve as a catalyst that impacts others. There may be spiritual histories where this level of depth was lacking or fraught with problems. Awakening is now involves revealing the darkness within and cultivating its power. Successful management of intimacy brings soul wisdom which may be applied to realms of our collective evolution.

Sagittarius is learning to *move with purpose from a position of spiritual understanding*. This sign aims to develop a mission which serves as a compass for the whole life. The lesson here is to "go for it" and spur others to similarly live life fully. Prior soul experiences may have lacked conviction or purpose. By loving and accepting the past, its lessons serve as the fertilizer for spirited action.

Capricorn is learning the *achievement of stature* and how to help influence evolution from positions of authority. The Goat is learning to trust its ability to manage important matters. Whatever contents are in the soul are ready to serve the collective in some way. Capricorn is figuring out how to awaken into prominence while preserving integrity and discernment.

The main lesson for Aquarius is to *bring us into the future through innovation.* By learning to breakthrough personal challenges and awaken to brilliance, Aquarius helps humanity tap Spirit's intelligence and connect the global world family. Healing personal issues and reaching non-attachment allows great skill in bringing groups or communities together in progressive ways.

Pisces is *developing love and compassion for everyone and everything.* All experiences can be held in gratitude, and forgiveness can be mastered as an art form. Pisces can assist others in cultivating a more loving vision for themselves and the world. Awakening here serves as an inspiration for us to feel our inherent interconnectivity.

Some people may be upset with the material I'm presenting here. It may seem as if the Moon is being labeled as "bad," while the Sun is promoted as being "good." As mentioned earlier, these value judgments belong to the ego. Instead, we can look at this situation from the position of the soul. All of us are awakening out of the unconsciousness that has typified our spiritual histories. Whatever is unresolved is carried along. We might view this unresolved material negatively, but that does not make the Moon "bad." Ultimately, we awaken and use the Moon as a vehicle for evolution. It becomes filled with light and presence, able to consciously bring Spirit into manifestation.

92

Chapter 4
The Moon & Sun: A Sacred Marriage

Historically, within the western tradition of astrology, the Sun and Moon are seen as the masculine (yang) and feminine (yin). They come together, as in a marriage, to create wholeness. From the transpersonal perspective, however, we see the Sun as our connection with Spirit, and the Moon as the representation of separation consciousness and our human physical form. The integration of Sun and Moon at this level constitutes a higher level of union—a sacred marriage. Judeo-Christian religions have a similar idea of "The Covenant," an agreement between God (or Spirit) and people to be in a divine partnership.

Unrequited Love

Like most other unions, this marriage has had a stormy history. The enormous disparity between the partners has been the main cause of their tension. Spirit is everything, and though we're precious, we're basically insignificant. Spirit is responsible for our existence, but it doesn't *need* us for its. Spirit has made love a part of existence, but we have not always been able to feel or express it. Many of us do not return love to the universe.

Imagine walking around in darkness. We might stumble around and think, "What's going on? What's that sound? Is there danger?" We are uneasy, anxious, and in need of help. It'd be nice to find a comfortable, safe place, perhaps something to

93

eat. In this moment of blindness, we might believe that the world is unfair. Since we'd like it to be fair, we set about to make it so. And this begins the venture of egoic survival and self-serving pursuits.

"I'm in charge of my life! I have every right to have life, liberty, and to pursue happiness." In the throes of establishing autonomy in an uncertain world, it's easy to disengage from our Source. We seek expansion and success—that'll be *good*. This tendency may go all the way to feeling invincible, entitled, and grandiose, striving for supremacy (God) in life.

This initial self-preoccupation becomes the perspective from which we understand the world and our place in it. We, of course, are at the all-important center of it. This view is reminiscent of the days before Copernicus when people believed that the Earth was central, with the Sun—and everything else in the sky—revolving around it. As our most immediate orientation informs us that there are two genders, the Sun and Moon become masculine and feminine.

The recent chapters of this marriage include our realization that the Earth is not the center of the universe, an external reflection of our collective readiness to move away from self-preoccupation. It also turns out that the Sun and Moon are not even close to being equal in size. Likewise, Spirit is getting "bigger," and our egoic selves are getting "smaller," as widespread interest in spirituality is flourishing.

Time moves on, and we learn more "bad news" about our position of supposed central importance. Quantum science has revealed that there's actually no solidity to us at all—we're made up of vibrating energy. Even "worse," spiritual teachers tell us that we live in the projection of our own imaginations. It's difficult for many to accept these notions—most would rather focus on the "real" world. This tends to be more comfortable, but it also has us renewing elaborate distortions.

94

Meanwhile, Patriarchy is tightening its grip on power. The industrialization and corporatization of the planet exaggerates the power differential between the sexes. Instead of us loosening control and accepting our "smaller" role, the egoic takeover is furthered by those in power. Men continue to dominate. Even now in the 21st Century, women work roughly 2/3 of the world's working hours, receive about 10% of the world's income, and own less than 1% of the world's property.

The more we have claimed the Sun as "the masculine," the more that Patriarchal rule has increased and perpetuated oppression. By accepting the position that the entire *human condition* is rooted in the Moon, we give the Sun back to Spirit. We make no pretentions that this is an equal relationship or that it represents an equitable relationship between the sexes. Instead, we can finally honor all other humans as we stand together on equal footing as vulnerable, emotional, imperfect beings. We can *receive* and accept the love that Sprit created and finally participate in this epic love story by loving the universe in return. We can fully love ourselves and let go of the egoic need to get bigger to control and dominate. We can partner with Sprit, awaken into its majesty, and consciously connect the divine with the mundane. The only way we can bridge worlds is if we retract the projection that the Sun is the ego or the masculine. This is our great moment to shine.

Bridging Worlds

In my book, *Between Past & Presence: A Spiritual View of the Moon and Sun*, I liken the Moon to the underground roots of a plant, and the Sun to the flower. We expand and awaken into our true self by integrating awareness into the unconscious. Just like flowers grow through the process of photosynthesis, we too are energized and sustained by the Sun that we grow towards.

We're also growing *in* to deeper levels of self love. The eventual goal might be to finish our work at this "school" and return to Spirit. However, as long as we are here, we mustn't evade the responsibilities of being incarnate. We grow *in* by being with the past and solidifying our roots to the Earth that supports us physically. We ground spiritual creativity into reality and bridge worlds.

There is an evolutionary movement from resolving the past (Moon) to the realization of the present (Sun), but this doesn't mean that the Sun is better or more important than the Moon. We are growing from the *unconsciousness in the Moon* to awakening and honoring the sacred marriage *by fully being in both worlds*. Though the Moon involves our lunacy or madness, the regressive parts of our nature, it's also full of beauty. Instead of any negative judgments about the Moon, it's more gentle and accurate to see it as a *less conscious* version of ourself. There is nothing wrong with being four years old, and our inner child remains with us too. The point is to move beyond the limitations of being like a four-year-old. We assist the Moon in *maturing*, so Moon seeds can sprout into Sun flowers. Plants continually need water—the Moon (seed) requires love (water), not abandonment.

The sacred marriage, this bridging of worlds, illuminates one of the greatest mysteries of all—the nature of consciousness. The issue is that most psychologists and "experts" only use the frame of reference of separation consciousness. We can understand consciousness as the integration of spiritual awareness and presence (Sun) with the personal well of the unconscious (Moon). Our consciousness is partly unified Spirit and partly the human separate self—a mixture of the transpersonal and the personal. St. Francis of Assisi said, "What you are looking for is what is looking." Our awareness is actually Spirit moving through our personal system. All we have to do is abide in this energy, and we are home. However, the egoic takeover has

96

defined the dominant paradigm in academia, science, mainstream society, and astrology. Now is the amazing time in history when we are awakening from its limitations.

Transmuting the Past ✳

The absorptive Moon holds on to the experiences that have made the greatest impact. We tend to hold on to what we have issue with, and because this material is often uncomfortable, it goes unconscious. As we are *energetic processing systems*, the very emotions which trouble us may potentially transform into the buried treasure that enhances us. As we'll explore, this is the gift of addressing our spiritual work.

We can release the contractive qualities of the Moon and expand. The Moon is like a gemstone with soot on it. The laser quality of the Sun can blast this soot away with its piercing light and heat—perhaps painful initially, but ultimately liberating. After the energy is freed, we are more able to connect with others and life. As we emerge from unconsciousness, we explore new frontiers of potential while illuminating the hidden gifts of the heart.

Along the spectrum from dark to bright, buried emotion can be used proactively in the present when we meet it with awareness and maturity. We see the lessons involved in the experiences, acknowledge our role in their co-creation, and have love for the entire process. Below is a chart showing how this plays out with each of the astrology themes. Part of the sacred marriage is to partner with Spirit in this project of recycling energy. By so doing, our "shit" becomes the fertilizer that helps awaken the world.

Sign	Emotional challenge	Empowered gift
Aries	anger, frustration	direction, assertion
Taurus	stagnation, gluttony	comfort, security
Gemini	disorganization	knowledge, curiosity
Cancer	upset, hurt feelings	heartfelt receptiveness
Leo	egocentricity	warmth, expression
Virgo	shame, guilt	competence, diligence
Libra	co-dependence	interdependence
Scorpio	intense wounding	power, impact
Sagittarius	dogmatism, grandiosity	spiritual direction
Capricorn	coldness, fear	mastery, wisdom
Aquarius	detachment	perspective
Pisces	sadness, grief	compassionate love

We must be willing to really *feel* our emotions, and have the know-how to channel these feelings consciously. This may sound basic, but the reasons why the material has gone unconscious need to be addressed. We have the choice to "clear it out or play it out." The Sun serves as a projector of the unresolved Moon whether we realize it or not. Once projected, we meet the energy in the external world. We're given another chance to choose to deflect it or love it.

When we do allow emotions to be felt, the hardened energy is released and given back to the universe. The internal pause button that kept part of us frozen in time is released as the underlying lesson is able to reach a conclusion. Sadness transmutes to compassion, anger to direction. We have access to unforeseen opportunities. We reap the rewards for doing this often difficult, if not outright painful, internal work. The Sun renews our hope and allows us to externalize who we are for both personal and collective reasons. Keeping unconscious defensive measures in place robs us of a lot of energy.

Emotions & Gender

We arrive closer to wholeness when we bridge polarities. We can stop projecting dualities on to the external world and focus on our inner experience. One of the clearest areas where we can take this step is with how we understand and manage emotion, especially in the realm of gender.

Regardless of chromosomal make-up, everyone has a Moon. When we look through the transpersonal lens, we see that the external world is a reflection of the inner. Therefore, we can't say that the Moon (or any planet) represents any other person than the self. From the evolutionary view, we have been around for eons. <u>The Moon pertains to unprocessed emotional dynamics that the soul wishes to resolve. We incarnate with the ideal situation to bring this up.</u> As we begin as infants in need of love, the mother is a natural projection screen of our emotional landscape.

This projection onto mothers—and more generally onto all women—has created a massive schism between the genders that we are beginning to repair. In general, the PVS conditions and socializes males not to be outwardly emotional, except in traditionally masculine ways (anger, bravado). Without owning and consciously managing the basic emotions of being human, they not only become projected on women but channeled unconsciously in a wide variety of destructive ways (substance abuse, workaholism, aggression, exploitation). As life is a co-creative arrangement, it's also true that women are responsible for coddling and enabling this emotional mismanagement, accepting projections, and, understandably, a fair bit of mishandling of their own emotions as well. All of us are learning how to live in a more awakened way.

The idea that women are emotional and men are tough has not only caused tremendous harm, it prevents us from progressing in our evolution. For us to reach wholeness, men must be emotionally intelligent, and women must access their leadership potential. Every man has the Moon (and Venus) in his chart, and every woman has the Sun (and Mars) in hers. It is possible for astrology and society at large to promote wholeness rather than dualism (Mercury), which keeps us eternally stuck in the Saturnian realm. As we move to integrate with the trans-personal, the relative level remains valid. We can certainly continue to celebrate and enjoy the dance and juicy spark of polarities. We are just opening to more of life.

As evolution progresses and life becomes more complex, neatly defined packages for the human experience become less relevant. When life was simpler, it was easy to classify the Moon as mother. Aside from the biological reality of nurturance, women took the lead in raising children, while fathers generally worked out in the world. Life today is not so black-and-white. Many fathers now equally share child-rearing duties. There are adoptions, sperm and egg donors, step-parents, children raised by relatives, homosexual pairings, and communal parenting arrangements. All of these situations (and more) potentially confuse who in fact is the mother and father (if the Moon and Sun are viewed as the indicators). You can have a woman donate an egg to a surrogate who incubates and delivers a child for a lesbian couple. Who's the mother?

An alternative to the simplification of dualistic designa-tions is to see the Moon from a broader context, that of the emotional unconscious. This foundation is then played out within areas of nurturing, including all caregivers, and the overall conditions of the early home life. The Moon, Cancer, and the 4th House covers 1/12 of life, and this terrain is certainly broader than just one person.

What is *familiar* in the soul history tends to play out in *family*, not only the mother. Nevertheless, it might sound

100

sacrilegious to some to suggest that the Moon is not "the mother," as this idea is so foundational in the astrological tradition. Making this leap, however, allows us to refrain from expecting women to carry the burden of our collective unresolved emotions. We accept responsibility for everything in the ego dream and receive the liberation that ultimately comes from doing so.

By securing a strong and loving foundation, we are able to hold up our end of the sacred marriage with Spirit. Our personal relationships (including marriage) become a reflection of our status in the sacred marriage.

Astronomical Organization

We can also understand the sacred marriage between Sun and Moon within the context of the Solar System and glean more information about their scope. First, a quick review: From our position on Earth, the Moon serves as our satellite illustrating how the past is continually surrounding us and influencing our instinctual behaviors. The Earth and Moon are a unit, suggesting physical incarnation (Earth) linked to unconsciousness (Moon). An astrology chart does not have the Earth indicated because we are on it. Though the Moon appears to be just another planet encircling the chart, the Earth/Moon duo is actually our reference point in the system.

The Sun is in the middle of the system, signifying its importance and centrality in our lives as the sustainer of life. The Earth (incarnation) revolves around the present reality (Sun) and pulls the Moon (past) along. The Sun is far grander than the Moon in scope and power within this system, and we are awakening into its magnificence.

From our perspective on Earth, the Moon is always seen in one of its changing phases. The majority of the time, it is only partially illuminated, suggesting that we have many degrees of unconsciousness. The Moon reflects light, just as the separate self is a reflection of Spirit. Furthermore, the reflection of light portrays the dynamic between the transpersonal and the relative worlds. Eckhart Tolle says,

> Past and future obviously have no reality on their own. Just as the moon has no light of its own, but can only reflect the light of the sun, so are past and future only pale reflections of the light, power, and reality of the eternal present.[xix]

The Earth/Moon unit exists within the orbit of Saturn, which structures time and the dimensions of mundane reality. Saturn (and all the planets) orbit the Sun (Spirit). Therefore, we are positioned within the relative world, though *sustained* by the transpersonal. Our efforts to leave planet Earth to travel through space is analogous to our quest to broaden our awareness away from the relative world.

The Nodes of the Moon   ☊ ☋

The Earth travels around the ecliptic, the revolutionary path around the Sun. The Moon orbits around the Earth and intersects with the ecliptic as it does. The two points of intersection are called the Nodes of the Moon, or the Lunar Nodes. The South Node is the point where the Moon travels from above to below the Earth's ecliptic, and the North Node illustrates the intersection from below to above. We see the theme of reaching down (South), as in exhuming the past, and rising up (North) into new and creative uses. The Nodes indicate where the past (Moon) *intersects* with incarnation (Earth) as we revolve around the present reality (Sun).

102

Since the Moon holds the impact of countless experiences, it would be impossible to resolve its voluminous scope in any one lifetime. The Nodes *of the Moon* tells us what is intersecting from the past to be resolved, which may then in turn also serve as a contribution to the world. If the Moon is like our roots and the Sun like our flowering, the Nodes portray the necessary gardening process. In order for our Sun to awaken, we must not only become conscious of and love ourselves (Moon), but also address the karma (Nodes) we created prior to that integration.

The Lunar Nodes suggest spiritual lessons. From the evolutionary view, we all have lived less consciously than we do now. We've created patterns and habits which keep us entrenched in particular ways of approaching life. Some spiritual teachers inform us that when we behave with awareness, we do not leave a karmic footprint as we are acting as vehicles for Spirit. Ramana Maharshi says, "After realization there is no karma." The Nodes may also illustrate past strengths and successes. However, as we are unfinished in our growth, we can always build upon the work begun in prior lives.

The Moon is pure feeling. Using words or ideas to capture its essence can actually bring us away from it. In contrast, the lessons of the Lunar Nodes are appropriately understood through language and analysis. The Nodes are points, and they point to what we're working on, the nature of the karma we're addressing.

The South Node is suggestive of familiar patterns and habits: skills, attributes, experiences, behaviors that come naturally. Unlike the inward emotional Moon, the South Node relates to how past lives were actually lived. Too much reliance on our habits prevents us from complementing our skill set through opening up to new challenges and experiences. Though many of us navigate the South Node with some measure of skill, very few of us actually know how to live it from the most awakened consciousness. The Nodal axis is a polarity, and reaching greater balance between opposing forces is work for us in the relative world.

The North Node provides complementary lessons and suggested areas of new discovery. When we have some facility with the North Node, we are able to bring in missing elements to the South Node patterns that provide greater wholeness—the sum becomes greater than the parts. As we are teaching what we are learning, the successful synthesis of the Nodes becomes a contribution we may offer the collective. The determining variable to our success is how we manage the awakening process.

If the awakening process gains momentum, attachments and defense mechanisms (Moon) gradually lose their grip and newer ways of operating emerge in the present (Sun). The gifts within the South Node mature and the intentions of the North Node become integrated. The Sun increases in luminosity, serving as the vital center to energize the soul work. If we stay in the darkness of unconsciousness, behavior remains motivated by ancient patterns and struggles. Events of the biographical life will thematically present the lessons depicted by the Nodes. The Sun then serves as a mere projector of the Moon, its more awakened potentials compromised by ego.

The Lunar Cycle

The Sun and Moon are involved in a monthly dance, a continual reminder of the cyclical nature of life. 12 times every year, we witness the full emergence of Luna into dazzling manifestation only to then gradually recede and again go dark. The New Moon illustrates the birth of the separate self from the Oneness of Spirit. In a complete lunar cycle, the Moon ventures out into life before returning back to the Sun—just as individuals enter the world to attain experience before returning to the

104

spiritual source. The amount of awareness (light) and vitality (heat) integrated during the lifetime is consolidated and carried forth into future incarnations, as well as our accumulated attachments and defense mechanisms.

The lunar cycle is often a secondary, and sometimes forgotten, variable in much of astrology discourse and practice due to the conventional undervaluing of a cyclical and evolutionary perspective. In the current astrological climate, the metaphysical is often marginalized in favor of a more practical, predictive, or personality emphasis. The gender-focused paradigm of the Sun and Moon does not translate well into a cyclical framework. How exactly would the masculine give birth to the feminine at the New Moon?

From the transpersonal viewpoint, the lunar phases teach us more of how the sacred marriage between the Sun and Moon takes form. Every part of the cycle has a unique way light is reflected. The waxing half features an upsurge of energy, like Spirit launching us into the world. In this hemicycle, the Moon is in eager pursuit of a goal. The waning half is often quieter, more invested in social or collective themes. In astrology charts, bright Moons tend to be more revealing and emotionally impactful, while darker Moons play their hands closer to the chest.

There are many factors to consider in getting a full understanding of how the position in the Lunar Cycle actually plays out. House and sign position, as well as the planetary aspects, are modifying variables. This discussion will be saved for *The Astrology of Awakening Volume 2: Chart Application*. For those who want more information in the mean time, please see *Between Past & Presence: A Spiritual View of the Moon and Sun*, which offers introductory information on all of the phases.

Solar Eclipses: The Egoic Takeover

The sacred marriage reaches climactic moments during eclipses. These are opportunities for growth if we can look at ourselves with humility and are willing to learn. We can take a leap in cultivating awareness or, alternatively, play out some pattern of unconsciousness in a more dramatic way. Sometimes it's essential to have a stronger wake-up call if we are in a deep slumber.

SOLAR ECLIPSE

For a solar eclipse, the Moon travels between the Earth and the Sun, obscuring the radiance of our source energy. We can see a sliver of light, a corona, around the Moon just like a king wearing a crown. As mentioned earlier, this alignment portrays the egoic takeover, the attempt to be royalty and have life cater to our needs. Unresolved and unconscious needs resurface, and emotion tends to overwhelm our awareness and ability to be present. There tends to be consequences, both immediate and karmic, when the ego is in control.

The Sun is overcome at this time by what is irrational and protective, so a regressive course is often set at these special New Moons. We do not realize what we are creating, similar to the beginning stages of life. We must learn by trial and error. As the lunar cycle moves around, we gradually learn to see what we are doing as more light is shed upon the emotional strategies.

Eclipses always take place near the Nodes of the Moon, indicating that these events deal with karma coming to a climax. It's as if we're getting a celestial progress note about how we're navigating life. The information is relevant at both the personal and collective level.

The ominous reputation that solar eclipses carry reflects how difficult and even painful it is for most of us to grow out of our unconsciousness. Awakening is the central process of spiritual growth, so these semi-annual events are truly markers of crisis and potential breakthrough. When a solar eclipse approaches, we know that particular facets of unconsciousness are ready to play out. We can take inventory on how we've allowed the ego to control matters and take conscious, corrective, action towards the resolution.

Lunar Eclipses: The Spiritual Giveback

Lunar eclipses occur at the Full Moon—awareness (Sun) strikes the Earth and casts a shadow over the separate self (Moon). We see the visual analogy of our fleetingness, how the Sun has the power to make us vanish. For those living in the throes of ego, this is a moment of accountability. After the Moon disappears, it reappears in a fiery red-orange hue. As we are made in the image of Spirit, the Moon temporarily dresses in colors of fire. At the lunar eclipse, we meet our creator inside the shadows.

While the solar eclipse portrays the "egoic takeover," the lunar eclipse can potentially be a "spiritual giveback," which has the possibility of correcting our egoic folly. The disappearance of the Moon symbolizes a potential cleansing and release of egoic tendencies. The reddish hue illustrates the emotional churning involved in removing egoic identification. The Moon is not only at peak emotional fullness, it appears to be exploding. Like a wound that is lanced, it can find release. In the next stage of the eclipse, the Moon disappears again, only to reappear in its fullness in its normal expression. Through this climactic process, we may realize our egoic tendencies and choose to make corrections in our navigation. For the remaining part of the cycle, we're poised to disseminate our newfound awareness in ways that are now more humble and learned.

If the path of growth is not taken, then unconsciousness may be played out climactically. This is when issues "come to a

107

head" or "reach a boiling point." <u>The disappearance of the illuminated Moon is like the complete disappearance of awareness to light our way</u>. The reddish hue becomes suggestive of the personal impact involved in holding on to what would be ideally let go of. The unconscious is distressed about renewing lunacy. With the reappearance of the Full Moon, <u>our unconsciousness is on display like the proverbial Emperor who is not wearing any clothes.</u> It's obvious that regressive tendencies need to be addressed. However, we might go on our way feeling a bit more comfortable as the light diminishes for the rest of the cycle.

<u>Eclipses are the season of high drama in developing consciousness and furthering our soul evolution.</u> The intensity of such times is consistent with how we're managing our lessons. The outdated view is that the gods are mad or taking vengeance. A more conscious view is that we take responsibility for our "madness" and potently partner with our development. Eclipses bring the process into sharp focus.

Chapter 5
The Inner Planets: Personal Orientation

The Sun and Moon form a sacred marriage, a bridging of worlds in facilitation of spiritual evolution. All the other planets function in service to this core. They can either reinforce separateness, or bring us to unity. We'll explore each of them in depth. We note how their physical characteristics suggest deeper meanings and glean insight about their spiritual purposes. We can see each of their roles in a spiritually progressive astrology. The extent of our awakening determines how each planet is approached and used. We'll look at each in terms of its role as a tool for the ego and as an expression of the soul's purpose in the manifest world.

We'll also discuss whether a planet's energy is *charged* or *neutral*. A thorough discussion of this concept can be found in Chapter 10. Since the idea is straightforward and easy for people to grasp, I've included it in these essays (though readers are welcome to read ahead to get the gist). The basic idea is that in addition to the yin/yang pairing, we can also classify facets of astrology in terms of being aligned with the left-brain (content) or the right-brain (process). This lens provides a deeper understanding of the scope and functioning of the planets and is an innovation for a renewed and transpersonal approach.

As we develop the inner planet functions, we are given the task to manage the fundamental areas of mind (Mercury), relations and sensuality (Venus), and action and libido (Mars).

These domains are so immediate in our development that it can be easy to stay focused on how personal they are. Indeed, astrological literature tends to view them only in this way, completely devoid of having any higher purpose. However, as we spiritually develop and bring soul to manifestation, everything about us is a part of this process.

We can awaken into the transpersonal and learn to attune to the inner planets in new ways. This synthesis literally brings Spirit down to conscious realization on Earth. Our task is to continually examine if we are serving the self, or moving beyond it. As vessels for Spirit, the inner planet frequencies may be distributed through our words, relations, and behaviors— throughout our entire body-heart-mind system, as souls having human experiences.

 Mercury

Mercury is widely understood as the intellectual and communicative function. It correlates to the left-brain—dealing with logic, reason, facts, analysis, and the transmission of information. The proximity to the Sun illustrates how close the thinking function is to our awareness. We tend to have that running chatter in the background commenting continuously on our experience.

The planet Mercury always has one side facing the Sun, while the other faces away. The hot side gets up to about 700 degrees Fahrenheit, while the cold side dips down to a couple hundred degrees below zero. This contrast vividly conveys Mercury's dualistic thinking: black/white, good/bad, male/female, etc. It tends to *separate* phenomena for understanding. As seen with the spectrum from dark to bright, having vast distinctions (and polarities) in the relative world sets the stage for our lessons to play out.

Mercury is a very small planet, indicative of being precise and to the point. Another way to see its diminutive size is as a parallel to how the intellect is a peon next to the enormity of Spirit. Through the use and ingenuity of the mind, we declared "The Enlightenment" as we moved out of the Dark Ages into science and greater knowledge. It seems we were a little premature with this title!

Mercury may not pertain to enlightenment, but it does move very quickly, just as our thoughts do. It speeds around the Sun in a brisk 88 days. The benefit of speedy information processing lies in reading, understanding, or talking swiftly. The down side is that whirlwind mental energy can lead us toward anxiety and imbalance as we spin away from our center. Its orbit is highly eccentric (second to Pluto), suggesting the unsteady nature of our thoughts.

The mind (Mercury) is intimately connected to our emotions and unconscious (Moon). If we have an experience that the ego classifies as "negative," then our outlook on life (Mercury) is colored by this interpretation. Though Mercury in itself is "neutral" (objective, detached, content-oriented), our underlying emotions influence thinking patterns. We become very passionate about our ideas and perceptions. Whenever we think of or see something as "good" or "bad," we can be sure that the neutrality of Mercury has been overcome by the ego.

The ego wants to survive, so remembering what is painful or challenging serves us. The cost of this strategy, though, is the mind's contraction into itself, an immersion in the personal story. Expansion into the transpersonal becomes quite difficult. We can see the ego's connection with the mind in the similarities between the Moon and Mercury. There is a strong resemblance, in both their cratered surfaces and comparable size.

Mercury   Moon   Size Comparison

The diameter of Mercury is 4,878 km, while the Moon's is 3,474 km. (The other planet of note which is around this size is Pluto, which has a diameter of 2,274 km – more on that later.)

The Egoic Mercury

From our position on Earth, Mercury is always seen near the Sun, never more than one zodiac sign away. For many, the mind is the centerpiece of identity. <u>Awareness is hijacked by the mind, which uses its light to illuminate thinking.</u> Descartes famously said, "I think therefore I am," a declaration of the egoic takeover. <u>Spiritual growth reverses this perception, as we come to see that, in terms of our identity, thinking is secondary to being.</u> We must reduce the importance we place on the intellect and become aware of its limitations. If not, then the tiny sidekick becomes our hero.

Mercury is easily fascinated and thinks that every whim is worth considering. <u>Jazzed with curious energy, Mercury endlessly searches for data</u>. The air side of Mercury (Gemini) is open to everything. The world is an endless playground for hypothesis and learning. Earth Mercury (Virgo) concerns the application of knowledge. As Gemini and Virgo are youthful signs, learning is a central focus in our cognitive development. The troublesome issue is overreliance on Mercury, which restricts further growth.

112

As we develop, we tend to become less binary and more nuanced—the lines between the "good guys" and the "bad guys" get more blurry, and sometimes they even change! When young children are asked how they are, or how school or a movie was, they tend to answer with "good" and "bad." The older they get, the more sophisticated the answers become. For the most part, astrology has a Mercury orientation and frames life at a simplistic developmental level.

In our development, it's necessary for us to use the mind to achieve a sense of order, a prime concern of the ego. We have named and categorized everything according to our limited ideas and frameworks. The mind has projected itself on the world, and we have all believed it to be true! Who says a stone should be called a stone? Certainly there is nothing wrong with understanding the world, but few stop to realize how relative this all is. We like to think we have it all figured out. Mercury is a prime tool of the ego.

The Awakened Mercury

With greater awakening, Mercury can play a more evolved role. Its proximity to the Sun allows us to send thoughts into the broader matrix which connects us. Our intentions have "wings" that inform the world of how we wish to direct evolution. Whatever we put out comes back to us in some way. However, if our thinking patterns are egoic or negative, that too radiates out to shape our reality accordingly. Ultimately, we can use our mind like it's a nerve ending of a much larger one, but Mercury must be open to this idea.

The relationship between the mind and the matrix goes both ways. Nikola Tesla said, "My brain is only a receiver. In the universe, there is a core from which we obtain knowledge, strength, inspiration." When we quiet the mind's chatter, we can

113

receive from the matrix, Developing contemplative or intuitive abilities strengthens our ability to partner with Spirit. The challenge in the present day is that anything that sounds "psychic" is often met with skepticism or scorn. The ego resists these possibilities because it wants to maintain control. As a result, great value is placed on practical matters, on living in the "real" world.

The conundrum is that there is no objective truth in the "real" (relative) world. Since we exist in the subjectivity of our consciousness, which is projected onto the world, we actually are investigating ourselves in our pursuit of worldly knowledge. Most are completely unaware of this and carry on with the thought that they can have certainty about life. The game of being "right" is often played out in dualistic ways: science/religion, Democrats/Republicans, or opposing countries fighting a war. In all of their respective minds, they are all definitively right, while their opponents just shake their heads. We might spend a lot of time convincing others how right we are, but when thoughts are entrenched in ego (Moon) there can be no persuading. Only when we diminish the passion or charge of ego can we begin to see another viewpoint.

Since there can never be an "Absolute Truth" in the relative world, we can grow to have less reliance on Mercury in understanding the *larger* questions. Part of the process is to dissolve old thinking patterns because they are conditioned by egoic patterns. Many spiritual teachers advocate "inquiry" into our thoughts to see that they can't be true in an absolute sense. In fact, when we turn them on their head and entertain their opposites, we might find truth there too. "I cannot change the world" and "I can change the world," are each true from different perspectives. When we see that the mind is an extension of the ego, we see its relativity.

Mercury potentially elevates us from our primal nature by dazzling us with complexity. It teaches us about Spirit, so we can understand how to become it. When we quiet the mind and dissolve thoughts through inquiry, we can find that Mercury is a marvelous *tool* for the soul to use in the relative world. Mercury is famous for being the *Messenger of the Gods*—it can give voice to the vast mysteries of the heavens. When we identify with our ideas we inevitably distort them. When we identify as vessels of Spirit, we allow information to move through us for evolutionary reasons. When we awaken from the dream of the separate self, we find that our thoughts are not *really* our own—they are a product of the sacred marriage.

Venus

Venus is sometimes referred to as Earth's "twin" or "sister" planet as it orbits close by and has a similar size. Venus gives us reflection, the encouragement to move beyond egoic identification and learn to spot the self externally. As is discussed in more detail in Chapter 10, Venus is a *neutral* energy, just like a mirror. It's concerned with concepts like justice, aesthetics, and the qualities of the sensate world. We often don't realize how charged we become by Venus, but that stems from us, not Venus. For more on this topic please see Chapter 10.

Conventional astrology designates Venus as a "benefic," as it provides comfort, pleasure, and company. Venus can be very benefic *to the ego*—a situation also responsible for the amplification of its darker and more devious side. The realms associated with Venus have become some of the main areas in which the ego plays out its dramas.

"Sisters": Venus's diameter is 12103 km; the Earth's is 12756 km.

From our perspective on Earth, Venus (like Mercury) is always located near the Sun, never wandering more than two zodiac signs away from its radiant manager. The inner planets connect awareness with the immediate environment, the consensus reality around us. With Mercury, our identification with the mind often leads to the negation of Spirit. The egoic takeover found with Venus positions us as *users* of both the natural world (earth Venus) and other people (air Venus).

Venus concerns beauty, and most consider this planet to be visually stunning. When we're seduced, we give our power away. We can admire Venus from afar, but if we get close, it would incinerate us in its steaming hotbed of noxious gases. Venus is famous for its volcanoes, which number around 170. There is also sulfuric acid raining in the upper atmosphere. This is not a hospitable planet! It's wise to maintain perspective and not get pulled in to Venus.

From the Earth, we can appreciate Venus for its magnificent illumination as it takes turns sparkling the morning or evening sky. After the Moon it's the brightest object the Sun illuminates for us. Since Venus is always near the Sun, we only get to see it for a little while in the sky, alternating from morning to evening. It can leave us wanting more, as we just get brief tastes and must go months at times without seeing it at all— good practice at not becoming too attached.

The Egoic Venus

Getting seduced by Venus has created a host of global problems. We have become addicted to this energy, which might lead to our collective ruin. We do not live in a world of unending resources. Sooner or later we must relax our attachment to *more* and live in cooperation with nature.

The earth side of Venus (Taurus) involves physical beauty and self-worth. The separate self requires physical materials to survive (clothes, shelter, food), and these have become injected with egoic urgency. We generally want comfort instead of pain, but the ego turns this "want" into a "need," and we use Venus only for self-interests. We may organize our entire life around securing enough money and possessions: "Whoever dies with the most toys wins!" We might choose a career based solely on potential financial gain instead of considering its contribution to others or the planet. We may equate having material possessions with happiness. Culture becomes materialistic and people are organized into financial classes (upper, middle, lower). The size of the bank account becomes a measure of a person's value. Slavery has even framed people as commodities to be bought and sold.

The air side of Venus (Libra) concerns social and conceptual realms. This is the energy of attraction, connection, and relation to the external environment. We learn to fit in with life and adapt to the norms of society. Libra is depicted as the Scales, the principle of balance. However, the egoic takeover creates havoc here. We might use the law to unnecessarily sue others. Many become preoccupied by their social standing and are continually evaluating their popularity. Style trumps substance, and we are caught up in appearances. Having delightful touches of beauty is endearing, but the egoic Venus transforms self-improvement into obsession, as seen with the booming cosmetic surgery industry. Nothing and nobody is "good" enough, which results in a wide array of psychological maladies including chronic anxiety, eating disorders, and depression.

In separation consciousness, the world is our potential Garden of Eden, full of abundance and delight. In the throes of unconsciousness, humans have exploited the Earth's resources and devalued the self as well. When we become more awake, we realize that an insatiable appetite is *self*-devouring. We may fall in love with our reflection in Venus's mirror, a beloved object, or something beautiful and hold on to it. It's quite easy for ego to latch onto Venus for security and connection in an uncertain world. We can realize that objects in the mirror are much closer than they appear.

The Awakened Venus

While it is Saturn that organizes the macro-structure of the physical world, Venus can be considered the *designer* who is responsible for aesthetics. In the movie *Inception*, the dream space requires an "architect" who creates the setting that a dreamer then fills with subjective processes. (Note: The name of "the architect" in *Inception* is Ariadne, which is also the name of a crater on Venus.) The movie explains that a dreamer is simultaneously perceiving and creating the dream. Venus filters how our surrounding reality is perceived, and therefore also *created*, in terms of individual meaning. This is how we're in contact with ourselves in the external world. As the movie illustrates, our minds populate the surrounding world so readily and continuously that most of us never have any idea that it is occurring.

In mythology, Venus emerges from the severed genitals of Uranus, symbolic of how beauty is connected to Spirit's intelligence (Uranus). In a sense, Venus, due to this connection with Uranus, is able to bring Uranian intelligence through the Saturnian boundary and into the manifest world. All color and aesthetics can be thought of as the "paintbrush" of Spirit. This is quite different from analyzing a "lifeless" world for its properties. We can appreciate the beauty of nature even more because we recognize how fleeting and precious it is. If we become attached, we are bound to suffer. Nature is a startling reflection of Spirit, and the greatest part of it is how amazingly intelligent it is.

Venus is associated with the absolute perfection of nature, which has miraculous aesthetic precision. There are patterns in nature which are anything but coincidental; chief among them is the "golden ratio." This mathematical ratio permeates nature, including sea shells, fruits, plants, a developing fetus, crystals, musical patterns, numerical sequences, and brain waves. Venus forms a conjunction with the Sun roughly every 1.6 years and completes a series of five conjunctions every eight years. A five-pointed star (or pentagram) is drawn in the sky, which has been called, "The Venus Star." The mathematical relationships of the star's segments reveal the golden ratio.

A rare event of the Venus/Sun conjunction pattern occurs when Venus transits across the face of the Sun (from our vantage point). This transit is similar to a solar eclipse (from our Moon), though Venus is far too small to obscure the Sun. These events occur in pairs, eight years apart, and these pairings happen every 120 years. At the time of this writing, we are in the midst of them (2004 & 2012). Considering what is happening on the globe regarding resources and money (Occupy Movement, income gap, dwindling natural resources, climate change), perhaps this event reflects a Venus version of the egoic takeover. Also, these transits occur in Gemini, suggestive of how dualistic thinking can obscure the radiance of Spirit. Our relationship with money, the environment, and our interdependence are all undergoing a major crisis point and reevaluation.

Arielle Guttman's *Venus Star Rising* is a wonderful resource. She writes that each of us has a "Venus Star Point," a personal relationship with the Venus Star. This pattern reveals another layer of Venus (arts, civilization, culture) pertinent for our collective evolution. The current Venus transits of the Sun may indicate that our relationship with Venus itself may be awakening (Sun) into a new expression. Perhaps Venus is inviting us out of separation consciousness and into broader connectivity.

The conceptual side of an awakened Venus may bring a more mindful and conscious form of civility and inter-dependence into our customs and laws. How can we live together in greater harmony? With Venus, we are able to understand the perspectives of others. The ego looks at others and thinks, "What can you do for me?" In contrast, the soul learns of itself *through* others. Just as Venus reflects the Earth as its sister or twin planet, other people teach us who we are by being "sacred mirrors."

Another spiritual purpose of Venus (its Taurean earth side) is about becoming poised, peaceful, and natural, more adept at using physicality (Moon) as a vehicle for spiritual evolution. We have the potential to give Spirit the arms and legs necessary to mold our surroundings according to its impulses. For many, the identification with the body becomes so strong that it seems ridiculous and implausible to suggest that it's not really ours. The transpersonal reality is that it's borrowed from

120

Spirit. It is only through this understanding that we can use it to bridge heaven and Earth.

Mars

Fiery Mars is learning to take risks in the development of will and courage. As seen with Aries the Ram, it plows ahead and learns through trial and error. Impulsive and imprudent action is just a part of the deal as we awaken to more informed ways of behaving. As the most active of all the planetary energies, Mars involves displays of personal power, desire, decisiveness, and force. The Sun is the energy of vitality, but it remains fixed as the hub of the cycles. Martial energy extends outward in service of competition, sex, and all forms of assertion. Mars energy is *charged*; it's passionate instead of reasonable. It's traditionally designated as a "malefic" because the ego prefers to not have to work through conflict.

Using the Earth as our reference point, the orbits of Mercury and Venus are tied to the movement of the Sun. The inner planets establish our orientation to the world, the consensus reality that surrounds us. Mars breaks free and represents the establishment of free will. It can have any angular relationship to the Sun — we can do anything we choose.

Mars is famous for its reddish color, suggestive of passion and often anger. It has the largest dust storms of any planet, indicative of a most turbulent temperament. These storms tend to increase when the planet is closest to the Sun. Likewise, we use the language of temperature when we speak of the intensity of our passions. The gift when our passions are "hot" is the opportunity to become more aware of them and express whatever has been suppressed or pent up.

Mars has the highest known mountains in the Solar System, as well as the greatest canyon, called The Valles

121

Marineris. It stretches more than 4,000 km long, is up to 600 km wide, and gets as deep as 8 km. In contrast, our Grand Canyon is about 800 km long, spans 30 km, and is only 1.8 km at its deepest. Mars's great canyon covers about a quarter of the circumference of the planet, resembling an enormous battle scar. Mars is our warrior spirit.

Mars

Mars has almost the exact same amount of land area as Earth. It just lacks oceans. It portrays our stripped-down glare of intensity. The Martian landscape is reddish, parched, barren—there is little sentimentality here. There are patches of ice at its polar regions, but this ice is frozen, not in flow. Other similarities include the length of a day—Martian days are slightly longer than the Earth's—and the angle of their axis—Mars at 25 degrees and Earth at 23. It's also interesting that Mars is half the diameter of the Earth and our Moon is about half the diameter of Mars. We are learning to see ourselves in, and ultimately own, our base passions. By so doing, we cease to create conflict and move toward greater intimacy.

Mars has two small, irregular shaped Moons named Phobos (13.5km) and Deimos (7.5km). Considering that Mars is close to the asteroid belt, these are thought to be captured asteroids, and their shape and size are consistent with this theory. In mythology Phobos pertains to fear, and Deimos to terror. Deimos is *the smallest known moon in the Solar System,* which is a metaphor to how terror may not have much actual substance to it. Perhaps it's an extreme egoic reaction to present stimuli based on prior unprocessed trauma. Phobos is destined to eventually crash into Mars, which may suggest that fear ultimately can be removed.

The Egoic Mars

It is all too easy for Mars to behave from ego. In fact, that's what most of us are doing almost all of the time. How much are we on auto pilot, behaving from instinct? How often are we reacting to the circumstances we find ourselves in, instead of consciously *directing* our lives? Many have had the experience of catching themselves in the midst of doing something unconscious: searching for ways to escape, subtly sexualizing connections, reaching for a bag of chips, or pushing someone around in some way. It can take years of cultivating awareness to act in alignment with soul intent.

Until we become aware of the nature of our unconscious, behavior is motivated by (and is a reaction to) our prior experiences and deeply ingrained patterns. We want to make sure the "bad" doesn't happen again, and we try to get more of the "good." Most behavior doesn't stem from choice, only the illusion of it. Here's the paradox of Mars—free will seems readily apparent to us, but only truly emerges when we resolve our past and can get ourselves out of the way. Then, our liberated behavior stems from our soul connection with Spirit, so it turns out not to be *personal* at all!

The cost of remaining unconscious is high. It is through our actual behaviors (Mars) that karma is created. When we behave in accordance to soul, there is no karmic residue because we are serving as instruments for Spirit—the ego (and its attachments and self-preoccupied agenda) is not involved. Sri Ramana Maharshi said, "Work performed with attachment is a shackle, whereas work performed with detachment does not affect the doer."[xx] We can understand this astrologically with the Moon's South Node, which reveals the *behavior* habits and patterns that we must learn to reconcile. Our internal worlds (Moon) don't necessarily create karma, unless we *act* unconsciously. What we put out into the world comes back to us in some way.

In order for us to achieve consistency of behavior with soul realization, we must bring presence and awareness to the unconsciousness of our egoic survival needs. If we don't, we have no idea that we are not *really* acting from freedom. The egoic Mars has unconsciously wreaked havoc on the planet—all the violence, wars, and sexual indiscretions. Any harmful and selfish behaviors have its fingerprints. We are collectively learning to tame this beast.

The Awakened Mars

We all must venture through the karmic patterns we have created. When we accept the past and take responsibility for our situation, we become able to live more freely in the present. It takes a lot of energy to keep issues buried or guarded. When we resolve our attachments and release our defense mechanisms, we have additional sources of energy to be used constructively. Martial energy becomes our ally as we learn to behave as a spiritual warrior. If we can face all of who we are, we can face anything in the world, as we understand that they are one and the same.

How do we know when the past is healed and behavior is free of creating painful karmic dramas? Awakened teachers describe how creative impulse emerges through them, and the

124

role on the personal level is simply to allow. Ideally, the fire of our Sun (connected to Source) becomes channeled in a certain direction through Mars. We understand and cooperate with what the energy is informing us to do. These impulses tend to be directed towards meaningful (fire) projects or connection. In contrast, when the ego is in control, our action is defensive and tethered to the past.

The spiritual warrior is willing to rise to the challenges of soul growth in a fearless way. The "high end" of any chart requires fierceness of intent and focus, the willingness to venture forth despite uncertainty and unfamiliarity. Ultimately, we can adeptly manage whatever challenges arise. Mars puts in place clear boundaries and is able to be an advocate of truth or freedom. It's not looking for a fight but is willing to stand for what the soul knows is right. Mars accepts positions where it can be a catalyst for change. When we are able to live the awakened Mars, we take charge of evolution on this planet.

Chapter 6
The Social Planets: Societal Organization

⚲ PALLAS- ATHENE   ⚳ CERES

Asteroids   ⚵ JUNO   ⚶ VESTA

As we travel beyond Mars and continue our exploration of the planets, it's a long way to Jupiter. In between these fire planets is an asteroid belt composed of thousands of boulders hurtling through space. Some of these are sizable and have attained significant astrological status, while others are less notable. One way to look at the asteroid belt is to view it as the milieu where the individual (inner planet functions) meets the broader social organization (Jupiter and Saturn) in the world. There are thousands of ways in which we take on various roles and personas in the world, such as "champion for peace" or "righteous politician."

It is only in the last few decades that the asteroids have started to be explored. Thanks to Demetra George and her landmark book *Asteroid Goddesses*, the focus has largely been along the lines of the social feminine. Many in the astrological community, particularly women, have considered this a most welcome addition to a system that is tilted in the direction of the masculine. The timing of this advancement parallels the feminist movement.

Some of the asteroids appear to address how the two sexes interact. Athena the warrior priestess is willing to fight anyone in support of justice. Juno addresses the dynamics of

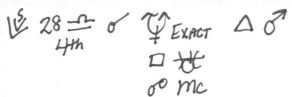

intimacy, how the bonds of commitment are managed and developed. Vesta concerns the process of tending to our inner fire for cleansing and inspiration—how we can purify in order to lead a sacred life. Her devotional nature finds roles in the world where the feminine safeguards what is pure.

Ceres, a grain goddess, oversees growth and the harvest. She is associated with nurturing, motherhood, and tending to the process of maturation. In recent years, Ceres has attained status as a dwarf planet. As the largest and most spherical asteroid, she resembles a planet more so than the others, and many astrologers have recently taken a special interest in her. The shift of Ceres into greater prominence is consistent with the reforms suggested in this book. Instead of viewing the Moon as "the mother" or "the feminine," our understanding of the Moon may change to the unconsciousness of the dreamer developing awareness of the dream. <u>Synchronously, Ceres is emerging as the archetype of the Mother, a *role* that the feminine plays. I have looked at Ceres in hundreds of charts of women who embody the archetype of "the mother,"</u> (Mother Theresa, Grandma Moses, Princess Diana, Ammachi, Golda Meir), and this association appears accurate.

The asteroids have been mostly linked to the feminine and its various roles. However, all males do have them in their charts. All of us address the social implications of gender and its various expressions in terms of child rearing, negotiating status, or in the details of relationship bonding. As society is becoming more egalitarian and open for people to have a variety of roles and identities, the asteroids are rightly becoming more instructive. As astrology continues to advance and reform, they are positioned to become increasingly understood and engaged.

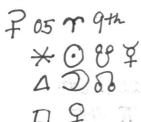

Jupiter

Jupiter signals a momentous departure from the inner planets. It orbits much farther away from the Sun than Mars— roughly a 12-year orbit compared to about 2 years for Mars. Jupiter encircles the smaller, personal planets (and the asteroid belt). It wants to direct them into something worthwhile and spiritually enriching. Its energy is carries levity and buoyancy, lifting us outside the parameters of the individual. Jupiter is a charged planet—our opinions, belief systems, and adventurous impulses stem from subjectivity and individual purpose. Jupiter is associated with the sign of Sagittarius, the Archer who shoots arrows towards long range goals.

Jupiter is colossal—it's the undisputed "King" of the planets. In fact, Jupiter is two and a half times larger than all the other planets combined (not including the Sun, which is a star). Jupiter's size is an irrefutable statement of how important it is for the psyche to grasp a sense of purpose. Jupiter embodies faith, the willingness to risk it all for something important. It governs the trajectory of the life force, a calling for the development of mission—connecting the individual to the collective.

With at least 64 Moons that orbit around it, Jupiter is holding court in the center of its own system. We see Jupiter's ability to wield tremendous influence. The shadow is an amplified ego which loves having many followers and sycophants who are non-threatening to his rule. Also, Jupiter/Zeus is famous for throwing lightning bolts, a parallel to the fantastic thunder and lightning activity around the planet. These bolts can be a sign of might, but can also mirror the ego's bombastic pronouncements and declarations of entitlement. Jupiter also has a faint ring system which is indicative of organization—in this case it's social and philosophical in scope, rallying together for agreed-upon causes.

Another noteworthy facet of Jupiter is the famous red spot, which looks like a bloody or blind eye. Every belief system is plagued by some form of blindness because Jupiter can't possibly know everything. It orbits within the separating force of Saturn and functions within social realms, not the transpersonal. Jupiter tries to make the spiritual understandable and is prone to simplifying its scope. The Earth could fit completely inside this enormous red spot, a reminder that our entire existence on our planet can be confused by philosophical blindness.

Earth & Jupiter

Jupiter is considered a fire planet, and it does radiate more heat than it receives from the Sun. It is a "gas giant," and Jupiterians are often accused of being full of hot air. The planet has no surface, symbolic of its speculative nature. Jupiter is notoriously difficult to pin down, always wanting to explore. It's also famous for being prone to excess, as depicted by its notable bulge around its center. Jupiter likes to live large and can be magnanimous like Santa Claus—the word jovial derives from it. Jupiterians are known for their charisma, which is reflected in the powerful magnetosphere, which is 14 times stronger than the Earth's.

The Egoic Jupiter ♃

Jupiter is called the "Greater Benefic." As discussed before, we can add the words "to the ego" to more accurately describe what this means. Jupiter potentially bolsters our self-interests, but can fall prey to the notion that having more (money, status, popularity, adventure) is always preferable to less. As a consequence, we might make unwise, possibly detrimental or immoral, decisions to see to this grandiose priority. The many moons orbiting Jupiter can indicate the lust for power of the Patriarchal King. Jupiter/Zeus is famous for volumes of infidelities, and his relationship with his wife Hera is like a grand template for the historical imbalance and tension between the masculine and the feminine.

As a social planet, Jupiter informs the direction of culture and society. Any area where a policy is implemented qualifies: politics, religion, education, and all of the committees which oversee the tenor of civilization. Jupiter involves the development of opinions and theories about what is best to do, and how to go about it. The egoic Jupiter may wish to set up culture and society around bounty, greed, and blind faith. Jupiter enjoys having philosophical consensus, all the Moons obeying its declarations. This agreement reinforces conformity, puffs up the ego, and limits progress. At the extreme, Jupiter might see one particular way of living as "the best" and see everything else as a threat. The egoic Jupiter justifies the launching of wars, sending planes into skyscrapers, or destroying our planet for self-interests. The harm it has done is incalculable.

Ideally, Jupiter invites the self to extend outwards, "How can I best serve the world?" is the healthy expression. If we stay within the grips of ego, Jupiter's energy is distorted into "How can the world best serve me?" Instead of rising to meet a life calling, the egoic Jupiter calls on the world to deliver benevolence. There is entitlement and expectation, backed by a belief system designed to affirm one's specialness.

These belief systems are broader than religious views, though religion is a main arena where ideology plays out. Most religions strengthen the ego with doctrine that promises some sort of salvation and confirms that the individual is living the "right" path. The ego is also given comfort and social reinforcement through membership in acceptable communal circles. Further, social/religious activity is a prime area for mate selection and business connecting—two of the prime concerns for the ego's survival. It serves the ego to affiliate with like-minded people—all made possible by *conforming* to a particular philosophy.

All belief systems are within Jupiter's domain, including atheism or any philosophy. In the case of non-belief, this stance too is governed by ego, which wants to claim superiority. It is quite threatening to the ego to surrender to something larger than it, so it looks for any evidence to support its own inflation. Whether it takes the form of atheism, being part of a "chosen" religion, or simply feeling entitled to maximize one's self-interest, the ego finds broad support with Jupiter.

The Awakened Jupiter

The more awakened response to Jupiter is to set a course that continues outward, away from self-preoccupation, towards the transpersonal. The arrows we launch with Jupiter can pass through the tests of Saturn (maturity, integrity, sensibility) and be seasoned enough to venture into egoless territory. If we don't continue to expand beyond the self, the arrows we launch may destroy the world. The frenzy of egoic entitlement and self-serving philosophies results in a magnificent clash of interests. The choice is to either come together (Oneness) or to come apart.

132

The awakened Jupiter walks a life path truly informed by Spirit (not just a mental philosophy). We can explore the transpersonal and become a vessel of inspiration. Contemplative experiences, adventures, and all sorts of journeys (both inner and outer) provide us with experiences and perspective about life. As we deeply engage these journeys, we end up moving beyond ourselves, which is what we find in the great stories and fables about "the quest." We initially set out for riches and instead end up with something more profound — well-earned insight about the world and our place in it.

Martin Luther King said, "If man is not willing to die for what he believes in, he is unfit to live." Our life direction can be in service to the greater purpose of our collective evolution. However, we also note that a terrorist might say the same thing! The difference is that a terrorist is serving a human (egoic) distortion of Spirit, while Martin Luther King was speaking about an authentic connection. The awakened Jupiter lives the life path as if every moment matters, fiercely committed to the expansion of consciousness.

Philosophy, religion, and higher education are some areas where this expansion takes place. It is helpful (perhaps necessary) to have the dominant organizational structures (Saturn) support, rather than inhibit, this movement. Too often churches, educational systems, and prevailing paradigms are entrenched in their own tradition and preservation. When there is institutional openness, Jupiter may fill our structures with a more informed approach. Operating within the orbit of Saturn, Jupiter brings broader understandings into comprehension and usefulness. The next Jupiter-Saturn conjunction is in Aquarius in 2020, which will present great opportunities for integrating the formidable energies of these two planets in new ways.

As with Mercury, Jupiter's truth is relative. Each person's path is unique. The astrology chart reveals the broad soul intentions for the lifetime (Uranus), and we get to sculpt how we live within the context of our circumstances (Jupiter). Similar to performing inquiry with our thinking patterns (Mercury), we can question our beliefs (Jupiter) and see that there are potentially many alternatives. Too often we are told we must live in a certain way. The awakened Jupiter is directed by Spirit, not necessarily by teachings.

However, teaching is also a part of Jupiter. We are challenged to find how belief systems can unite around a core set of universal principles. *The Perennial Philosophy* is one such attempt. It will be discussed and illustrated through astrology in a later chapter. Jupiter has the potential to inform us about the universe and its unlimited possibilities—the only thing that gets in the way is the egoic Saturn.

Saturn ♄

With Saturn, we have come to a very important juncture in the planetary order. Saturn is the final stop before the transpersonal planets, which are hidden from our usual perception. Famous for its rings, Saturn's jurisdiction is the landscape of the visible world and the role of containment and structure within it. It's the principle necessary to make existence grounded and practical, the overseer of consensus reality where the separate self exists within the relative world. Saturn (aka Chronos the Timekeeper) is associated with the organization of time. It remembers what has gone before in order to serve what is to come. Saturn is appropriately cautious about moving forward too quickly. It initially resists change due to the unpredictability that sudden variations may produce.

Saturn's energy allows objects to maintain form. Since matter and energy are essentially reversible, Saturn is responsible for keeping the material world intact. People tend to trust that the physical world will be the same from day to day, and most of the time it's a sure bet. Saturn is naturally aligned with the status quo and stability. Like its associated sign Capricorn, virtues such as persistence, determination, and integrity are part of its scope.

Saturn's most notable characteristic is its assemblage of rings. Aside from their striking intricacy and beauty, they signify order, containment, and precision. The various particles, rocks and ice which compose these rings are elaborately orchestrated by the planet's energy. No other planet can claim such sophistication with any of its features. They illustrate that order can in fact be marvelously elegant. Indeed, Saturn is widely considered a stunning planet—many consider it to be the most beautiful in our Solar System. Its appearance contrasts with its grim reputation and its traditional designation as a "malefic."

Similar to Jupiter, Saturn has a large collection of Moons. Its 62 known satellites are like faithful workers serving a larger manager. They dutifully move around their orbits in lockstep precision—a reflection of adhering to the reality principle and authority. Of particular note is Titan, the largest Moon in the entire Solar System and the only one with a major atmosphere. Here we see Saturn's ability to bring the conditions for others to grow and thrive. Paradoxically, Saturn is the only planet of the Solar System that is less dense than water, which conveys that the manifest world actually has very little substance to it.

Saturn has a hexagonal wave pattern of clouds around its north polar region that has a larger diameter than the Earth. The atmospheric conditions allow this to be persistent and relatively stable. Again, we note structure, order, and reliability.

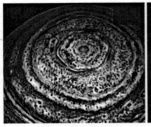 

The hexagon pattern   Gorgeous Planet

The Egoic Saturn

The ego has a complicated relationship with Saturn. On one hand, they get along great. The ego strategizing with Jupiter becomes concretized into society through Saturn. Policy driven by ego takes form in institutions, organized religions, and social systems. We can actually create an infrastructure tilted in our favor! As men have largely controlled the levers of power and authority for many centuries, Saturn does correlate with Patriarchy. Through organization and hierarchy, the kingdom becomes complete at Saturn—now the task is preservation, and this is where it gets complicated.

Ultimately, the only constant in life is change, and astrology vividly reveals this. The planets move into new signs and make an assortment of aspects to each other—all of them designed to spur evolution. The outer planets specifically concern change and transformation. Saturn is located in the middle of this energetic carnival. If it cooperates, then it must yield control and flow with evolution—this is how Saturn can be instrumental to progress. If Saturn chooses to deny the reality of change, then the clashing begins. Saturn turns defensive and vigilantly protective of its boundaries and walls. It focuses its time and efforts in warding off any perceived threats. <u>Outer planet stimulation can puncture or even destroy what has become outdated and in need of transformation. If Saturn gets</u>

stuck in attachment, life can turn into a marathon of resistance. The very things the ego wanted to erect eventually turn into burdens to preserve. This is partly why Saturn is malefic to the ego—reality can be harsh.

In states of protection, the ego (Moon) resists maturation (Saturn). This dynamic is seen with the natural opposition Cancer (Moon) has with Capricorn (Saturn). Beyond Saturn is non-attachment and self-transcendence, so evolution is threatening to the ego! The egoic Saturn inhibits spiritual growth as it holds on to the familiar and a sense of control. Though it is we who resist growth, Saturn is blamed for being the jailor that keeps us contracted. Most do not fully accept reality (our karmic predicament, the fact we're going to die, or how we can't possibly attain eternal happiness in an uncertain world), and Saturn receives the projection of being malefic.

Those who take responsibility for the conditions of their lives and accept the limitations of being incarnate are able to forge an effective partnership with Saturn. A healthy ego structure that is durable but not overly-attached, can learn lessons, attain wisdom, and evolve into being an elder. Saturn/Capricorn develops social responsibility and receives the natural consequences of doing a job thoroughly and adeptly. With the structure of earth, these people are natural managers and leaders. Jupiter brings broader potentials to our awareness; Saturn decides what is worthwhile and hammers it into form. This energy allows us to *amount* to something—and if we do it right, we outgrow the need to take credit for it. We can have a relationship with Saturn that is as beautiful as the planet itself.

137

The Awakened Saturn

What happens is the best thing that can happen. People who can't see this are simply believing their own thoughts and have to stay stuck in the illusion of a limited world, lost in the war with what is. It's a war they'll always lose, because it argues with reality, and reality is always benevolent. What actually happens is the best that can happen, whether you understand it or not. And until you understand it, there is no peace. --Byron Katie [xxi]

Saturn is most certainly malefic *to the ego.* Anyone seriously interested in spiritual growth would find that to be most welcome! It gets us to see that continually trying to satisfy the ego is a dead-end street. The world is not set up for our enduring satisfaction, and eventually we may see how destructive the ego can be. Though the ego is a manifestation of Spirit like everything else, our *misuse* of it is indeed malefic. We must get *beyond* ourselves to do Saturn well. In fact, we must submit to the so-called Reaper (a common version of Saturn) which holds the reality that we are going to die. Then we can awaken to our spiritual selves through the transpersonal planets.

We can grow to see how futile the act of preservation is when life's design includes continual change and evolution. Accepting this reality takes humility, maturity and perspective— the gifts of Saturn. We may actually find that feverishly trying to meet egoic needs can paradoxically lead to non-attachment. After reaching the supposed pinnacle of success (making millions of dollars, gaining enormous popularity, etc.), now what? We might see how hollow the whole game is if it's not being informed by broader spiritual nourishment. This theme is

138

captured in the famous story of the Buddha, who leaves a life of external riches and splendor to discover Spirit.

Saturn does involve life in the manifest world, and we can sculpt a contribution to society that serves more than our self-interests. When we free ourselves from the egoic takeover, we feel honored and humbled to use our Spirit-given gifts to benefit evolution. With Saturn, we know that success in life is measured over the long haul. We are blessed to have a viable, functional container to play out this evolutionary project and make the most of our time here, for our own evolution and that of others.

Saturn is a neutral energy, as it relates to structure, not process. It's largely responsible for setting up the consensus reality in the four-dimensional world. Nature has many laws that prove solid to the test of time as seen with classical physics. However, when we arrive at the transpersonal we find that these laws can be transcended. For instance, with quantum physics, we know that electrons can move backward through time and be both particles and waves simultaneously. However, most of everyday life is necessarily under the auspices of Saturn, but *it is not the final authority on what is real or how things work.*

The gift of Saturn is wisdom. This energy is mature and solid, comfortable with the limits of reality. One common attribute that all wise people or elders embody is the integration of Saturn's energy with other frequencies. Within the limits that Saturn imposes, mature individuals have been able to preserve the radiance of the Sun, the heart of the Moon, and the inspiration of Jupiter. Saturn is like a grandfather clock. It adds the dimension of fortitude and the precious commodity of being classic. When Saturn's energy is successfully integrated to the other frequencies, we take them more seriously.

139

Interlude: The Great Divide

Saturn structures consensus reality, the organization of our existence within separation consciousness. Until Uranus was discovered in the 18th Century, Saturn was the outermost planet. In Saturnian fashion, a dominant emphasis in history has been on tradition and the maintenance of societal and familial order. We have clocks and calendars to keep precise track of time and the seasons. Interestingly, the 7 days of the week were named after the 7 visible planets which were known then: Sunday (Sun), Monday (Moon), Tuesday (Mars), Wednesday (Mercury), Thursday (Jupiter), Friday (Venus), and Saturday (Saturn). As we now venture away from Saturn, let's put its realm in perspective. Saturn is about 870 million miles away from the Sun, and has a 29-year orbit. Pluto is 3.7 billion miles away and has a roughly 248-year orbit. Eris is 9.7 billion miles away and orbits in 557 years. (Other objects in the Kuiper Belt which have recently been discovered include Sedna, Quaoar, and Orcus.) In fact, scientists believe that there are at least 70,000 small objects that orbit our Sun in this belt.

All of this activity occurs within the parameters of our Solar System which, in astronomical terms, is miniscule. Our Sun is one star of billions in a galaxy that is only one of billions of galaxies! It's tough to wrap our brains around this scale, and certainly too much for any workable astrology. The point, though, is to see the limitations of orienting consciousness only within the orderly parameters of Saturn. The familiar tends to be comfortable, but Saturn can keep us confined. The plethora of discoveries in recent years that stretch our conceptions of our Solar System is an invitation for us to further expand the parameters of our usual consciousness.

The great task now is to more fully take steps in bridging the relative world (Saturn) with the transpersonal (Uranus).

Saturn's orbit is 29 years, which signals an end to youth. As mentioned previously, youthful Mercury has been the usual energy employed in astrological study and practice, which anchors us within Saturn's realm and limits astrology's capacity for maturing. Uranus orbits the Sun in 84 years, which matches the natural human lifespan more so than any other planetary orbital period. The suggestion here is that as we further evolve, we naturally arrive at the Uranian or transpersonal perspective. This is not to exclude what comes afterwards—Neptune, Pluto (and beyond) suggest further spiritual *processes*. The movement from Saturn to Uranus conveys the central and essential shift, the transition of our default orientation from only the relative to the inclusion and eventual prioritizing of the transpersonal. I believe we are collectively at this point of making the transition. There has been a lot of recent chatter of a "global shift in consciousness," some sort of collective awakening.

There is a lot of space between Saturn and Uranus. In this vast region, many objects called "centaurs" reside. As seen with Sagittarius, a centaur is part horse (physical) and part human (intellectual)—they concern the bridging, or integration, of worlds. Centaur-logic is a term used by Ken Wilber who writes, "the observing self is beginning to transcend the mind and the body, it can for just that reason begin to integrate the mind and body. Thus, 'centaur.'"[xxii]

On our way to the transpersonal, we must achieve a sense of wholeness, a strong foundation for the transcendence to come. It makes sense that we each have to first become somebody before we can become nobody. Authentic spiritual growth builds upon first being an integrated self with a *healthy* ego—which brings us to Chiron.

Chief among the centaurs orbiting outside Saturn is Chiron, the most well-known, and the only one to be used regularly by a majority of astrologers. Chiron wasn't discovered until 1977, which is somewhat surprising since Uranus was discovered two hundred years earlier in 1781. Chiron relates to health, getting our system in alignment. <u>Sharing the same root as chiropractor, it has to do with making the necessary *adjustments* for maximal well-being</u>.

In mythology, Chiron is known for his skill in medicine and healing, which was instrumental in aiding his own debilitated condition. As we teach what we are learning, Chiron is often discussed as the "wounded healer." It is appropriate for us to give the world a product of our growth. <u>Wherever we have been wounded is where we can help heal others, and this is in any realm of life, not just with physical health.</u>

Chiron is a "Renaissance" figure who is learned in many crafts, wise in many ways. As we saw in the late 1970s, interest in the healing arts exploded (crystals, aromatherapy, biofeedback, acupuncture, Reiki, etc.). Visit any metaphysical fair and you will see a large buffet table of supportive methodologies and techniques to assist you in arriving at your center. As Chiron orbits beyond Saturn, many of these methods go beyond conventional medicine and paradigms and bridge with the transpersonal. Interestingly, Chiron was opposed Uranus for many decades of the 20th Century (roughly from the 1950s through the 1980s), so a large segment of the world's population has the task of bringing these alternative therapies into the mainstream.

With its focus on separation consciousness and survival, the ego tends to take us away from the reality that we're souls having human experiences. <u>Chiron addresses the egoic splintering away from Source</u>. <u>We all carry a toll from repeated incarnations and are in need of connecting the heart back to Spirit</u>. It can feel lonely and vulnerable here in separation consciousness!

142

Working on our Chiron (perhaps with some of the methodologies mentioned above) not only brings us healing amidst the challenges of separation, it grants us the accompanying wisdom from our experiences. Chiron is a mentor and teacher. It was my mentor, Steven Forrest, who taught me that with Chiron we can whine about what is broken or we can take measures to heal. Staying within the confines of Saturn will ultimately make anyone whine. Our collective healing is accelerated by continuing to venture onward.

Chapter 7
The Outer Planets: Spiritual Attunement

Our planetary exploration now presents us with the movement from Saturn to Uranus, which can feel like breaking out of prison. It's the titanic step from being locked into a personal identity to being able to also indentify with the transpersonal. Saturn would have us believe that when the lights go out, that's it, goodnight—the Reaper comes for us. With Uranus, we see that as a silly cartoon. It turns out that death is the recycling of energy. When we accept that our energy belongs to Spirit, we are renewed to be in service to our Source.

Each of the outer planets plays a significant role in the awakening from separation consciousness. Uranus serves as the metaphysical organization, a matrix that connects everything together. We can picture this matrix as being a gigantic nervous system, an elaborately sophisticated brain. Neptune relates to the dream space set within this structure where we co-create our reality with Spirit. Pluto plays a complicated role. A representative of the shadow, it involves the psychic material disowned by the Moon, which is banished to the outer regions of the Solar System. If we mismanage our dream through lack of awareness, then it could turn into a nightmare (the dark Pluto). By embracing the shadow, we can retrieve what has been disowned, discover buried spiritual treasures within it, and give this wisdom to the world.

Since the transpersonal planets orbit the Sun, they are secondary to the great sustainer of life. Ultimately our spiritual growth involves soul realization, which connects to the Oneness of Spirit. Transcending the ego to participate in transpersonal processes is not an endpoint of evolution. The outer planets involve further reconciliation of the ego (Moon).

The outer planets tell us that we have to deal with life *far away* from our Source energy. This is why spirituality is often discussed as a journey. Part of the process in "coming home" to Spirit is to engage in *all of life* from awakened consciousness. We must address and resolve our karmic bank account, which doesn't magically disappear when Saturn is transcended. The cultivation of awareness allows us to meet our spiritual lessons more adeptly. Addressing these lessons opens a gift to assist in collective evolution. The more we realize the Sun, the more effectively we navigate all the energies in the system.

Spiritual awakening opens the door beyond Saturn, the crucial ticket into advanced levels of growth. We take full responsibility for our situation and consciously work at the resolution. Addressing the terrain of the outer planets is an exciting, though challenging, program of liberation (Uranus), conscious dreaming (Neptune), and fearless empowerment (Pluto)—all of which further allows us to successfully *bridge worlds* for our evolution.

Uranus

As told in the famous mythic tale, Saturn castrates Uranus, rendering the transpersonal inaccessible. These mythic gods are caught in an epic story of brutality and estrangement, but there are always roads toward integration and ways to heal.

Uranus (and its associated sign Aquarius) compels us to break through personal limitations and seize greater possibil-

146

ities. It can be exciting, but also destabilizing. Since Uranus goes beyond what is understood, Uranians are often considered "loose cannons" or threats. Revolutionaries can be aggressive and create an aura of fear. With maturation, Uranians learn to harness this jazzy energy with mastery and firmness. Over time, society learns to adapt to new realities—what was once outrageous becomes commonplace.

Uranus was the first planet discovered with a telescope, and its scope does include technology. Although most inventors like to claim ownership of their ideas, discovery is just *discarding the cover*. We are learning to tap into the intelligence of nature, which has always been there and always will be.

Uranus brings us to non-attachment as we consider life in terms of soul evolution instead of merely seeing to ego needs. Uranus has the coldest planetary atmosphere, hardly radiating any heat at all. That's quite a difference from the fire planet Jupiter, which radiates even more heat than it receives from the Sun. The coolness of Uranus (air) is objective or neutral. Likewise, when we cease to judge the world, we can be open to whatever comes our way. A pitfall for Uranus is when non-attachment turns to detachment, which is a disconnection from life.

Uranus has an axial tilt of 97 degrees, so it appears to roll on its side instead of spinning. Its north and south poles lie where most other planets have their equators, so Uranus makes us rethink our normal sense of orientation or direction. Uranus is considered "The Great Awakener." Interestingly, its south pole points at the Sun, which suggests how the metaphysical organization which envelops us (Uranus) can lead us toward spiritual realization (Sun).

Another peculiarity is its magnetic field, which does not originate from anywhere near the planet's geometric center. It's highly asymmetric, about 59° from its axis of rotation. Unlike the relative order and normalcy we find with other planets in this regard, Uranus again breaks the rules.

Like the other gas giants, Uranus has many moons, 27 in all. We might be tempted to see these Moons like the followers who devote themselves to Jupiter and Saturn, but again, there's a twist. The Uranian satellite system has the least amount of mass among the gas giants. In fact, the collective mass of its five *largest* moons is less than half of Neptune's Moon Triton. The largest of the Moons, Titania, has a radius of about 789 km, which is less than half of the Earth's Moon. There is a sense here of diminishment of stature, the reduction of self-importance, as we get involved with the transpersonal.

Second only to Saturn, Uranus has a magnificent ring system—an illustration of order and elegance. Here, the rings suggest metaphysical organization compared to Saturn's jurisdiction over the physical world. This organization is seen through the intelligence which permeates nature, astrology, and other systemic functioning of the universe. Rings are circular, portraying wholeness.

Uranus

With its linguistic closeness to the word "anus," even its name is Uranian! In addition to the discomfort and laughter that can arise in saying it, there are several ways to pronounce it. The naming of the planet itself had to go through an individuation process. First, they wanted to name it after King George, then in

148

honor of its discoverer, William Hershel. It was rightly named after the Sky God Ouranos and avoided these other egoic namesakes.

The Egoic Uranus

Uranus, like the other transpersonal planets, is often classified as a "generational" planet due to its huge orbit, and this is certainly a relevant factor. At the individual level, Uranus points to phenomena which have been "out of bounds" and difficult for a person to claim and use effectively. Sometimes this material is disruptive, even traumatic. As we break through prior limitations and prior egoic confines, we individuate into new ways of being. We align ourselves with a soul potential that was previously unrealized.

Self-alignment is prone to the egoic takeover. We may intuit what we need to do in order to be "true to the self," then stick it to the world as we pursue it. Self-alignment devolves into justified selfishness, even grandiosity. Taking pleasure in being ornery, counter-cultural, or rebellious is not transpersonal. These behaviors stem from a need to prove something, get back at someone, or cause mayhem. Many comic book villains portray this attitude with their eccentricity and brilliance. Many have some form of condition or life circumstance which makes them "unacceptable" to others. They are motivated by the unhealed ego.

The crackling busyness of this energy requires an outlet. Ideally, we partner with it for the sake of global advancement— to usher in the future for all to benefit. It has been all too common that brilliance has been used for personal gain, which can actually sabotage what is beneficial for all. We erroneously assume that we alone are responsible for our novel abilities and take maximal advantage of it.

149

The egoic Uranus may drop out of society altogether. Those who identity as different—from the mainstream culture, consensus reality, or dominant paradigms—might reject Saturn and render the self impotent and disconnected. The result can be problems in the "real world," the very place they wish to leave. In some cases, they might actually harm or disrupt society as seen with the example of the Unabomber. Mental instability can be part of the ego's distortion of Uranus. Without consciousness it can manifest as many forms of pathology, all of which challenge us to release the need to have an "easy" or "good" life.

The Awakened Uranus

In contrast to villains, superheroes often portray the awakened Uranus. They usually hide their personal identity and refuse to take any personal credit for assisting the world. Their talents and capacities are beyond what is "normal" in the everyday world. Plot lines involve saving the world and other acts of heroism. Though Uranus is not about "saving the world," we note the need to address the forces which limit and threaten evolution. The awakened Uranus is willing to put the self on the line (even die), as there is no investment in personal outcomes, just service to evolution.

The condition of Uranus in the natal chart indicates extraordinary potential. There are social, cultural, communal, and other collective extensions too. Since Uranus resides in a sign for 7 years, we can join with others in our Uranus genera-tion to create additions to culture and society. However, groups or communities can also have ego-filled agendas and demands.

The collective level is different from the transpersonal, which includes the transcendence of ego and experiencing interconnection with life. To restate Deepak Chopra, "The tree is my lungs; the earth is my body; the waters are my circulation."

150

The ego no longer holds identity confined within the body-emotion-mind system. With Uranus everything is just energy, and astrology charts depict particular patterns of it.

The Uranian matrix is the nervous system of a cosmic mind. Everything in the relative world is like a nerve ending connected to this mind. Just as a tiny sample of DNA would reveal volumes about a person, everything has the broader intelligence of nature within. Transpersonal psychologist Stanislav Grof says, "The human psyche shows that each individual is an extension of all of existence."

The Uranian matrix functions on every conceivable level. Every branch of science and mathematics, from the realm of astronomy to the intricacies of the quantum world, are part of its creative brilliance. The scientific law of the conservation of energy affirms that energy can never be created or destroyed, only transformed. At the micro-level, quantum physics reveals a world that boggles our everyday notions of space and time. Time has been found to be neither linear nor unidirectional; space is curved; and all measurements of space and time are relative. Subatomic phenomena can appear as either particles or waves. There are no definite places or times for matter to exist. Even more puzzling (and Uranian) is that everything is connected non-locally, which means that there are imperceptible connections among *everything*, through all space and time.

At the biological level everything is part of the great web of life, an interconnected ecosystem, sustainable and efficient. Underlying the biological level is our DNA, the genetic code— another example of a vast intelligence of breathtaking proportions. At the psychological level, we are connected to all of humanity, not only around the globe but also throughout history and into the future. The matrix is like the behind-the-scenes coordinator of our spiritual growth. Everything may catalyze greater awakening no matter how difficult, perplexing, or camouflaged it may appear.

One way the universe gets our attention is through synchronicities, which bridge our familiar experience with the numinous. They're a multi-leveled connecting principle that echoes our consciousness back to us. Synchronicities bring us exactly who we are, ready or not. They are the signs on the road towards wholeness. The universe is fully engaged in our spiritual growth; we just have to pay attention.

Albert Einstein's famous equation E=mc² is helpful in understanding the interface between the matrix (Uranus) and our everyday reality (Saturn). Einstein suggests that matter (m [Saturn]) is a crystallization of energy (E [Uranus]). Anything material (m) is impermanent (E), and will eventually perish. The speed of *light* squared (c^2) goes with the Sun. So *E* (Energy, Uranus) = *m* (Saturn, reality) c^2 (illuminated in the present). Everything in our awareness is the universal intelligence taking some particular form. Uranus needs Saturn for relevance in the familiar world, all made possible by the constant of light. The mythic castration is mended by fully cooperating with reality, by being with what Spirit is illuminating. Much of this process involves the reconciliation of our karma, which is brought directly to us.

Karma means that what we put out comes back to us, often in mysterious and perplexing ways that transcend time, space, and the immediate reality—perhaps even the present lifetime. We reap and sow in an endless exchange. The matrix delivers our consciousness back to us so that we can learn to navigate it skillfully through clear intentions. Sol Luckman says:

Contrary to popular misconception, karma has nothing to do with punishment and reward. It exists as part of our holographic universe's binary

152

or dualistic operating system only to teach us responsibility for our creations—and all things we experience are our creations.

Neptune

Neptune is the emotional dream space that permeates the Uranian matrix. <u>As a transpersonal and water planet, it's the spiritual love that nurtures life.</u> <u>The Moon is the individual heart, while Neptune is the heart of Spirit</u>. Removed from separation consciousness, Neptune carries an ecstatic feeling of lightness and return—a selfless merging with the numinous. <u>While Jupiter aspires to new heights, Neptune is the experience of transcendence once the heights have been attained.</u>

Neptune (and Pisces) involves the love that exists both inside us and all around us. Its evolutionary purpose is to facilitate and support growth though benevolent, compassionate acceptance. It is part of every person's evolution to love the collective through the momentum that self-love creates. It is hard to approach the gifts of Neptune when we feel empty within ourselves.

Neptune has a "Great Dark Spot," comparable to Jupiter's "Great Red Spot." Different images from 1989 and 1994 show similar spots in different areas on the planet. Certainly it wasn't the same spot mysteriously moving around, or could it be? The planet features many smaller dark spots, which shift around and disappear—activity indicative of the uncertainty and nebulousness of dreams.

Neptune

Neptune has a faint ring system composed of fragmented and unstable rings. Some are in a state of decay, and one in particular will eventually disappear. This too portrays the fleeting, mirage-like dreamscape of impermanence and illusion. The contrast between Neptune's rings and Saturn's durable orchestration is strongly symbolic of their energies.

Neptune's winds are the strongest in the Solar System and have been recorded up to 2,100 km/h. Uranus, by contrast, was visually quite bland when the *Voyager 2* spacecraft flew by (1986). Neptune features a whirlwind of activity—everything about this planet is in flux, indicating Neptune's unstable processes.

Though Neptune has 13 known Moons, its largest, Triton, comprises more than 99.5 percent of the mass orbiting the planet. Unlike any other large Moon in the Solar System, it has a retrograde motion compared to the planet. It's locked into a synchronous rotation with Neptune, so Triton always keeps the same hemisphere pointed at Neptune, just as the Moon does for Earth. Its retrograde motion portrays how time is distorted, while the enduring synchronous rotation invites a steady point of focus. In myth, Triton is known for his trumpeting sound which calms the seas, a helpful reminder that we are dreaming. Triton is slowly spiraling inward to be eventually torn apart, illustrative of the impermanence of the dream state. Another Moon of note is Neried, which has one of the most eccentric orbits of any satellite in the Solar System—another nod toward wildness.

Due to its relatively large size, Neptune's orbit has a profound impact on the region directly beyond it, known as the Kuiper belt. It has a series of "orbital resonances" with these bodies that follow precise mathematical ratios. Neptune and Kuiper Belt objects are locked into patterns so the traffic runs smoothly. Though Pluto sometimes moves within Neptune's orbit, they will never collide. We can trust that we'll be safe in the dream—Spirit has it all set up for us to surrender to the experience.

The Egoic Neptune

As the dreamer can get lost in the dream, the ego's relationship with Neptune can be most challenging. Neptune's selflessness can turn into identity confusion, victim and martyr issues, or the many avenues of escapism. The ego might use Neptune as the rationale to destructively disobey the laws of order and rationality. We might get caught up in a trance or swept away in ungrounded experiences or seduced into addiction. Lost in Neptune's trance, some ask why one reality is preferred to another—resignation, despair, and even suicide can result.

Perhaps the greatest ego trap with Neptune is the confusion of Neptune with enlightenment. One of the main points that spiritual teachers emphasize is that awakening is not about having positive or peak experiences, but rather about presence and awareness, being clear and attuned to life. Many seekers are interested in experiencing ongoing bliss as a balm against egoic pain or suffering. Feeling "good" is pleasurable but strengthens the ego's need for it. A criticism of the New Age movement is that its culture can be syrupy and loving to the

155

point of lacking authenticity and ignoring the shadow. This "spiritual bypass" can be appealing, as it avoids emotional pain and interpersonal tensions. The ego adapts a Neptunian orientation and enjoys the social and sometimes professional rewards this bestows.

For many, the illusion of separateness is the only reality. Indeed, it can be extremely convincing! The realm of dreams may seem unable to impact the "real world," and being "a dreamer" usually implies the inability to actually get anything accomplished. There is little awareness that we actually exist *in* the dream space. Lacking this awareness, we stay indentified in the physical realm and try to master its workings. To move beyond, we must take responsibility for the dreaming process and shift our governing paradigm to include the transpersonal.

The Awakened Neptune

Eckhart Tolle says, "Most humans alternate not between consciousness and unconsciousness but only between different levels of unconsciousness."[xxiii] The inability to consciously dream has contributed to our collective reality being in the mess it's in. A review of history reveals enormous strife, suffering, and a multitude of ways we've been imprisoned in the ego. The awakened Neptune helps us release attachments and see the physical world as the illusion. Neptune infuses a vision and provides us with hope. We can augment this through any spiritual practice (lucid dreaming, chanting, meditation, prayer, etc.). Contemplation can remind us that the ego is a tool and help loosen our preoccupation with it so we can increase our awareness of the dream space.

The dream space is a formless, invisible, interactive field of timeless possibilities co-created between the dreamer's consciousness and the world. The multiple dimensions of

Neptune must pass through Saturn's gate, which always entails some kind of negotiation. Much has been said in recent years about "creating your reality," and it can be a controversial and confusing idea. What is often left out of this discussion is that we are *co-creating with Spirit*; the world is not a blank and open canvas for us to use. Only phenomena consistent with reality come to being. A 63-year-old frail woman is not going to manifest a basketball career in the NBA no matter how much she focuses on this outcome.

There are many ways to dream. Nighttime dreams are often unconscious and may not be backed by intention or any co-creative process. They are rich for delivering unconscious messages to the conscious mind. We can develop the ability to dream consciously at night and use the time constructively. There are fantastic tales of exploring consciousness from sorcerers and shamans, but these inter-dimensional experiences often seem out of reach. Neptune can feel like an inner longing that is unspecific or lost. When this desire is investigated, we might find that it seeks to be at peace and in a shared experience with everything—to actually awaken to experience Oneness.

When we acknowledge this desire from our emotional foundation (Moon), we can consciously co-create our dreams (Neptune). The dream space is where the ego can get lost in unconsciousness, and it's also where we can awaken. The ego must release control and learn to trust and accept all of life. We can develop love and compassion for the self, the dreamer, who has not always dreamed consciously. The clearest way to dream is to be in the loving heart center (Moon) and consciously radiate (Sun) this into the world. The more genuine we are in our prayers and intentions, the more the world intimately connects with us.

Neptune can feel nebulous, like we're lost in a sea of possibilities. Yet at times, life unfolds in ways that make it obvious that we are playing a part in its creation. Events are too "on story," coincidences and collaboration with *seemingly* external events are too perfect. In these moments it can feel as if we are peaking behind the curtain of reality. And now we have the technology (Astrology) to navigate the dreamland. When used as a tool for awakening, we have the map, the guide that takes us through the organization of the dream. We can watch the astrology events that are transpiring and willingly attune our consciousness to what is really going on.

In order to get a picture of how well we're dreaming, we can just look at our lives. There it is—the results of what is being held in consciousness are manifest all around. We are not more advanced than where we are—you can't argue with reality.

Pluto

When the fledgling Moon is young in its evolutionary journey, it necessarily needs to contract to feel *solid* and self-reliant; however, anything physical has a shadow. Imagine light (Sun) hitting the Moon (physicality, ego), which then casts a shadow ending at a small point (Pluto). We noted earlier that the Moon's diameter is 3,474 km, while Pluto's is 2,274 km. It's the only planet smaller than the Moon. Pluto suggests where the Moon's shadow ends, at the furthest reaches of the system.

Whereas the Moon feels familiar when it is illuminated, Pluto holds the material we refuse to own. Pluto is often correlated with the soul because our spiritual healing requires an engagement with this material. Considering that the shadow is related to the lunar unconscious, it's more appropriate to think of Pluto as the terrain of ego healing. When we're integrated with what has been split off, we can more fully realize our soul connection (Sun) with Spirit.

Pluto, and its associated sign Scorpio, brings the dreamer into the darkness to engage with its deepest layers. Relentlessly psychological, Pluto territory is the proverbial sewer or bowels: the most hurtful, wounded, simmering, intense, raw, throbbing, unspeakable, problematic contents buried in the egoic unconscious. There are many gradations of severity to Pluto, but everyone has this planet in their charts—we all have been roughed up by life.

Pluto concerns the use of power, and is associated with what many call hell. Whatever hellish stimulation impacts us most strongly resides in us with great intensity. Ignoring Pluto creates a continual, increasing need to face it. When we do address it, we become empowered, wise, and fierce. The conscious Pluto doesn't get much press, largely because so few know of its territory. Since Pluto is about extremes, the "high" Pluto contains some of the most ecstatic experiences available to us—from the incredible exhilaration of psychological break-through to the intimacy of sacred sexuality.

Much was made of Pluto's recent "demotion" in status from planet to dwarf planet, but this has absolutely no bearing on its functioning. As discussed earlier, our naming and classification of the world's phenomena is our projection. If we were to call a "rock" a "gurk," it makes no difference to the rock. What matters is our *relationship* to the world. The spiritual relevance of Pluto's reclassification is the reflection of our collective discomfort with the shadow, particularly among those who prefer rationality (as generally seen with scientists who "demoted" the planet).

Just as the shadow can be elusive, there were sixteen known pre-discoveries of Pluto without it being known for what it was. It was officially discovered in 1930, which coincided with the rise of Hitler, the beginning of the formulation of the atomic bomb, the Great Depression, and the rise of modern psychology—all Plutonian in nature. Its discovery was made public on 3/13/1930, 149 years to the day after the official discovery of Uranus (3/13/1781).

Pluto has an axial tilt of 120 degrees and, like Uranus, spins on its side. Its relatively small size makes it prone to orbital disruptions. It's impossible to predict if it'll be at perihelion or aphelion at specific times in the distant future. Its orbit is extremely eccentric and highly inclined, so it varies from all the other planets nearer to the Sun. Pluto resides in the Kuiper Belt, which is a region beyond Neptune. All of these factors suggest that the Pluto realm is like no other.

Pluto has four known moons at this time—all discovered recently; Charon (1978), Nix and Hydra (2005), and a moon which is currently unnamed (2011). The largest is Charon, which forms a binary system with Pluto, the barycenter of their orbits lying between the two bodies. They are tidally locked to each other—both present the same face to each other at all times. In myth, Charon is the ferryman who takes the dead over the river Styx into the Underworld. He's associated not only with literal death, but any death and rebirth we go through. Charon invites us to relinquish our resistance, and escorts us through transformative experiences, psychological processes, extreme altered states, or some rites of passage. We encounter Pluto when we go to war, get married, engage in sexuality, face our death, or have shamanic experiences.

Pluto and Charon

Pluto's surface is remarkably varied. It features dramatic changes in both brightness and color, with black, white, and orange the most pronounced. Resembling a marble, Pluto's color mixture suggests a higher degree of complexity compared to Mercury's tendency to see things in black and white. One fourth of Pluto's surface is in permanent daylight, while another fourth is in permanent darkness. In between, half of the planet is a mix of the two extremes.

Pluto's eccentric orbit takes it closer to the Sun than Neptune for part of its cycle, which illustrates how our shadow emerges in our dreams, both sleeping and waking. The psychological is a part of the transcendent. The last time Pluto was closer than Neptune was between February 7, 1979 and February 11, 1999. This time frame brought a significant emphasis on Pluto in our collective consciousness (AIDS, sex abuse scandals, Cold War, nuclear issues, pornography, etc.), as well as major works on Pluto in the field of astrology.

The Egoic Pluto

The attachment to ego preferences potentially creates Plutonian material. If the Moon insists on staying in ego-friendly territory, it will strengthen unresolved issues through its resistance to them. As a result, they fester unconsciously and impact our well-being in a variety of physical or psychological ways. Or they might reach some crisis point and explode into the world.

As the universe is a reflection of the psyche, we have plenty of opportunities to bring Plutonian material to consciousness just by living. We often adopt a defensive stance against the world. This strategy tends to drain our energy and is absolutely futile anyway. Pluto always has us in the end. We're going to die, and we know it. The great game of protection and preservation is rigged—we'll never succeed! Nevertheless, we build elaborate defenses thinking that we can safeguard ourselves from the inevitable. <u>Staying within a fortress of our disowned shadow is a prison.</u>

While in this prison of unconsciousness, the egoic Pluto acts unconsciously. The places we have Pluto issues (sexuality, power, interpersonal hurt, abuse) are where our blind spots play out. Within the frame of reincarnation, we see that this hellish dance could go on for eternity. Internally, we might have fear, grief, or anger which remains unprocessed and out of reach. As a result, we stay unwise, unbalanced, and ineffective until we are ready to meet Pluto. We may unwittingly become the very thing that we have objection to: emotionally difficult, unable to perform sexually, avoidant in relationship. It turns out that we ARE Pluto, and have been all along. This is not to suggest that we have been "bad," rather we've been *unconscious*. We didn't know what we were doing in these realms and created some tough lessons. As we mature, we accept our prior unconsciousness and shadowy behaviors as part of our ego's curriculum. In fact, we learn to love them.

Until we are able to love and integrate Pluto into the light of our soul, the egoic version controls life on the planet. Pluto puts the maniac in egomaniac. All the dictators, power-grabbers, manipulators, users, criminals, the insane and deranged—every *pathological and abusive* behavior we see stems from here. The egoic Pluto is found in the rapist and murderer, the guru who sleeps with his disciples, or the gold-digging vixen. It's not always so dark or dramatic either. The emotionally absent parent, garden-variety neurotic, or run-of-the-mill porn addict are some other faces of it. The people who have truly healed are few. Loving and accepting the self is most helpful in reducing the charge of this energy.

162

Unhealed, the egoic Pluto will annihilate us all. The collectively repressed Pluto can ruin the planet through catastrophe, such as nuclear war. Pluto is like a self-destruct mechanism if we fail to grow. If we perish through our unconscious ways, Pluto transforms our energy like a restart button. The alternative is awakening, which is not something optional, luxurious, or for a select few. It's a necessity for everyone.

The Awakened Pluto

In order to retrieve what has been banished, we must be willing to go there and feel what we couldn't or wouldn't feel at the time of initial impact. We can learn to *honor* the experience and cultivate the deep wisdom in it. When we contact our anger, pain, sadness, or fear, we can transform it. What is usually needed is some form of deep dive into the unconscious to tap into it. Many therapeutic modalities are out there to help us. In the last decade, shamanic practices such as ayahuasca and other plant medicines have become increasingly popular routes of healing. We need to purge what we've been holding on to—not so different than defecating after holding it in. Yes, Pluto is our "shit" and we need to release it. Ultimately we find that shit is fertilizer for the collective. Like the fables show us, there is beauty within the beast.

We can search for anything at all still lurking in the shadow—internally or externally, as they are ultimately the same thing. We can be open to whatever unfolds, willing to surrender to any process. We maintain our connection to personal will, but the personal will is connected to transpersonal will (Pluto). As we become the awakened Pluto, we direct evolution. Whereas the egoic version wants to control the planet for personal gain, the awakened Pluto takes control for completely selfless reasons. We fiercely "be the change we wish to see in the world," as Gandhi encouraged us, and sometimes we end up dying for it.

The awakened Pluto has psychic dimensions. As with shamans and fabled sorcerers and alchemists, there's the ability to move between worlds, to alter the relationship between energy and matter. Carlos Castaneda's books are one popular presentation of this material. Such abilities are found in many cultures, though the practitioners tend not to advertise, preferring some measure of secrecy (Pluto).

The awakened Pluto overpowers Saturn's temporary structure. The changes it instigates can be ruthless. It makes sense that Pluto is usually feared and demonized. It's relentless but has a profound evolutionary reason for every transformation it activates. Pluto is our connection to the *evolutionary intelligence* that permeates the cosmos. This intelligence is aware that a virus, earthquake or famine can have enormous evolutionary importance for the survival of the collective. Those who learn to authentically embody this wisdom become our greatest catalysts for change. As a *charged* energy, Pluto's extreme nature captures the unforgettable and truly transformative moments of the spiritual drama.

Beyond

As technology advances, so does our understanding of the Solar System. In the 1990s the Kuiper Belt was discovered, a region beyond Neptune that has some similarities to the asteroid belt between Mars and Jupiter. There's over one thousand known objects in this area, and some scientists speculate that there are many more thousands. Pluto orbits in this region, as does the dwarf planets Makemake and Haumea. All of these discoveries led to the rethinking of what constitutes a planet,

164

which then led to the reclassification of Pluto by the scientific community.

Due to its size and gravitational pull, Neptune has a profound impact on the objects which reside in the Kuiper Belt. As mentioned before, it has orbital resonances with them, a discernible pattern in their organization. Many have a 1:2 or 2:3 ratio between Neptune's orbital pattern and the smaller, more distant objects. This illustrates that there is a connection between our dream space and what lies beyond it.

Beyond the Kuiper Belt is the "Scattered Disc" where Eris orbits, and the "Oort cloud," which holds the boundary of the Sun's gravitational dominance. Some scientists believe the Oort cloud contains trillions of objects! Below are the larger objects orbiting beyond Neptune.

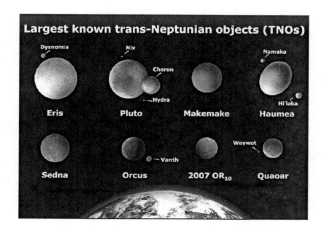

We live in a time of thrilling expansion and discovery, and it will take many years for astrology to catch up. We must figure out how to study these objects. How do we not clutter our charts when there's so much available? Due to the extremely long orbital periods of these objects, it is reasonable to suggest that they're not going to be *major* players, as some won't even change signs in a person's lifetime. However, some may hold great fascination in the collective imagination like the outer planets have. Just as the asteroids give us more tools, the trans-Neptunians similarly portray that there's no end to our inquiry into the universe. The expansion of consciousness continues.

Chapter 8
Consciousness, Evolution & Revolution

The expansion of consciousness is central for a progressive astrology. We've increasingly become more aware of the universe beyond planet Earth—our exploration into space is illustrative of awakening. In this chapter, we'll discuss the evolution of consciousness and its significance for astrology.

Saturn orbits about 870 million miles away from the Sun. For almost all of human history, we've understood it as the outermost planet. Our reality has largely been framed in terms of separation consciousness as we've oriented ourselves to the relative world. We've also believed until fairly recently that everything revolved around the Earth. The egoic takeover enjoyed this misbelief that we were at the center of the universe. The heliocentric view was offered in the 16th Century and was initially met with great resistance. As is generally the case with innovation and new paradigms, it takes some time to achieve broad acceptance.

We discovered Uranus (18th Century), Neptune (19th Century), and Pluto (20th Century)—a striking progression of expansion. Already in the young 21st Century we have gone much further. The world of the Kuiper Belt has come into our awareness, and many new celestial bodies orbiting our Sun have been found. This bounty of new information will take some time to sort out in terms of its astrological relevance. Two of these "new" planetoids, Eris and Sedna, have already made significant strides towards being integrated into our astrological canon.

Eris orbits the Sun from almost 10 billion miles away! That's well over 10 times farther than Saturn. Clearly, we greatly limit ourselves when we stay only within the Saturn realm. Farther still is Sedna with its highly irregular orbit, which resembles a paper clip. Sedna comes "near" to our Sun in its perihelion (about 2.5 billion miles beyond Pluto). Then, for its aphelion, it ventures way out to somewhere around 84 billion miles away—*that's about 100 times further than Saturn*! We are clearly being invited to greatly expand beyond the boundary of the relative world.

Some might say that we are indeed integrating with the celestial phenomena beyond Saturn. The outer planets are already valued and engaged by most astrologers. Many are even beginning to use trans-Neptunian objects and other phenomena such as The Galactic Center or The Great Attractor. However, the question is whether phenomena beyond Saturn are approached in egoic or transpersonal ways. As illustrated in the chapters on the planets, everything is prone to the egoic takeover.

The Evolution of Consciousness

Albert Einstein said, "No problem can be solved from the same level of consciousness that created it." The idea is that only by climbing to new perspectives can we resolve our difficulties. The inability to raise our consciousness leads us to repeat our issues indefinitely. He also said, "Insanity: doing the same thing over and over again and expecting different results." The implication is that *the failure to evolve consciousness ultimately leads to insanity.*

It's appropriate to ask whether consciousness really does evolve. And what exactly does that mean? Though this sounds like a weighty question, it's actually rather simple. We can easily see how we're more conscious than we were earlier in our lives. As we develop, we are more aware about the self and the world. There are distinct stages that our consciousness goes through, from complete unconsciousness to what Jean Piaget called "concrete operations," to more abstract levels. As we grow, we learn important lessons, cultivate wisdom, and see life differently. The modern mind might see this as basic, but this understanding is *relatively* new. It was only 150 years ago that Darwin put forth the theory of evolution which brought the idea of progressive development to the forefront. The field of psychology is even more recent. Within it there are countless models of how consciousness evolves. In addition to Piaget, Erik Erikson, Sigmund Freud, and Abraham Maslow are some of the more famous developmental psychologists.

Astrology predates these developments so it's understandable that advanced notions of consciousness weren't incorporated in it. Early uses of astrology reflect the consciousness of those times. The question for us now is whether we will continue to perpetuate the non-evolving approach or reform astrology to include evolution.

As mentioned earlier, there are a couple of ways to approach this question. The first is to see astrology like *every other field*—it grows and changes over time. There is a foundation that adapts to new understandings and continually becomes renewed over the generations and centuries. The innovations that become included are well thought out and are designed to make reasonable updates to ensure the continual relevance and flourishing of the field.

The other approach is to see astrology as unalterable—a perfect system that would be soiled by any tinkering. This level of strict adherence to a set of guidelines is only found in extreme orthodox religions. Astrology initially developed when Saturn was the outermost planet, the final authority. Inside Saturn's orbit is Jupiter, the planet of belief systems. Together they can concretize philosophy as a governing paradigm and oversee its preservation through history—not so different from a religion.

Uranus's discovery in the 18th Century signaled our collective readiness to question what had been concretized. Since then, we have seen dramatic acceleration of advances across the board, an explosion of technology, and the proliferation of human rights. Life has become more sophisticated, cultured, and diverse. The changes that Uranus awakens are wisely brought into the prevailing structure and methods in every field. In the 21st Century evolution is moving so rapidly that there is very little tolerance for lagging behind. The inability to innovate casts businesses, teachings, or cultural attitudes as being irrelevant and dogmatic.

Astrology is not a religion. However, many who adhere to Saturnian models and methods insist that they have the "pure" or "real" astrology. Students may lack the awareness that what is being taught is *one way* to approach the system, not the only way. Many astrological tenets are not questioned—they become a part of the canon, which perpetuates the consciousness which founded them. Being able to see that our view of astrology is the view of the self can ultimately free us.

We now know that consciousness is not contained within the boundary of a person—it gets projected into the world. We can see ourselves in the cosmos, a view in contrast to the Biblical notion that the divine *hands down* a set of principles for us to follow. This externalization of control is consistent with the focus on the "car" to the exclusion of the "driver." The result is being bound by our charts, and the planetary placements become deterministic. As we move from a Saturn-controlled existence to

170

one that is integrated with Uranus, we reclaim our power from forces beyond us.

Awakening brings freedom. When bound to unconscious reactivity, we have little choice. The world is going to trigger us, and there is nothing we can do about it (unless we resolve underlying issues). As we become increasingly more aware, *we're able to use the creativity in the present moment.* However, if we view the Sun as "the ego" or "the masculine," astrology may inhibit spiritual realization and the freedom that it offers. With this view, charts convey an unalterable destiny that we have to accept.

The implication is that we're enveloped within a pre-determined, mechanized universe that is beyond our consent. The egoic reaction to this rather bleak outlook would be to make the best of our situation by maximizing personal power. Astrologers have largely approached the situation like a pirate holding a treasure map. On the fortune hunt, the ego wants to move to where the "goods" are, safely escaping what could be "bad."

We can accept that we're co-creators of evolution, which is exactly what we find with our DNA. Though we have a specific genetic code, including predispositions and inherited traits, we can *choose* to live healthily or not. Behavior choices impact how genes manifest, and our conscious decisions also activate our charts in a wide variety of ways.

One of the greatest surprises I have found is that many people interested in awakening and the evolution of consciousness are dismissing astrology. In fact, this trend is quite pronounced with those involved with Integral Theory, a movement which promotes the integration of knowledge and wisdom traditions for spiritual growth. In *Integral Astrology,* Armand Diaz writes, "Consider how rare it is to see even the most prominent astrologers speaking at a meeting on transper-

171

sonal psychology, consciousness studies, or global change." In order for astrology to catch up, it must fully incorporate the idea that consciousness evolves.

Levels of Consciousness

Ken Wilber studied wisdom traditions and philosophy cross-culturally in order to assemble the most thorough model of how consciousness evolves. In *A Brief History of Everything* he puts forth a comprehensive understanding of consciousness with the broadest possible consensus. His model has nine distinct stages, which mesh well with what I'm proposing for astrology. Though Wilber says that there is great individual variation to how personal evolution progresses, there is a general, discernible pattern that can help us map the territory. He writes, "Evolution is best thought of as Spirit-in-action, God-in-the-making, where Spirit unfolds itself at every stage of development, thus manifesting more of itself, and realizing more of itself, at every unfolding."[xxiv]

Level 1 (Physical Self): The first stage is typified by infants, who lack a boundary with the external world. This level is described as "physiocentric," with the body being the locus of orientation. In order to move beyond this level, we differentiate between self and world. We learn to identify as a physical, separate self.

Level 2 (Emotional Self): Here we experience an emotional fusion with existence, a "biocentric" orientation. As we develop, we learn to differentiate from the external emotional environment and establish identification as an emotional, separate self.

Level 3 (Conceptual Self): At this cognitive level, there is identification with the mind's images, symbols, and concepts.

172

Here, we begin to use language and develop the intellectual separate self.

Level 4 (Role Self): At this stage, the broader structure of the world and others' perspectives are brought into awareness. We understand how people take on various roles and follow a set of rules. There is an emphasis on doing things right in order to obey and conform to the immediate organization of reality. We begin to develop identification as a social separate self operating from a moral code.

Level 5 (Mature Ego): Often called "formal operations," at this level there is more internal process about the complexity of life. A "worldcentric" orientation emerges whereby the roles and rules previously accepted are now questioned. There is a deeper awareness of the uniqueness of all people—the relative truths of divergent paradigms and cultures. Rankings of what and who is "better" or "worse" give way to equal consideration and opportunity for all.

Level 6 (The Centaur): Typified by a synthesis between body and mind, the self becomes "integrated in its networks of responsibility and service." The body and mind are understood as "experiences" or "tools" for specific uses. Less identification with the body/mind system is the beginning of egoic transcendence. At this level, our "authenticity" is championed, and we are poised to contribute to our collective evolution.

Level 7 (The Psychic—Nature Mysticism): At this stage, awareness is no longer confined within the separate self. The ego is transcended and *one identifies as nature*. Everything external is perceived as a reflection of one's consciousness. From prior levels, this level of consciousness might be seen as regression into having no boundaries. However, it's a conscious expansion, or awakening, into all of life. Everything to do with being a separate self (body, emotions, mind, ego) is now fully understood

173

and utilized with the identification of a soul having a temporary human experience.

Level 8 (The Subtle—Deity Mysticism): Wilber describes this level as "interior luminosities and sounds, archetypal forms and patterns, extremely subtle bliss currents, and expansive affective states of love and compassion."[xxv] Building on the psychic union with nature, we are now fully connected to "the interior bliss body or transformational body, which transcends and includes the gross or natural domain but is not confined to it." We are connected to the archetypal mythology that pervades all of humanity. Mythology is seen in terms of Oneness instead of organizing the various myths in separation consciousness. This level also addresses "the subtler pathological states of what can only be called Kosmic terror, Kosmic evil, Kosmic horror."

Level 9 (The Causal—Formless Mysticism): A state of awareness at its source of Emptiness, which is paradoxically full of creative potential—one becomes the "seer that cannot be seen." There is *no identification with any form*, just eternal presence. Mastering this level is to continually "abide in awareness," to allow everything to rise and fall without any attachments. We experience that this awareness and presence has existed throughout all previous levels, which brings one to the Nondual.

The Nondual: The formless gives way to the Nondual, which connects to absolutely everything (empty or form). Wilber does not assign this as a level because it underlies it all. "The pure *Emptiness* of the Witness turns out to be one with every *Form* that is witnessed." Oneness is directly experienced without any compartmentalizing whatsoever. "The entire universe is a transparent shimmering of the Divine, of primordial Purity." The relative world arises within the Nondual, which remains non-attached to it all.

174

At each level there is a decline in egocentricity and the evolution of a more expansive and inclusive experience. Growth through these levels is highly unique with many ups and downs, "peak experiences," and periods of regression. However, Wilber states that there is a consistent development of the self's "center of gravity" through this structure of spiritual evolution. We may touch in and experience any level at any time, but evolution tends to go through these distinct broader stages and their discernible pattern.

The first 3 levels establish the egoic center of operations (physical, emotional, intellectual). Level 4 brings a social component, but there is still a preoccupation with the self, an evaluation of differences between self and other, strategies of competition and survival. There is the tendency to see the self in positive ways and anything that is a threat in some way to be negative.

Level 5 is the first level of spiritual maturity—a shifting of focus from self-interest and personal agenda to prioritizing greater connectivity. However, one of the issues at this level is the need to make everything equal, which carries the potential to sabotage further evolution. There is truth that nothing is better than anything else (Gemini), but there is also truth to different levels of consciousness (Sagittarius) and moral distinctions of "right action." Being unable to integrate the vertical axis of greater heights has resulted in what Wilber calls "flatland"— consciousness is deprived of depth, and meaning collapses.

As a remedy to this conflict, many people strive to heal and grow to bolster the efficacy of the self. The movement towards integration is the spirit of Level 6 (Centaur), but the challenge is remaining unclear or unable to venture completely into the transpersonal. This is the level of our great existential

175

questioning, where we sense there is more. Wilber says, "The personal has gone totally flat." There is a growing hunger for even greater connection. To continue onward, we relax the identification with the mind.

Wilber says that the percentage of people who advance to Level 7 is quite small. He says, "We have a rather small pool of daring men and women—both yesterday and today—who have bucked the system, fought the average and normal, and struck out toward the new and higher spheres of awareness."[xxvi] At this level, there is often a confrontation with the consciousness that does not understand or resists further progress. Those working at this level may become overly-excited about their awakening and slip back into ego to promote it. Upon experiencing the transcendent, the ego can get caught up in a zealous agenda. In this pitfall, we believe that everyone should take this sacred medicine, or meditate, or sit with this teacher, or study astrology—basically do whatever we're doing. With non-attachment, further advancement is more possible.

At Level 8 there is a deeper immersion in transpersonal experience. Wilber mentions that a pitfall of this level is confusing the transpersonal with the collective. We might approach mythology and archetypes in ways that don't fully grasp their *transcendent* scope. If this happens, then we may (consciously or not) culturally identify with particular arche-types. "We are Dionysian." Ideally, these archetypes provide spiritual guidance or wisdom, a metaphysical connection to the One like strands in a tapestry. Instead of conflating "collective" with "transpersonal," the integration of Level 8 involves the experience of archetypes emerging out of Emptiness. Wilber writes, "There is a Light of which all lesser lights are pale shadows, there is a Bliss of which all lesser joys are anemic copies, there is a consciousness of which all lesser cognitions are mere reflections, there is a primordial Sound of which all lesser sounds are thin echoes."[xxvii]

At Level 9 (Causal), there is further elevation from the consciousness of the separate self to ultimately identify as spiritual awareness and vitality. Wilber mentions Patanjali, who describes bondage as, "the identification of the Seer with the instruments of seeing," the egoic takeover. At this level, we resolve any lingering beliefs that we are responsible for, or have ownership of, our own awareness. The idea that we are only vessels of Spirit is now fully realized.

Wilber mentions that the transpersonal is not concerned with resolving dualities and allows the relative world to be as it is. Problems are "dissolved, in the primordial state, which otherwise leaves the dualisms just as they are, possessing a certain conventional or relative reality, real enough in their own domains, but not absolute."[xxviii] He says, "all of those little selves and subjects that held open the gap between the seer and the seen—they all start burning in the freedom of nonduality."[xxix] Interesting that he uses the word "burning," as the realization of the Sun is the astrological correlation. The spiritual work is ultimately resolved when there is an ongoing abiding in the Nondual, and the ability to bridge the transpersonal with the relative—full participation in the sacred marriage.

Levels of Consciousness and Astrology

The levels of consciousness are stages of growth within the relative realm. We may think of the process of incarnation and our subsequent development as venturing through these levels. We can also think of them in broader terms of spiritual development from lifetime to lifetime where the "center of gravity" of consciousness gradually evolves through these stages. We can find correlations of the various levels of

177

consciousness with astrological factors. First, we'll focus on the correlations between the planets and the elements with these levels, and later we'll address different approaches to the discipline of astrology based on these levels of consciousness.

ℏ

EARTH

    Level 1 (Physical Self): Incarnation occurs within the Saturnian (earth) realm, which sets up the conditions for existence as a separate self. The first level correlates to the earth element, the great foundation from which everything sprouts. When we are born, we enter the material dimension, which is made possible by the structure of Saturn. Our initial orientation is a complete identification in the relative world, which explains much of our subsequent attachment to it and the conditions for autonomous life that it makes possible.

☽

WATER

♂

    Level 2 (Emotional Self): At this instinctual level, the emotional body connects to the surrounding world. The Moon (the dreamer) comes alive, activated in the setting of another incarnation for continued spiritual evolution. In addition to the Moon, this stage correlates with the element of water, which activates and nourishes life. In addition, Mars, the other planet of instinct is aroused. This level is resolved upon the differentiation of the self from the environment. By so doing, we begin to develop behavior choices (Mars), which stem from the urge and necessity to satisfy our underlying needs (Moon). Together, the Moon and Mars have to do with survival and protection.

☿

♀

AIR

    Level 3 (Conceptual Self): This level brings a more sophisticated relationship with the surrounding world. Consciousness begins to identify with the mind (Mercury), which connects to the aesthetics of the immediate environment (Venus) it perceives. The two inner planets hold the neutral structures of concepts, language, and the form in which the consciousness of the dreamer (Moon) projects upon. We can see this level in terms of the air element (which both Mercury (Gemini) and Venus (Libra) have connection to).

Level 4 (Role Self): This social level involves the asteroids, the various roles we take on in our identity. In addition, Level 4 and Level 5 (Mature Ego) can both be seen in terms of Jupiter and Saturn—the planets most relevant to our social and collective interdependence. At Level 4, we establish an ethical code (Jupiter) and understand that the separate self fits into the broader fabric of society (Saturn). Here we want to follow the rules and behave with "right conduct," which stems from some particular guiding philosophy (Jupiter). We play our role in the world, and expect others to do so, or face the consequences (Saturn) of justice. There are many opinions about what is suitable or not in social settings, and therefore many hierarchies are erected to illustrate these principles. The broader world is now engaged, but the ego is using the external structures of life for its agenda and advantage.

Level 5 (Mature Ego): The evolution here is a more conscious use of Jupiter and Saturn. At this level, there is greater awareness of our social interdependence and the needs of others. The relative nature of personal preferences is understood, which allows us to connect with others not for self-gain, but for mutual benefit. There is respect for the realities of our collectivity, and we feel an impetus to contribute to its preservation and prosperity. No longer is everything judged for its value in meeting ego needs. Instead, this "worldcentric" orientation is able to question underlying self-serving motivations as being detrimental to our collective survival.

Level 6 (Centaur): Chiron (fittingly, a Centaur), involves the integration of the body/mind system, and ultimately the transcendence of them. Through this integration, we begin to move beyond Saturn and its jurisdiction in separation consciousness. We take measures to heal the wounding entailed in separation so that we can reach greater wholeness and approach

179

the transpersonal. We leave behind vestiges of a false self and call forth our authenticity.

Level 7 (Psychic): We identify as part of the inter-connected matrix (Uranus) that envelopes us—the *apparent* boundary between self and world is permeated. We understand that synchronicities reveal our consciousness, and we see ourselves in everything. There is no more jockeying to get ego needs met. Instead we learn to live with non-attachment and cooperation with whatever unfolds. Our experiences inform us we are a part of Oneness, and we feel the necessity to live in accordance with the underlying intelligence of nature. The separate self is no longer completely in charge. Like having a GPS, we are now connected in to divine guidance, to the world itself.

Level 8 (Subtle): This level involves both Neptune and Pluto. Here we have a profound engagement with transpersonal experiences, both the advancement into deeper mystical union (Neptune) and the reconciliation of the shadow (Pluto). The dreamer is consciously able to navigate within the dream space. Much of the work involves advanced spiritual evolution: the resolution of karma and the claiming of soul intentions. By exploring the heights (Neptune) and depths (Pluto), the curriculum of the human condition nears completion. Any technique that accesses these areas of consciousness would be appropriate (hypnosis, shamanic practices, dream work, some forms of meditation, etc.). We become fluent and wise about all of life and then able to serve as a catalyst for evolution in various ways. When the lessons of this archetypal level are successfully cleared, we are left to dwell in the underlying Emptiness that makes it all possible.

Level 9 (Causal): The eternal awareness and presence of the Sun. The Sun literally causes life to occur, and we are able to fully connect with, and identify as, our Source energy (enlight-

180

enment). Wilber says that from this level, <u>we have the experience</u> <u>that spiritual awareness has existed at all the prior levels, though</u> <u>hidden in the blindness of ego.</u> We no longer have any pretentions that we own our energy; rather there is only the allowance of the great dance between emptiness and form. The unbounded creativity that permeates existence is experienced without any divisions or machinations relevant in separation consciousness. This level correlates with the fire element, the energy of life.

The Nondual ties it all together. The Sun (Causal) connects everything in this Solar System, and perhaps we move beyond. We fully realize Spirit, all that is.

Consciousness and Approaches to Astrology

How might we apply these different levels to how we understand astrology? At what level of consciousness has astrology functioned, and where can it grow?

Every level of consciousness has a different view of the world, set of values, and underlying motivation. We note this at a personal level in our own development as our prevailing philosophy, values, and motivations tend to change drastically as we age. Similarly, it would make sense that astrology too would change over time to adapt to the collective growth of consciousness. Let's explore the 9 different levels in terms of the various approaches to astrology to more fully comprehend where we've been, where we are, and where we're going.

There are many types of astrology, as most cultures throughout history have developed some version of it. My focus here is on a general overview of Western Astrology. For more reading on pairing astrological traditions with different qualities of consciousness please see *Integral Astrology* by Armand Diaz.

The first 3 levels (Physical, Emotional, Conceptual) are grouped together as being foundational for the separate self.

181

There is no broader outlook in the process of developing a personalized relationship with one's body, heart, and mind. The 4th Level (Role Self) is the first which has awareness beyond the immediacy of self—how the individual relates to the world. It is an understandable step in our collective evolution for us to initially approach life from the position of ego. The universe is perceived in strictly personal ways (gender, dualism)—the endeavor of astrology is a giant canvas for our projections.

The "Role Self" is the consciousness we find in many role-playing and board games, which are quite common in years of social development. We can draw a parallel with the most popular game in history, *Monopoly*. The object of the game is to succeed. We move around the board (venturing through life) in linear fashion, one turn at a time. We are looking out for our own interests and see others as competitors and potential threats. We are prepared to play by the rules, and we expect others to do the same (or go to Jail). Money is the measurement of success—with every turn, we can either gain (good) or lose (bad) some. The object is to take over the world and best one's opponents.

In the mindset of conquest, a map to guide the treasure hunt is very valuable. Astrology becomes an instrument for self-gain. The ego looks at the various parts of the system and decides what tends to be advantageous and what isn't. There are positive and negative designations for various planets (benefics, malefics), their residence in particular signs (exaltation, fall) or houses (strong, weak), and aspects (good, bad). Everything is judged for how it *serves* the character on the board. There is no emphasis on the consciousness of the player; the focus is only on the game. Everyone is assumed to be of equal status. Individual variation (consciousness) is not a part of the equation. The game comes alive with a tumble of the dice.

This "Monopoly Mentality" of Level 4 is the Patriarchal Value System discussed in Chapter 1, the prevailing way astrology has been developed and used throughout history. As Level 4 is a very domination-focused mentality, it's not likely to admit its limitations, level of conscious development, or yield to a more conscious way. Like the bankers who monopolize wealth, this consciousness remains focused on its agenda and justifies the pursuit of personal happiness. The only way this level moves forward is if it matures—it fiercely resists external persuasion.

Level 4 is interested in making astrology profitable. If money, status, and celebrity comes with doing the craft well, then why not! The value system is driven by financial gain, status, and social influence, so commercializing astrology would be quite natural. The issue is that astrology *at this particular level* becomes standardized. It proliferates through the entire astrological culture—groups and organizations, publishing houses, conferences, and everything else associated with Jupiter and Saturn. The mindset is continually reinforced, and variation from it is marginalized. Those who differ tend not to be published or respected, invited to groups and conferences, or given the coveted name recognition which garners influence.

The concretization of Level 4 consciousness in astrology (in the United States) occurred in the 1960s when the field surged in popularity. It quickly learned to cater to egoic concerns and became simplified to reach the greatest audience (which goes along with the greatest profit margin). Astrology filled newspapers and magazine columns. Attendance at astrology-related events soared. The map for the treasure hunt suddenly became widely available. We can now understand our personality, relationship prospects, and appropriate career. There is nothing "wrong" with asking these questions, for the ego's need for survival and happiness is legitimate; but a more spiritually meaningful astrology is available.

183

Level 5 (Mature Ego) is not so concerned with domination. It genuinely wants to grow and live in a peaceable world where everyone is valued and respected. The development of psychological astrology with its humanism and optimism fits here. This movement places less emphasis on good/bad designations and understands that consciousness is the determining factor in how astrology manifests—the focus is now on the driver rather than the car. All of this does show evolution, but Level 5 is not the endpoint. What's missing is a true transpersonal orientation. Most psychological astrology promotes spiritual growth in the abstract (a wonderful goal for someone to have), but does not really inhabit a spiritual paradigm. There is a secular trend in this movement—the goal of which is to make astrology universal. It's a laudable goal, but the by-product is staying limited in ego.

Psychological astrology renewed dualistic designations. The favored split is no longer good/bad, it's now male/female. The Sun is masculine, the Moon feminine—men are from Mars, and women are from Venus. The interest in psychodynamics, parental influences, relationships, and sexuality are of paramount concern in healthy psychological development. Psychological astrology reflects the movement towards gender equality going on at the time. The 1960s is when Level 5 consciousness was individuating from Level 4, and psychological astrology's emergence out of traditional forms mirrors this.

Astrology at Level 6 (Centaur) is the first development to move beyond Saturn. As mentioned earlier, there are many modalities associated with Chiron at Metaphysical Fairs, and astrology usually has a table there too. Astrology is used like a diagnostic tool to suggest where energetic imbalances lie. The human body is seen as a collection of energies that we can work with. Astrology became used by healing practitioners (acupuncturists, body-workers, etc.), and many astrologers take on the role of healer.

More progress, yes, but Level 6 is not the endpoint. Furthermore, Level 4 and Level 5 consciousness fills the literature referenced for Level 6 uses thereby stunting further expansion. Individuals at Level 6 tend to be free thinkers, and many arrived at creative uses for astrology. Astrology can be correlated with just about anything (colors, chakras, numbers, the Enneagram, and other systems), and it has been. Without a guiding paradigm for these uses, astrology can veer into a mishmash of speculation. The criticism from traditional astrology in this regard is appropriate. However, a return to more rigid uses is unwise as well. What Level 6 lacks is the transpersonal, but when it's developed at Level 7, those who wish to use astrology in the healing arts will have more to draw from.

Level 7 (Psychic), associated with Uranus, brings us to the transpersonal. The dividing line between this level and prior ones is the full implementation of the idea of spiritual growth. The developing field of "evolutionary astrology" is most aligned with this notion. This term is used here not to suggest one particular approach (or teacher), but rather any astrology that sees the chart as being pertinent to the lessons of one incarnation. The view is that we are souls having human experiences. Everything to do with the separate self (body, emotions, mind) is in service of soul intentions. Instead of astrology addressing the question of *how* we are, the focus is on *why* we are a certain way. Astrology gives us questions for us to address in our growth, not definitive answers about what will happen.

Though psychological astrology promotes growth, the tendency for secularization in the field has steered the conversation away from reincarnation. Many astrologers are skeptical about soul evolution, and some claim it to be

185

disingenuous, if not fraudulent, to accept money to discuss a person's past lives. Spirituality is not only nebulous to consciousness prior to Level 6, it can be threatening. Many do not want to entertain the idea that somebody else can be more evolved. Therefore, the playing field is leveled, and flatland astrology results.

Since the advancement to Level 7 in the field is so recent, it is currently figuring itself out. The major issue is how to renew and refresh astrology for this level of consciousness. What leaves, and what stays? If Level 4 and Level 5 consciousness pervades earlier uses, and some of these tenets become renewed, then a new direction might not be new at all. For instance, if the Sun is renewed as ego, instead of awakening from ego, then is that Level 7? How is the Moon, its Nodes, or Pluto seen? There are many questions to consider. Certainly awakening beyond egoic confines must be the central component here. This book is an attempt to address the issues in this development and to add to the discussion. Chapters 10 and 11 will explore some ways how astrology can be operable at this level.

Level 8 (Subtle) correlates with Neptune and Pluto, a deep encounter with *experience*. Writing about these planets, or such processes, is not the same as being immersed in them. The prior level (Psychic) correlates to the mental energy Uranus, and is suitable for the mind to be a part of. Level 8 is watery, the terrain of spiritual processes. In order to go there, we must relax the mind and become absorbed in experience.

Level 8 astrology is currently even less developed than 7, but there are some seeds beginning to sprout. Some astrologers *invoke* the planets through various practices. Others work with them through techniques like Holotropic Breathwork[xxx] or in guided visualizations. No longer is astrology just a "symbolic system." It reveals nature and crackles with vitality.

One of the recent cultural buzz words is "shamanic." It's getting used all over the place. Its true meaning is often distorted or watered down. However, the purity of what it means to be a shaman correlates to this level. Level 8 would be direct engagement with astrological energies in profound and transformative ways. Shamans are able to travel through consciousness and connect with the archetypal energies at a subtle level. They facilitate cleansing, purging, and visioning.

Whether they know of astrology or not, shamans work within consciousness at the Neptune and Pluto frequencies, which often entail altered states of consciousness. Hypnotists, alchemists, mystics, sages, and others could also be facilitators or practitioners of astrology at this level. The facilitator must be sufficiently "empty" to serve as a channel or vessel for energy to flow through and direct it consciously for spiritual healing. The younger people currently on this planet seem especially equipped with this capacity, as many have the transpersonal planets in transpersonal signs.

As for Astrology at Level 9 (Causal), we can only speculate. What will it be like in the hands of someone who is fully enlightened? It's an interesting question to ponder, but as with Level 8, it is purely experiential. At Level 9, consciousness abides in the emptiness of pure awareness, the creative potential (Sun) which underlies existence. Though enlightened people could certainly use astrology as a craft, wouldn't they be dipping back to prior levels just as we might dip back into ego to use it skillfully? Or could there be some kind of way astrology is used experientially here, similar to what was discussed at Level 8? At this time there are far more questions than answers available. We will look at Heliocentric astrology in Chapter 10. Though this is a mental exercise, it might be a peek into astrology at Level 9 for the time being.

187

The Nondual appears to be completely beyond astrology, which is a system based on various parts. Oneness transcends and includes astrology. The goal of having a "Nondual astrology" would be impossible for the very reason that using astrology must be from the position of a separate self.

The Structure of Evolution

Through extensive cross-cultural and historical research, Wilber found nine levels of consciousness. He also explains how evolution itself (not just consciousness) unfolds. His work seamlessly relates to the four elements found in astrology, and my book, *Elements & Evolution: The Spiritual Landscape of Astrology*, addresses this theme in great detail. What follows in this section is a brief recap of some main points from this earlier book of mine. This information is key in understanding how awakening fits into a broader structure.

The basic idea is that evolution moves from matter (earth) to life (water) to mind (air) to soul (fire), the last being our connection with Spirit. There is liberation from separation consciousness back to unity consciousness. The evolutionary picture also includes a manifesting channel, by which unified Spirit is brought down into the material world as individual souls.

This ascending/descending movement of Spirit manifesting in matter only to venture forth in its liberation back home is termed "The Perennial Philosophy" and is found in many philosophical, spiritual, and religious traditions—from ancient Greek and Eastern philosophies to the great Western religions. Aldous Huxley writes, "Rudiments of the Perennial Philosophy may be found among the traditionary lore of primitive peoples in every region of the world, and in its fully developed forms it has a place in every one of the higher religions." Though there

188

are many versions of the philosophy, there is a common thread of evolutionary progression through broad stages.

Liberation

The liberating channel begins with the earth element, the physical substance that supports life. Like the bottom of a pyramid, everything stems from this widest and most mundane level. Next, life (water) emerges from this foundation in the form of autonomous beings. Fittingly, membership at this level requires water for sustenance. The next movement is the development of intellectual and communicative (air) skills. Membership at the air level requires some form of nervous system. The air level is more exclusive than the water level, which is more exclusive than the earth level.

Finally, the next step of growth is to realize that our energy (soul) belongs to Source (fire), and consciously reunite with it. Membership at this level is made up of those who seek spiritual realization, a subset of the wider mental level. The zenith of the pyramid would be the full illumination of Spirit, or enlightenment (fire). Since our individual souls are eternally linked to Spirit, we can think of Spirit as where the evolution is "complete," though that is a linear notion from separation consciousness. When we get to the transpersonal, linearity gives way to timelessness. Spirit is not seen as a "level" since it envelops everything. Oneness eludes systems of classification and division. Each level builds upon the previous, while also moving beyond it. This movement from evolutionary level to level assumes a pyramid form (see graphic below). It's important to note that some tend to view what is higher as "better," a by-product of Saturn's reliance on hierarchies. Instead, we view this as movement from the physical to the nonphysical. Up is not "better" than down—we can remove value judgments and see this strictly in terms of direction.

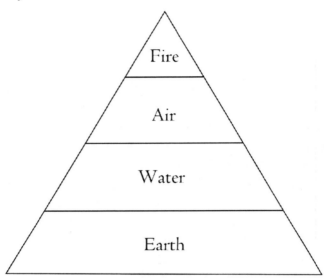

The Liberating Pyramid

Like the tendency of heat to rise, our souls seek to elevate and return. The natural motion is towards Source, just like flowers grow up to the Sun. The issue is to *cooperate* with this unfolding. The PVS places great value in mastering and benefitting from the physical world. We are conditioned to become attached to the earth realm because it's the most tangible level of egoic success. Voltaire said, "It's difficult to free fools from the chains they revere."

We can stay restrained by an attachment to the physical. An insistence on rationality can also impede our progress. At this time of evolutionary unfolding, we have been enamored with the mind. In fact, the epoch called "The Enlightenment" is the time of dramatic *intellectual* advancement and achievement. In the last few hundred years we have more fully civilized the planet and have even ventured into air and space. Now there is a growing hunger for soul realization. We may be at the cusp of collectively upgrading our consciousness to the mystical and mysterious fire level. Then, we may implement more sustainable ways to live on this planet. It appears that if we do not move beyond the immediacy of personal desires (which lead to pollution, resource depletion, climate catastrophes, etc.), we may destroy the Earth foundation which hosts us. There has never before been such a pressing need for our collective evolution. The critical step is to recognize the egoic takeover, and give back the fire level to spiritual realization.

Manifestation

James Hillman says, "As Plotinus tells us, we elected the body, the parents, the place, and the circumstances that suited the soul and that, as the myth says, belongs to its necessity."

The manifesting pyramid is upside-down (relative to the liberating one). The process begins at the top, the fire level and the vast oneness of Spirit. Everything originates from this unified source. As the manifesting channel moves down the elemental levels, there is a narrowing process which eventually leads to membership on the earth level.

The fire level is an endless field of creative possibilities that transcends the mind and human limitations. This is where souls connect with Spirit, like individual flames of a larger fire. Seen when we bring two candles together and then apart, fire can both separate and also reunite into one flame. Our souls can venture into separation while simultaneously maintaining a connection to, and identity with, the broader fire source.

191

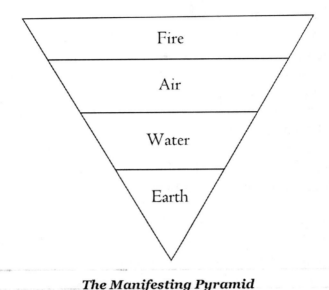

The Manifesting Pyramid

From the fiery source, souls choose to incarnate for their evolution to proceed. The next advancement is to the air level and a specific *comprehension* of the spiritual mission; creative possibilities are narrowed into a specific plan. Astrology is at this level, and one's chart depicts the soul's plan. Next, the soul ventures towards life, to the specific human conditions for a particular incarnation. In the gestation period in the waters of the womb, a body is formed. The water level brings us familiarity with the physical world. Our autonomy is initiated at birth, the earth level is engaged, and we begin our evolution in separation. We learn to orient to our body, our emotions and our mind as we move through the liberating channel.

Personal to Transpersonal

Recall the 9 levels of consciousness described earlier. We can correlate the first 3 levels with the first 3 broader stages of evolution. The Physical Self is paired with earth, the Emotional Self goes with water, and the Conceptual Self relates to air. Not until Level 9 do we fully arrive at fire. Evolution involves a rather quick orientation to body, heart, and mind before far longer periods of addressing Levels 4-9, the different stages in further egoic development and its eventual transcendence. It appears that much of our evolutionary work involves the passage from air to fire.

Our great lesson involves the shift in consciousness from solely identifying as ego to incorporating the soul. Our usual consciousness is anchored to the familiar dimensions of our everyday world. Upon raising consciousness to the transpersonal, we break through the walls of Saturn and address the lessons of the outer planets, which may bring us to soul realization. If our focus stays within the relative world, then that is where we stay. The classical "rulerships" illustrate how the scope of the transpersonal becomes reduced to the relative world, and these will be reviewed in the next chapter. Also, seeing the Sun as "ego" or "the masculine" is reflective that spiritual realization has not been promoted or understood.

A shift to the transpersonal does not compromise our membership in the relative world—they occur simultaneously. The outer planets correlate with further liberation into the transpersonal. Participation in the sacred marriage bridges these worlds. Wilber writes "Only when Ascending and Descending are united, we might say, can both be saved. And those who do not contribute to this union, not only destroy the only Earth they have, but forfeit the only Heaven they might otherwise embrace."[xxxi]

193

Chapter 9
Astrology & The 21st Century
Part 1: Deconstruction

Shifting astrology from being primarily used as a tool for self-gain to one that promotes spiritual growth requires reform. In this chapter, we'll further explore how the egoic takeover and the Patriarchal Value System can be found in the conventional approach. We will deconstruct the system in these ways and the next chapters will then clarify how we can reconstruct astrology in tandem with more universal principles of spiritual evolution. The crux of the matter is a shift from Saturn to Uranus as the planet associated with the system's functioning.

Uranus wasn't discovered until 1781 so of course it wasn't a part of the formation of astrology in the early days. The course of evolution is a continual expansion into new frontiers and the subsequent integration that creates a new world. In considering reform we'll look at the various parts of the system and put everything under the microscope: planets, signs, houses, and aspects. Much of the process will involve shifting from seeing the system only dualistically (Mercury) and from the PVS (Saturn), to Uranian equality, universal principles, and transpersonal awareness. In particular, judgments (good/bad) are leveled in order to promote spiritual relevance. The first issue is to address Saturn and Uranus in more detail.

Ultimately, the two titans must work together, but there is a contentious history. Saturn castrated his father Ouranos, which symbolizes how the mundane world can appear separate

195

from the transpersonal. How do we organize life (Saturn) in ways that continually adapt to our broadening of consciousness (Uranus)? To heal the castration, *Saturn must be willing to change.* If not, end of story—evolution does not proceed, and we stay in the past. In turn, *Uranus must be willing to compromise.* It can't expect the evolution of consciousness relevant to the year 2500 to instantly appear on the stage in 2012—everything in its own time (Saturn).

Here in 2012, it seems appropriate for Saturn to *fully* acknowledge that Uranus is the organizing energy of astrology. Saturn is earthy and structures the *material* world. It has to do with architecture, infrastructure, tangible connections—the prevailing order *on the ground.* It exists within time, the relative world, and follows the rules of classical physics. Uranus is airy, intellectual, and metaphysical. It relates to space, distances, invisible connections—the structure *in the air.* Uranus provides order for the transpersonal and follows the perplexing, paradoxical "rules" of the quantum world. Astrology is clearly Uranian. The mystery of Spirit (transpersonal) is responsible for its functioning—astrology is not common sense. It's beyond our conventional (Saturn) understandings of how the universe operates and is largely rejected by the "experts" in mainstream academia, science, and religion.

Though astrology is Uranian, astrologers have historically tried to make it Saturnian. Though applying the vise grip is necessary, we must look to how broader possibilities have become compromised. How can we move the vise grip down the evolutionary line?

We can refrain from judging the various parts of the system, for these judgments stem from ego preferences. Saturn tends to organize with hierarchies; it sees some facets of the system as more important or better than others. With Uranus, we understand that everything is important and has evolutionary value and meaning. From the Saturnian view, astro thought to portray the positive or negative things tha happen. In contrast, Uranus sees astrology depicting opportunities to realize greater wholeness.

Whereas Saturn concerns the finite world, Uranus brings us to the infinite, the endless recycling of energy. It's inclusive of the transpersonal, including reincarnation, which is a form of recycling. Saturn is interested in actual events that are observable and register in the manifest world. It likes to have certainty—*this* particular chart factor or transit means *that outcome.* Uranus asks us how we are going to manage the energy. Any particular chart factor or transit has unlimited possibilities for how it plays out—all contingent upon the consciousness of the chart owner.

Saturn would prefer that astrology be precise, orderly, and specific. Uranus understands that consciousness cannot be understood logically, so we must resist simplification. We can understand general themes, not specific meanings, as free will and choice are part of the equation. Astrology can only be predictive at the archetypal level. It portrays the broad energetic dialogues taking place, but cannot reveal exactly how these energies might manifest due to the co-creative relationship with the chart owner.

From the viewpoint of Saturn, it's appropriate for astrology to inhabit the mainstream. Astrology can enter business and commerce and be profitable. Uranus might warn that when astrology becomes standardized it will perpetuate a certain paradigm and level of consciousness. Upon commercialization, it enters a world of marketing, profit margins, popularity, and egos. It is prone to distortions in the direction of pleasing people or "selling out" for gain.

Ancient vs. Modern Dispositors

Conventionally called "rulerships," we'll now look at the issue of ancient and modern dispositors. As the word "rulership" has connotations with domination, the use of dispositor (a more neutral word) is increasing. Since the discovery of the outer planets, many astrologers have chosen to use the modern dispositors. However, a significant portion of astrological discourse in literature, lectures, and practice perpetuates the ancient ones. The intention here is to explore the underlying mindset of the dispositors so we can have more clarity of what paradigm we'd like to follow. I have found that the movement to modern dispositors is consistent with the expansion from a Saturnian (PVS) orientation to Uranian (spiritual evolution).

Scorpio: Mars (ancient) or Pluto (modern). Scorpio involves power, sexuality, and fierceness (Mars), but also psychological dynamics, making sacred contact with others, and resolving the shadow (Pluto), which have increased relevance in modern times. Scorpio is a sign of *depth, process, and complexity*. The shaman, hypnotist, psychologist, or researcher aim to get to the bottom of things. Mars is not interested in these processes, as it's *the most self-aligned energy in the entire system*. Scorpio is relentlessly *interpersonal* in scope, continually monitoring and evaluating interactions. Mars operates in a blunt and unsentimental manner, while Scorpio involves layer upon layer of psychological complexity and emotion.

Though everyone has a Mars, the traditional mindset is that it's masculine, and the glyph for Mars is the masculine symbol. The PVS mentality is that men control sex and power. Whereas sexuality is actually a *shared* experience (Scorpio), the Patriarchy insists that men call the shots. Men are conditioned to initiate sexual advances, and a man's stature is often measured

198

in terms of his success in this realm—the ability to secure a mate and propagate his genes. Much of the "locker room" male culture includes not only comparisons of sexual conquest, but also the ability to dominate (muscles, penis size, etc.). Scorpio involves sharing resources and deep bonding which is *mutually* rewarding. Men, though, have set it up whereby they ask for a woman's hand in marriage, and she is expected to assume their name.

Mars ruling Scorpio diminishes the role of female sexuality, assertiveness, and leadership. It leads to seeing intimacy and sexuality (Scorpio) as a battle (Mars) and, due to biological reality, men conveniently often have the upper hand. Men have far outnumbered women in crimes of passion (rape, murder, abuse), which correlate with the darkest potentials of this combination. The PVS sees strong women (Hilary Clinton for example, a Scorpio) as cold, calculating, bitchy, and unfeminine. Due to the imbalance and distortion of healthy Scorpionic sharing, women (unconsciously or not) have used sexual and/or emotional tactics to claim their power and partici-pate in the battle. The domination (Mars) mentality extends to other Scorpio areas, including controlling others. The PVS rewards the power grab of other peoples' resources (Scorpio). Successful imperialistic political systems and aggressive busi-ness practices like corporate raiding are applauded.

In contrast, Pluto, so-called "Lord of the Underworld," is a perfect fit with the sign of the underworld. Linked to the transpersonal, Scorpio takes on a whole new world of meaning. Sexuality can be sacred instead of just about domination and libido (Mars). The sexual act can consciously connect partners with Spirit as co-creators of life. Pluto invites us to reveal the shadow and work with others for psychological and spiritual growth. Ideally Scorpio wants to *share power*, and Pluto invites a deep dialogue of how that can play out for everyone involved.

Scorpio also involves death, and Mars tries to conquer this by claiming enough power to secure a legacy and for offspring to carry out a lineage. Instead of the futility of trying to be immortal, Pluto holds the knowledge that after death (both psychological and physical) we rise again like the phoenix from the ashes. We willingly honor our impermanence because we know we are forever connected with all that is. With all of its layers, only Pluto has the *depth* worthy of this complex and mysterious sign. Accepting Pluto as the dispositor of Scorpio is itself an act of transformation. It portrays the willingness of the masculine to put down its sword and surrender into the inevitable abyss of intimacy with all of life, which, it turns out, is filled with ecstasy.

Pisces: Jupiter (ancient) or Neptune (modern). Pisces swims in the ocean of consciousness and experiences the One-ness of Spirit. It is selfless, compassionate, and visionary. Jupiter is interested in spiritual/religious matters, but orbits within Saturn's domain. When the scope of Pisces stays within the PVS, we must go through organized religion or clergy to contact the divine. Religious institutions have cultural norms, expectations, and often social and political agendas that adherents are expected to follow. Salvation (Pisces) is promised by following church doctrine (Jupiter), not spiritual development (Neptune). At the extreme, Jupiter can be dogmatic, full of fire and brimstone, a far cry from the unconditional love of Pisces. Jupiter narrows the infinite (Pisces), and men are the self-appointed representatives of God. Women have overwhelmingly had second class status; even today women can't serve in the highest ranks in many organized religions.

Neptune informs us that we do not need anyone, anything, or any particular ideology to experience Spirit. It is universally available and everyone's birthright. The sea (Pisces) refuses no river—all of us are connected through consciousness.

Neptune is Poseidon, "God of the Sea," a perfect match with Pisces the Fishes. Instead of trying to understand the ineffable with philosophy (Jupiter) or scripture, Neptune invites us into experience. We are able to transcend the conceptual mind and learn to identify *as* Spirit. Whereas Jupiter might have you believe there is one "right" religion or way to live, Neptune dissolves man-made constructions to directly engage the dreaming process.

Ironically, it does not serve the church's interests to have people actually develop spiritually, because they may grow out of needing the church! Most conventional churches in the West do not promote meditation and spiritual practices and tend to marginalize their contemplative wings (if they have one). The Gnostics, Sufis, and Chasids have all been swept to the side by mainstream Christianity, Islam, and Judaism, respectively. Jupiter ruling Pisces ties spirituality in the knot of religion. Neptune as the dispositor frees spirituality (Pisces) to be transpersonal (Neptune), instead of being governed by a philosophy (Jupiter) within a Patriarchal organization (Saturn).

Aquarius: Saturn (ancient) or modern (Uranus): Both Saturn and Aquarius have to do with systems, societal organization, and the collective milieu. Saturn is the "Lord of Time," and Aquarius deals with the future, which is a part of time. However, as discussed before, earth organization of the visible world (Saturn) is far different than air, the invisible (Aquarius). Past (Saturn) is related to the future (Aquarius), but should there be a sense of *rule* here? It's as if the present moment serves as a step for the past to perpetuate its control endlessly into the future. The more awakened view is that the present has unlimited creative possibilities, which become possible when we're able to learn the lessons from the past and *let it go*. Saturn ruling Aquarius is about eternally holding on.

Aquarius is the sign of change, while Saturn is all about tradition. Aquarius pulses wildly with freedom, Saturn tends to be controlling. Saturn separates, while Aquarius wants everyone and everything to join together. Aquarius can be counter-cultural, unconventional, and wild, while Saturn is conformist and restrained. This "rulership" quells rebellion, stifles original thinking, and punishes variation. Aquarius levels the playing field and makes no judgments about anyone's worth—we're all in this together. Saturn organizes hierarchies and carefully oversees who can advance based entirely on status and support of the system. Saturn ruling Aquarius makes evolution and advancement impossible, grinding innovation (Aquarius) to a halt (Saturn). Reform (Aquarius) is under the auspices of those entrenched in power (Saturn), who would never want to undermine their interests.

Uranus is the Sky God, the ideal energy to be paired with this *transpersonal air* sign. The main argument I have heard against this pairing is that Aquarius wants consensus, while Uranus is "ornery," unable to truly connect because it insists on unrealistic ideals. The problem with this argument is that Uranus is neutral and detached; giving it a temperamental disposition might say more about us than the planet. As the matrix of Oneness, Uranus holds everything in connection! Uranus makes potentially workable connections in everyone's chart, and with every Uranus transit we are able to grow and connect with life in new ways. The issue is us, not Uranus. We must be able to stretch in novel ways to integrate with it. If not, then *we* become ornery and difficult.

In order to embrace Uranus as the dispositor of Aquarius, we must release our control (Saturn) of the world and give it back to the transpersonal intelligence that envelops us. This is an act of our personal freedom as we no longer have to take on the responsibility that wasn't ours in the first place. It's an indication that we trust the universe and are willing to abide in its natural rhythms instead of trying to control nature with our own designs and ego preferences. It's an acknowledgement that the PVS is ready to transform.

Patriarchal control of sex and power (Mars/Scorpio), religion and spirituality (Jupiter/Pisces), and progress and reform (Saturn/Aquarius) is now woefully outdated to modern consciousness. Switching to modern dispositors is consistent with releasing the egoic takeover and participating in the spiritual giveback with the outer, transpersonal planets.

Some astrologers argue against modern dispositors by saying that the outer planets are "generational" and therefore shouldn't be seen as personal in the chart. As discussed in the sections on the planets, we all have an *extremely personal* relationship with the process of individuation (Uranus), connection with divinity (Neptune), and our shadow (Pluto). These may be peripheral to the mundane tasks of survival, but they are nonetheless incredibly important and enriching parts of life. The negation of the outer planets having personal relevance reflects the broader negation of spirituality—again echoing Saturn's castration of Uranus. If we are souls having human experiences, then *our primary orientation is the transpersonal*, with life in the relative world arising in proactive relationship with our necessary spiritual lessons and processes. Instead of just seeing the outer planets as generational, we can understand that these energies have many facets and dimensions depending on the *context of consciousness* that is relating to them.

The issue comes down to what actually works in terms of chart interpretation. In my experience, the modern dispositors clearly work, but we must be able to meet them. When we engage the process of spiritual awakening, we consciously work with the outer planet energies, and they become more potent in the chart. It may be hard to believe that different people could

203

have different dispositors in their charts based on the quality of their consciousness. With Uranus, we understand that the driver is in control, not the car. Transpersonal consciousness activates the transpersonal planets.

Since most people are primarily identified with the Saturnian realm, it might seem more sensible and practical to just use the classical dispositors in order to meet people where they are at. However, we unwittingly perpetuate the PVS with these associations and limit the transpersonal possibilities within the chart. Here's one possible resolution: Since we are bridging worlds, essentially acting as a soul in a body, we can *primarily* advocate the awakened potentials of the modern dispositors. Then, we might also promote *the most conscious expression* of what the ancient dispositors are suggesting. This way the chart owner becomes a catalyst for igniting greater consciousness in the relative world and thereby helping the world heal from Patriarchal control. Instead of being bound by Saturn, we infiltrate its walls and act as a force of evolution within.

Astrology has not developed with the understanding that the quality of consciousness is the central variable of how a chart manifests. As a replacement, the various facets of the system are ranked as being "good" or "bad." We see the unmistakable fingerprints of dualistic Mercury, which is connected (though mostly unconsciously) with our ego needs.

We'll now explore the ways in which good/bad designation(s) permeate the astrology we've inherited. They're found with the classification of benefics (Jupiter, Venus) and malefics (Saturn, Mars), and with planets having exaltation, fall, dignity, or detriment—all of which have connotations with good or bad. In addition, there are "good" aspects (trine, sextile) and "bad" ones (opposition, square). Planetary residence in particular houses also carries value judgments.

Benefics & Malefics

This issue was discussed in Chapters 5-7, so this review will be brief. The essential point is that planets are energy, which has a broad spectrum of potential uses. The planets are like different colors of a rainbow, and all colors are illuminated by light (Sun). When the planets are met with awareness, they bring us closer to spiritual realization. Enter the ego, which has less lofty aspirations. It looks at the rainbow and decides, for instance, that it likes blue better than yellow. When a planet is not valued and used consciously, its darker facets emerge.

The Patriarchy has played out the shadow of the so-called "malefics" through tight-fisted control (Saturn) on all facets of society (economically, politically, socially), backed by the willingness to use brute force (Mars) in order to subdue any opposition. Most wars are initiated by men driven by egoic desires (wealth, power, fame, etc.). Saturn and Mars have been used by the Patriarchy as a double punch in the gut to anything and everything that gets in its way.

Part of its arsenal is the projection of dualistic categorizations, the creation of "bad guys." Battle lines are drawn, and our authorities are, of course, always the "good guys" who are going to protect us as long as we give our power away to them. "Our side" holds the righteous and virtuous principles of liberty, justice, and democracy (Venus) stemming from the "right" use of religion (Jupiter). The "other," the enemy, is evil or at least guilty of gross distortions of all that is good in the world. All the while, each side is a mirror reflection of the other. The polarizations keep all players perpetually battling one another, and everyone ends up suffering as a result. (George Orwell's classic *1984* illustrates this dynamic in dramatic fashion). The only way to dissolve this manufactured polarization is to accept that others are not only a reflection of ourselves, *they actually are us*. In the end, there is only the One.

This issue comes down to the question of whether there are good or evil forces in the world. We can shift our framework instead to one that describes a spectrum of unconsciousness and wakefulness. There is a dark, unconscious Saturn and Mars, as well as bright, conscious versions. The same is true for the all the planets. Furthering good/bad classifications tells the universe that we are abdicating our responsibility to evolve. Upon the development of consciousness, we are in charge of how energy manifests. We can throw out value judgments and refrain from labeling unconsciousness as bad or evil, for those are dualistic (Mercury) terms connected with ego. As we further awaken, we can understand the mismanagement of energy as *lessons* in our spiritual curriculum. Just as it's not "bad" to be a 1st grader, we can soften our judgments about those who are undeveloped and struggling in unconsciousness. In fact, it's more helpful to show compassion.

Planetary Placements in Signs

Imagine a geometrical structure composed of 10 sides, a decahedron, like an enormous 10-sided die. Each of the sides represents one of the 10 planets. The 10 sides are further split up into 12 smaller windows, which represent the 12 signs. Imagine a source of light inside the decahedron, which shines through the structure to make 120 different colors. All are a necessary and valid expression of Spirit, and collectively *we must attend to the programs of them all to live consciously on this planet.*

Let's see how these designations actually work by looking at some examples of well-known people who have a planet in exaltation, fall, dignity, or detriment. Some may argue that these examples are cherry-picked to illustrate my point and

206

that other chart factors must be considered. I completely agree that we cannot possibly tell the entire story of a chart by isolating any one factor! However, there is still something worth noting here, which can shift our habit of holding rigid good/bad judgments about sign placements.

Five examples are given for each designation. Shining, conscious examples are listed for every "negative" categorization (detriment, fall), while shadowy, unconscious examples are listed for the "positive" (dignity, exaltation). Of course, the point is not to suggest that the so-called "good" placements are really "bad," and the "bad" ones are "good." It's to illustrate that *every placement has a wide spectrum of potential uses* and that the chart owner is responsible for how they might manifest.

In working with my clients, I regularly hear concerns such as, "I hear that I don't have a good Moon..." These designations do reach a wide audience, leading many people to believe that there is something "wrong" in their charts. Some have responded with a bleak outlook on how their lives can go. It serves us well if we can legitimately let go of classifications that undermine our empowerment.

The Sun

Fall in Libra: Mahatma Gandhi, John Lennon, Johnny Carson, Sting, and Bruce Springsteen have all developed social visibility, especially in artistic and diplomatic (Libra) arenas.

Detriment in Aquarius: Michael Jordan, Ronald Reagan, Oprah Winfrey, Paul Newman, and Sheryl Crow have all attained megastar status and have used their visibility to advance humanitarian (Aquarius) causes.

Exaltation in Aries: Julian Lennon's fame pales in comparison to his Libran father. (He also has artistic Venus exalted in Pisces, while John has Venus in Virgo, sign of its fall).

207

Joseph Fritzl was the monstrous father who kept his daughter as a sex slave for decades. Others include Vincent Van Gogh (suicide), tennis player Jennifer Capriati (drugs), and Rodney King (police brutality victim).

Dignity in Leo: David Koresh was a cult leader who led 75 people to their death. Fidel Castro and Benito Mussolini were oppressive dictators. Monica Lewinsky and Amy Fisher are both famous for participating in underhanded sexual indiscretions.

The Moon

Fall in Scorpio. Bono, Elizabeth Taylor, Jennifer Lopez, Raquel Welch, and Rod Stewart are all seen as incredibly magnetic, having achieved wild success and popularity.

Detriment in Capricorn: George Clooney, Abraham Lincoln, Federico Fellini (cinema), Maria Sharapova (tennis), and Indira Gandhi represent the very best in their fields and hold many awards and honors.

Exaltation in Taurus: Figure skater Tonya Harding's Olympic scandal involved an attack on her main rival. Lyle Menendez is a convicted murderer, while "Grizzly Man" Timothy Treadwell was eaten alive by a bear by putting himself at grave risk. Jackson Pollock killed himself, as well as another person by drunk driving. Bernard Madoff is synonymous with greed.

Dignity in Cancer: Jimi Hendrix, Janis Joplin, and Kurt Cobain all died at the age of 27 from dangerous self-abusive behaviors. Cho Seung Hui was the Virginia Tech (2007) gunman, and Roman Polanski experienced the Holocaust, his wife was murdered, and he had to flee the United States due to criminal allegations for pedophilia.

Mercury

Detriment and fall in Pisces: Thomas Jefferson, Nicolaus Copernicus, Galileo Galilei, Rudolph Steiner (metaphysician), and Maya Angelou (poetry)—all visionaries.

Detriment in Sagittarius: Far-reaching intelligence as seen with Isaac Newton and Marie Curie (science), Robert Hand (astrology), and Paramahansa Yogananda (spirituality). The New York Times has claimed that Noam Chomsky is "arguably the most important intellectual alive."

Dignity and exaltation in Virgo: Albert DeSalvo ("The Boston Strangler"), singer Amy Winehouse decided she didn't need to go to rehab and subsequently died at age 27, River Phoenix died at 23. Wilt Chamberlain claims to have slept with 20,000 women, a poor decision for anyone's health. Hugh Grant faced public humiliation and relationship woes due to poor choices with intimacy.

Dignity in Gemini: Ted Kaczynski ("The Unabomber") used his intellect to kill people, as did grotesque murderer Jeffrey Dahmer. Mark David Chapman had highly unstable thinking patterns, which led to the decision to kill John Lennon. Others include John Dillinger (crime) and Traci Lords (underage pornography).

Venus

Fall in Virgo: Artistic perfection noted with Academy award winners Robert Redford, Kate Winslet, and Julia Roberts, *Harry Potter* author JK Rowling and opera singer Luciano Pavarotti.

Detriment in Scorpio: Magnetic celebrities Jodie Foster, Leonardo DiCaprio, and Denzel Washington are standouts on a very long list. Steven Spielberg is responsible for putting some of the most compelling dramas on the silver screen. Bill Gates amassed a fortune and became a philanthropist.

Detriment in Aries: Audrey Hepburn, Jack Nicholson, and Jennifer Anniston have all been immensely popular cultural icons who have influenced cultural trends. Michelangelo and Auguste Renoir are known as two of the finest artists in world history.

Dignity in Taurus: Adolph Hitler (genocidal maniac), Jeffrey Dahmer (cannibalistic sexual maniac), Louis Farrakhan (hatemonger), John Hinckley (obsessed Ronald Reagan assassin), and John Bobbitt (whatever one does to have his wife cut his penis in half).

Dignity in Libra (dignity): Nazi mass murderers Joseph Goebbels and Ivan the Terrible, Jesse James, Dylan Klebold (Columbine killer), and Woody Allen, who seduced his step-daughter.

Exaltation in Pisces: Richard Nixon, Sirhan Sirhan (murdered Robert Kennedy), Betty Ford (alcoholism), David Letterman (sex scandal), and John McEnroe, who holds records for paying fines for temper tantrums on the tennis court.

Mars

Fall in Cancer: Roger Federer (considered by many the best tennis player in history), Michael Phelps (record-breaking Olympian swimmer), Jean Claude Van Damme and Keanu Reeves (action movie stars). Pablo Picasso led an artistic movement.

Detriment in Taurus: Michael Jackson and Madonna have been called the King and Queen of pop music, Muhammad Ali (boxing champion), Harry Houdini (legendary escape artist), and Eva Peron, who fearlessly led Argentina into a new era.

Detriment in Libra: The Dalai Lama is a leader for millions. Nelson Mandela led South Africa out of Apartheid, and Winston Churchill led Great Britain in times of war and great tumult. Kobe Bryant has led the NBA in scoring as well as several teams to titles, while Elvis Presley led culture into a new form of music.

Exaltation in Capricorn: Lizzie Borden (axe murderer), Lynndie England (infamous maltreatment of prisoners at Abu Grahib in Iraq), former lead singer of INXS Michael Hutchence (suicide), and Lindsey Lohan (reckless behavior). Mars can be obsessed with self-gain or status in Capricorn. Model Anna Nicole Smith married an octogenarian tycoon and received a huge sum of money upon his death.

Dignity in Scorpio. Managed poorly, this combination leads to blood, excessive violence, and death as seen with dictators Joseph Stalin and Mao Tse Tung. Martial artist Bruce Lee was dead at the age of 32 with controversy surrounding his death. Hunter S. Thompson committed suicide, and musician Marilyn Manson is infamous for glamorizing depravity.

Dignity in Aries: Reinhard Heydrich was the Nazi architect of the Holocaust, while Hermann Göring was a chief military commander who executed the plan; others include Slobodan Milosevic (Serbian dictator) and Jared Lee Loughner (murderer). The term "sadism" is derived from Marquis de Sade, who liked to mix violence with sexuality.

Jupiter

Fall in Capricorn: Ludwig van Beethoven, Walt Disney, Charlie Chaplin, Steven Forrest, and Mark Zuckerberg (Facebook creator) have all made a substantial impact in their fields.

Detriment in Gemini: Oprah Winfrey, Alexander Graham Bell, Thomas Edison, Charles Dickens, and Stephen Hawking have expanded communications and knowledge.

Detriment in Virgo: Bob Marley, Thomas Jefferson, Ralph Waldo Emerson, Niels Bohr (physics), and Guglielmo Marconi (invented the telegraph) are all visionaries.

Dignity in Sagittarius: Robert Mugabe (Zimbabwe dictator), Ayatollah Khomeini (religious fundamentalist), Heinrich Himmler (Nazi commander), Eva Braun (Hitler's wife), and Silvio Berlusconi (corrupt Italian Prime Minister) have exercised great entitlement for their own aims.

Dignity in Pisces: Rush Limbaugh (right-wing ideologue), Karl Rove (George W. Bush's "brain"), Augusto Pinochet (Chilean dictator), Roger Clemens (suspected steroid user), and Tom Cruise (religious fanatic) have all been accused of being corrupt or misguided in their aims.

Exaltation in Cancer: Cult leaders Jim Jones and Marshall Applewhite used religion subversively. Niccolò Machiavelli's philosophy is defined in the dictionary as "the employment of cunning and duplicity in statecraft or in general conduct." This approach was also employed by Benito Mussolini (fascist dictator) and Mike Tyson (convicted rapist).

Saturn

Fall in Aries: Leaders with this placement include George Washington, Albert Einstein, Florence Nightingale, Kofi Annan (Nobel Peace Prize), and Will Smith, who has been called "the most powerful actor on the planet."

Detriment in Leo: Popular celebrities include Arnold Schwarzenegger, Kareem Abdul-Jabbar, Hillary Clinton, Steven Spielberg, and Danielle Steel (best-selling author).

Detriment in Cancer: Dolly Parton, William Shakespeare, John F. Kennedy, Bob Marley, and Patch Adams (health care) all put their hearts into their careers.

Dignity in Aquarius: Criminals Charles Manson and John Dillinger were denied freedom, while Donald Rumsfeld, Jerry Falwell, and Sarah Palin support policies designed to do so.

Dignity in Capricorn: Jeffrey Dahmer, Jim Jones, David Koresh, Ayatollah Khomeini, and Ike Turner (wife batterer) is a collection of undignified people.

Exaltation in Libra: Includes Eric Harris (Columbine killer) and David Berkowitz (serial murderer), as well as Communist dictator Mao Tse Tung. Roseanne Barr and Pee Wee Herman have made headlines for their lack of tact and civility.

Exaltations and the Patriarchal Value System

The definition in the American Heritage Dictionary of exalt is, "1. To raise in rank, character, or status; elevate. 2. To glorify; praise; honor. 3. To increase the effect or intensity of; heighten. 4. To fill with an intensified feeling such as joy or pride; elate."

Who decides what is exalted? What is the mindset that underlies it? Does it make more sense that it's Spirit that favors certain facets of the system, or that it is we who do so? Does the light shine equally through all sides of the decahedron, or not?

As evolution unfolded through the centuries, the spirit of conquest filled explorers, politicians, businessmen, and others eager to sculpt the world anew. The exaltations portray this spirit of seizing the day. It is a step in our collective evolution to potently assert ourselves in order to create functional civilization. This sentiment is captured in a verse from *Cortez the Killer* by Neil Young.

He came dancing across the water
With his galleons and guns
Looking for the new world
In that palace in the sun[xxxii]

What happens when we find the palace in the Sun? Is it appropriate for men to claim a throne there or rather to put down the guns and humbly ask Spirit for entry? The humility needed for spiritual awakening is not a part of the mindset found in the exaltations. They're a perfect reflection of the PVS—so much so that we can just import the content from Chapter 1 that describes the PVS (in italics) and just add the astrology correlations and additional commentary.

Sun in Aries: *The world is seen as a place to conquer, and the mindset is that men are most qualified to perform this task...the masculine tends to become enthralled with absolute supremacy, even to the point of believing it can be God. Kings, dictators, and certain clergy members are just a few examples of men who have brazenly declared they are infallible.*

The Sun's exaltation in Aries is reflective of the egoic takeover. Instead of seeing the Sun as awakening from ego, the sign most about the autonomous self (Aries) is thought to be where we shine brightest. Aries is the most conventionally masculine sign in its expression, and the most about separation consciousness. We also find the value of competiveness in the sports industry and the huge sums of money paid to those who achieve in this arena. This combination also includes the preoccupation with military power.

Moon in Taurus: *A central Patriarchal value is to control resources, be it money, commodities, or natural resources such as land or oil...the mindset of "the more money the better"...The PVS expects women to be stable nurturers in the family system.*

214

The Moon's exaltation in Taurus portrays the attachment to wealth and material objects, an emotional allegiance with earth and the status quo. Furthermore, as the Moon is traditionally seen as "the feminine," we notice the PVS preference for women to be stable, sensual, beautiful, and peaceful.

Mercury in Virgo: *As men tend to identify with the left-brain, the PVS promotes reason, practicality, results, and precision. The valued mindset is skeptical and insists on tangible and definitive proof before changing positions. The sensory, physical world has the least ambiguity to it, so working effectively in this realm is championed. Figuring out how to do things well is what serves society, not pie-in-the-sky abstractions.*

The intellectual conservatism of the PVS does not promote questioning or innovation. There is a fascination with conquering the earth realm. The mind is in tune with what is tangible and known (Virgo) instead of what is beyond—the transpersonal, the ineffable, the mysterious.

Venus in Pisces: *The PVS expects women to yield to men's decisions and position of power. Receptive and docile women are seen as attractive, and the proverbial "trophy wife" is highly valued. The PVS demands that women accept their subservient role. It welcomes their seductive flair and mystery, but makes no space for them to be competitive with men.*

Conventionally Venus is paired with women, and the exaltation in Pisces shows conventional attitudes towards them. Beauty is idealized, and the women who are powerless, receptive, and docile are seen as most attractive. This attitude has led to the proliferation of pornography, sexism, and the consciousness that "the feminine" includes some degree of disempowerment or victimization (Pisces). Venus in Pisces values the absence of conflict in relationships, everything looking good, and plenty of cash (Venus) flow (Pisces). Venus in Pisces also correlates with the glamorization of the supernatural.

215

This has led to many artistic (Venus) portrayals of spirituality (Pisces) found in culture, but the divine tends to be dressed up in idealized and fantastic ways that are unreal. This portrayal shows up throughout the history of European art and on up to modern cinema.

Mars is exalted in Capricorn: *Men are expected to be focused on their career and the outer world, to work hard and achieve status. And the best way to be a good provider is to excel within the prevailing systems, to climb the established ladders of success. Endurance, attaining experience, and achieving status are championed values. There is pressure to strengthen the system, honor its history, and promote the possibility that any man who climbs the ladder with these values should have his eventual turn at the top.*

Mars in Capricorn is the dutiful soldier or successful athlete, the mighty machinery that tears into the earth for corporate gain, or the power broker on Wall Street. This value of fighting for corporate gain, financial interests, or societal status can be very difficult on men. They end up being conditioned to lose themselves in the system, convinced it's the "manly" way. The universal yearning for spiritual evolution remains within men, but it becomes distorted and/or repressed, resulting in alienation, depression, stoicism, stunted emotional development, and the condemnation of spirituality. The drive to excel in and influence mainstream consciousness (Capricorn) reinforces the value of the earth realm, particularly how it can be profitable.

Jupiter is exalted in Cancer: *The PVS wants to maintain tradition, values home and hearth, reveres patriotic and nationalistic sentiments. Creating communities and having like-minded and agreeable people as neighbors strengthens the fabric of society. In fact, the PVS likes to expand community through sports leagues, church activities, and other ways of bringing people together. Family values are championed, such as getting married, being heterosexual, and*

216

having children. These values aren't necessarily "old fashioned."
They're what support a stable society.

Expansive philosophy could bring us to further heights, but Cancer values the tried and true old ways. The United States has Jupiter in Cancer (conjunct the Sun), and we see the valuing of "mom, apple pie, and baseball." Though there is an old-fashioned charm in this placement, it also expects conformity. The vibe is non-threatening and pure like 1950s culture, the simplicity found with *Leave it to Beaver*. The darkness is the undercurrent of patriotic and nationalistic sentiments, the promotion that our way is the best. Jupiter in Cancer can be self-congratulatory and nearsighted. Great value is placed on enlargement, on owning a huge house on a large plot of land, on being the big fish (Jupiter) in the local pond (Cancer). Family vacations or celebratory occasions in the home (such as holidays) are supersized (Jupiter).

Saturn is exalted in Libra: *The PVS instills many norms for society. Men govern systems of laws, and should someone break these laws, there are rightful punishments. It serves everyone to maintain social civility, so being respectful of others, and especially authority, is valued. The cultural norm is that men propose marriage and women are expected to take their name. Culture and the arts are welcome, but they should be tasteful and reflect the values of society. Commerce is especially important—the buying and selling of goods benefits everyone, so the PVS promotes materialism and consumption. Status equates to having the finer things: expensive wine, trendy name brand products, luxury accommodations, season tickets, etc.*

Saturn's exaltation in Libra shows Patriarchal (Saturn) ideals (Libra), social conformity, and adherence to established laws and protocol. These values maintain maximal stability while also inviting everyone to engage with the mainstream culture. We can believe in the courts, the government, the police, and the authorities—they have our best interests in mind (or so we're told). The shadow of Saturn in Libra is institutional corruption, a system that rewards "kissing ass" and elitism. Professionalism is valued and promoted, and those who do not rise to meet particular standards are judged to be second rate. Saturn in Libra puts forth traditional views of relationships and marriage, oppresses (Saturn) equality (Libra), and frowns on social deviation. The primary value is on appearances and adhering to conventional roles.

We notice an emphasis on earth with the exaltations. Though there are four elements, almost half of the exaltations (three of seven) are in earth, and each of the three earth signs has a planet designated as exalted. Here we see the focus on the mundane world and the marginalization of what lies beyond it. It serves Patriarchal interests to not have people undermine the power dynamic, but rather serve as rank and file soldiers (Mars in Capricorn) who obediently follow a god-king (Sun in Aries).

It is especially revealing that Mercury is exalted in Virgo, one of its associated signs. This is a further exclamation of the intellectual attachment to the earth realm, which keeps our heads (Mercury) in the sand (earth). The promotion to exaltation, when no other planet is similarly exalted in its own sign, shows a deep alliance between the mind and the tangible. The sign of innovation and genius (Aquarius) would seem appropriate for Mercury's elevation, but Aquarius (fixed air) insists on perpetual questioning of what has come before, and the *reformation* of our acquired knowledge for what's to come.

In Virgo, the mind becomes ensnared in a trap of scientific materialism, a condition so pervasive that even questioning it is an act of intellectual destabilization. If one criticizes the PVS, the Mercury in Virgo defense is to discredit the author by attacking credentials or their knowledge base — basically saying they don't know what they're talking about.

218

Virgo claims precision and expertise, with lots of minutia as evidence of intellectual accuracy.

The emphasis on mental precision sets the terms of discussion. Whoever has done the most research and has the most experience must be the most qualified. An elaborate infrastructure is erected to hide behind—the supposedly illustrious halls of academia, professional conferences, tightly controlled publishing and media corporations. The mind (Mercury) is in the role of slave (Virgo) to the system. There is no awareness that Virgo's scope of knowledge might be limited or biased. Virgo employs logical routines and methods, narrowing the dialogue to particular areas that lack ambiguity—it's "down to earth" and abides by "common sense," notions that are hard to disagree with. The shadow of its diligence is rigidity. Jiddu Krishnamurti said, "A consistent thinker is a thoughtless person, because he conforms to a pattern; he repeats phrases and thinks in a groove."

The exaltations illustrate the PVS in all four elements. Instead of energy (fire) being transpersonal and universal, Sun in Aries illustrates the masculine takeover of Spirit and the focus on separation consciousness. Earth is the overwhelming focus of life—to connect the will (Mars) with mainstream consensus (Capricorn), mind (Mercury) with materialism (Virgo), all driven by the personal need (Moon) for security and comfort (Taurus). The benefics (Jupiter, Venus) are exalted in water signs (Cancer, Pisces) indicating the ego's preference for only "positive" emotional experiences. Air concerns innovation, new ideas, and possibilities. The only planet exalted in air is Saturn, the one most about suppression and control. The exaltation of Mercury in Virgo (instead of Aquarius) also goes along with the PVS discomfort with change.

The Falls

The designation of a planet being in "fall" is considered the "worst" possible placement. As we saw earlier, this view is not borne out with chart examples, since an individual can respond consciously to any chart factor. As we'll explore, when we are able to manage these designations intentionally, they illustrate how we can correct the historical imbalances of the Patriarchy. We can bolster the areas that have been less valued and create a more integrated world civilization. It turns out that the falls have important meaning—whatever has been marginalized or repressed can serve as keys for liberation and spiritual evolution.

Sun in Libra: Here is the movement from separation consciousness (Aries) to valuing interdependence, from domination to collaboration. We are developing the awareness that we must honor and rely on each other for evolution to continue. Instead of the individual (Aries) taking on the role of Spirit, we can learn to see Spirit in each other. This is the sentiment of the Sanskrit word "Namaste," holding the awareness that everyone is a sacred mirror to us.

Moon in Scorpio: The PVS wants to avoid emotional turmoil, psychological issues, and the shadow. Our task now is to make this terrain a top priority. First, the PVS can acknowledge that it has projected emotional instability on to women, as with its view that the Moon is exclusively feminine. Now, we can all acknowledge that we are rooted in the Moon and work to resolve our issues and become more conscious. The current culture does not like painful emotion and most look for ways to avoid or medicate these feelings. A new value could be to work profoundly with this material, to see the value of catharsis and release, and to bond with others by working through the dark.

Mercury in Pisces: To balance the attachment to the left-brain, we can intentionally engage the right-brain and see its scope as equally relevant. Efforts to develop intuition, psychic ability, musical and artistic intelligence, and abstract thinking are called for. We might heed the message of intellectual advancement given by Einstein, "If you want your children to be intelligent, read them fairy tales. If you want them to be more intelligent, read them more fairy tales." In addition, contemplative practice that calms intellectual restlessness can be helpful in loosening our attachment to the left-brain. We can support people in "living their dreams" and understanding the dreaming process. Further evolution involves having the mind (Mercury) fully involved with transpersonal processes (Pisces).

Venus in Virgo: Instead of promoting the ideal that relationships should be easy and flowing (Pisces), we can take on the responsibility that they are work in the trenches of soul evolution. We can invite others to reflect back to us (Venus) what we need to work on (Virgo). When we see others as a mirror of the self (recall the Sun in Libra), we become very interested in the messages they have for us. Venus in Virgo holds the value of being helpful to others. Our evolution is furthered when we set up services for the poor—electricity and utilities, condoms to limit the spread of disease, quality health care, etc. With the intention to assist others, we tackle the social problems that plague the planet and thereby usher in a new day.

Mars in Cancer: Instead of directing energy into the promotion of the status quo (Capricorn), we can value introspection and feeling. We can develop the ability to live (Mars) with greater sensitivity (Cancer) and strengthen unconditional love of self. We can also learn to see that whatever conflict (Mars) we have experienced in family contexts (Cancer) was actually there to help us become emotionally stronger. The PVS might suggest that we can grow out of our past, leave it behind, and seize a new day. A new value might be that we can grow *into* our past and learn to love everything we've been through. Then we can approach the world as a warrior (Mars) connected to heart (Cancer).

Jupiter in Capricorn: We can bring greater purpose into the dominant power structure, enlarging (Jupiter) the mainstream (Capricorn) to include more philosophies and perspectives. To balance the value of community and loving thy neighbor (Cancer), we can also put forth the notion of discovering greater meaning (Jupiter) in the everyday world (Capricorn). How can we create greater purpose in our governing and dominant institutions? Instead of being driven by corporate gain, businesses (Capricorn) may become motivated by spiritual concerns. Jupiter in Capricorn challenges the Patriarchy to expand beyond its prior limits and into greater possibilities.

Saturn in Aries: This is quite the reversal of values from the exaltation of Sun in Aries. Instead of promoting the self as being God-like (Sun in Aries), we can do the self-work to achieve greater mastery and maturation. Instead of creating social norms that value sophistication (Saturn in Libra), living the ideal of high culture, we can value individual differences (Aries). We can place less emphasis on conformity and more on self-development. As we move towards the value of appreciating (and celebrating) our interdependence (Sun in Libra), the bolstering of Saturn in Aries is most necessary. It invites us to mature into greater levels of self-respect, conduct our behavior responsibly, and embrace our individual program of evolution. If we want to steer from the soul, we have to mature the ego and become solid (Saturn) in the separate self (Aries).

Dignities & Detriments

The exaltations portray the preferences of the PVS, and the falls help us balance that value system by incorporating the polarity of it. The only issue with the dignities and detriments is to remove the good/bad suggestion in the vocabulary of these classifications.

Planets are rightfully paired with signs. Aries goes with Mars, Taurus with Venus, and so on. The astrology system boils down to the repetition and variation of 12 essential themes. Having a planet in its home sign focuses the spiritual work in that theme. Jupiter in Sagittarius is not "stronger" than Jupiter in Scorpio or Gemini, but rather suggests that the chart owner is learning to expand further (Jupiter) in areas of philosophical understandings, adventure, and purpose (Sagittarius). With Jupiter in Scorpio, the focus shifts to address another theme. Here, Jupiter is bridging theme 9 (Sagittarius), with theme 8 (Scorpio)—a situation no less desirable than working only in theme 9 (Sagittarius). Every soul is enrolled in a different curriculum.

One way people attempt to stretch past the good/bad judgments is to suggest a better fit between planet and sign. Venus just "fits" better in Libra than Aries is their mindset— there is room to allow a conscious expression of Venus in Aries, though Libra would be more ideal. However, saying that the fit is better (or more ideal) is still claiming that a particular placement is preferable. Mere word substitutions fail to shift our fixation on the car to the exclusion of the driver.

Another approach is to embrace the spiritual value of each of the planets in each of the signs. When value judgments are set aside, we create more room for a deeper engagement with our curriculum.

Aspects

Conventional astrology also has judgments about the aspects. In particular, the trine and sextile are considered "good," while the opposition and square are "bad." Again, this mindset has the assumption that the chart, rather than the chart owner, is responsible for how the astrology plays out. Many now use the terms "hard" and "soft" aspects, but if the soft aspects are seen as preferable, we're just dealing with another word substitution.

Aspects are like connecting cords between planets, like phone lines that make the energetic dialogue possible. However, the phone line doesn't *participate* in the dialogue. Some use astrology with the belief that the type of aspect influences the planets in question. Transiting Pluto moving into a trine with the natal Moon may be seen as a "good" thing. Pluto pertains to shadow material while the Moon is our emotional unconscious. Any interaction between these planets is going to bring out buried material that the person is uncomfortable with. I have repeatedly seen crisis and great challenges with this, and similar, "soft" aspects—both in natal configurations, as well as with transits and progressions.

The difference between the hard and soft aspects is friction or flow between the planets. Sometimes we have a challenging phone connection and other times its smooth sailing. Sometimes friction is needed to catalyze evolution. At other times, it's appropriate to learn lessons through flow. In either situation, we may or may not manage the lessons consciously. Many astrologers have noted that some of the greatest breakthroughs come with managing hard aspects effectively. With the mindset of spiritual evolution, we can be especially excited about the opportunities these bring.

Houses, too, carry the historical good/bad judgments. "Accidental dignity" occurs when a planet is in a house it's naturally associated with—for instance Mercury in the 3rd or Moon in the 4th. Once again, there is a judgment that this situation is preferable, as the term "dignity" has positive connotations. Among its definitions is, "nobility or elevation of character."

Angular planets (on the MC/IC or ASC/DSC axis) tend to be thought of as "stronger" than others. The same issue applies once again—it's how the person lives the planet, not the placement itself, which determines how strongly it manifests. That being said, the nature of angularity tends to be more pronounced in expression. These planets are generally active and amplified, both in natal charts and by transit or progression. We also see this relevance with Astrocartography, which illustrates on the globe where planetary energy activates a chart angle. When we are near these lines, the planet in question tends to become central and immediate in our experience.

The question is whether increased activation, as conveyed by the chart angles, is in any way advantageous. In the West, there is a value on doing. In the East, there is more a value on *being*. I heard a teacher once say that in the West we are taught, "Don't just sit there, do something," while in the East it's, "Don't just do something, sit there." He was trying to show us that our tendencies for action are only one way to live, one *value system* in approaching life. When we develop our ability to *be* (in contrast to always doing), we cultivate mindfulness, a more centered and clear way to handle life. Imbalance, though, can also be created by only "being" and not also "doing." Quantum physicist Amit Goswami says that the brain functions optimally when "doing" and "being" are completely balanced. He suggests we, "do, be, do, be, do, be." This dynamic follows the rhythm of having yang and yin houses (and signs) alternate around the wheel.

With a value system focused, instead, on learning and growth, we might develop a bias towards planets in the cadent houses: knowledge (3rd), skill development (6th), philosophy and expansion (9th), and spiritual practice (12th). In contrast to the more immediate areas of personal behavior (1st), family (4th), relationships (7th), and career (10th), the cadent houses have more to do with personal growth. However, angular planets are preferred as they're seen as "strong," while planets in cadent houses are often seen as "weak." They're sort of like the guy who chooses to meditate instead of joining his buddies to watch the football game, a "weakling" in their eyes. The PVS does not support spiritual seeking, and the promotion of the angular houses is a symptom of it.

We can honor the reality that angular planets are more active than others without having any judgment on this. We can also honor the important roles cadent planets have, especially their significance in spiritual evolution. Most people are going to hear strong/weak and interpret this along the lines of good/bad, so these designations are unhelpful for soul evolution. We can remove this judgment and appreciate the value of everything in the system.

Patriarchy & The Planets

Another area where we find a Patriarchal bias is with the planets, as a great majority of them have masculine mythological underpinnings. Although the Sun is our spiritual source energy, it's conventionally seen as "the masculine," and is associated with the masculine god Apollo. Some people see Mercury as androgynous, but in myth Hermes (Mercury) is clearly masculine, the son of Zeus. Hermes and Aphrodite had a child named Hermaphroditus, who is the androgynous figure.

Venus (Aphrodite), Goddess of love and beauty, is considered feminine. The Earth correlates with Gaia, who is also feminine. The widely used standard set of 10 planets does not include Earth because it is our point of reference. It will not be counted here as a feminine archetype that is actively a part of astrology. However, the Earth's Moon is conventionally seen as "the feminine."

Mars (Ares), the God of War, is masculine. The social and outer planet energies broaden from the personal to involve worldly matters. All of them are masculine: Jupiter (Zeus), Saturn (Chronos), Uranus (Ouranos), Neptune (Poseidon), and Pluto (Hades).

Out of the ten standard planetary energies used in most astrology, eight are considered masculine and two feminine. Women are basically given the task of looking good (Venus) and incubating children (Moon), both of which at least in part serve the masculine. Furthermore, Chiron (a masculine figure) is now included on most astrology charts and is discussed widely in astrology literature. With his inclusion, the masculine tally increases to nine.

A relatively recent development is the popularity of the "Asteroid Goddesses," which does provide some much needed gender balance. However, most astrology throughout all of history has not included the asteroids. Furthermore, there are thousands of asteroids, many of which are paired with masculine figures. If we include the four major asteroid goddesses (Vesta, Ceres, Juno, and Pallas Athena), the total is now a more respectable nine to six, a 3:2 ratio favoring the masculine. However, the asteroids are given second class status, which is another reflection of Patriarchy. Athena especially stands out in this respect, as she was a major goddess in Grecian mythology (Athens is her namesake), but is merely an afterthought in how most astrology is practiced.

Eight out of the ten major planets used in astrology are associated with masculine mythological figures. There is clearly a Patriarchal bias, but there is no condemnation here; it is just a byproduct of where the course of evolution has taken us. As a reflection of the consciousness of the times, astrology couldn't have developed otherwise. Another test to see if there's been a historical Patriarchal bias: Can you name one female astrologer whose work shaped astrology prior to the 20th Century? Very few can.

Astrology & Gender

Oneness divides into duality, forming the polarities of yin and yang. There are times for rest (yin) and times for action (yang). The tides ebb and flow. Day alternates with night, life with death. The yin-yang dichotomy can be seen throughout nature in millions of ways.

The feminine is only a part of the yin, and the masculine is but a part of yang. Gender is certainly an area in which we see this division. However, yin and yang energies in nature *rarely have anything to do with gender*. For instance, inhalation or listening (yin) and exhalation or talking (yang) are not feminine and masculine. They involve the flow of energy either inward or outward. Making gender associations with these things is not useful—in fact, it's potentially confusing.

There's the tendency in our thinking and our language to pair things dualistically. There is nothing *wrong* with this, but we need to remember that making simplified, black/white pairings can distort and conflate phenomena which do have differences. The way that yin and yang are discussed and used in astrology tends to include the notion that yin IS the feminine and yang IS the masculine—that they are synonymous. Therefore, everything in astrology is seen through the filter of gender. This has created some distortions.

The polarity of Cancer/Capricorn is often discussed in terms of the traditional gender stereotypes of home vs. career. Capricorn is often seen in paternal ways (iron-fisted control, CEOs, authority), but it's categorized as a "feminine" sign because it's of the earth element (yin). If we remove the association with earth/yin and actually look at how Capricorn functions in the world, would we truly think of it as feminine? On the other hand, the sign most about relationships, harmony, and togetherness (Libra) is a "masculine" sign (air). Venus is thought of as feminine, but it's associated with a masculine sign. In the current way of classification, the archetype most aligned with career, tradition, and authority is feminine, and the one most about relationship, aesthetics, and art is masculine. Could there be a better way to organize the system? In the following chapter, we'll be doing exactly that.

Chapter 10
Astrology & The 21st Century
Part 2: Reconstruction

In this chapter we'll address issues of integrating the transpersonal perspective into astrology. There are a number of reforms we can implement so that astrology can more explicitly promote spiritual growth instead of catering to ego preferences. The criteria for these reforms should be that they rest on common sense, have a sound theoretical underpinning, and appeal to universal sentiments.

First, I'll introduce a new classification for the elements. Understanding earth and air as neutral, and water and fire as charged adds an important nuance, providing a more complete way to understand the characteristics of each element. As we'll explore, it also invites us to see things from a less egoic perspective. With the inclusion of this important variable, I'll provide a brief summary of the 12 facets of the system, including both their awakened and egoic expressions. Then, we'll address some classification issues that arise with these innovations, and further suggestions for grouping the system in terms of the elements. Finally, the chapter ends with a summation of the universal principles of *The Astrology of Awakening*.

Charged & Neutral Elements

Changing the way we categorize the elements is the foundational piece to this "reformed" astrology. This new method provides greater nuance and perspective—a revolution that can change our understanding of every planet, sign, and house.

The conventional organization is to pair earth and water as the yin (receptive) elements, and air and fire as the yang (active) elements. This classification has been around for centuries. In my previous book, *Elements & Evolution*, I proposed an additional way of organizing the elements—framing water and fire as the "charged" elements, and earth and air as the "neutral." Below are some of the main points of this issue. Check out the *Elements* book for a more thorough discussion.

The standard yin/yang format of pairings deals with the vertical dimension. Earth and water are solid, physical elements—they conform to gravity and take tangible form. In contrast, air and fire are not tangible or grounded. So on a vertical axis, we can picture air and fire as located above earth and water.

Looking at the elements on a horizontal axis creates the new grouping. In fact, a division into left and right fits perfectly, as the elements will be organized into what is widely discussed as left-brain and right-brain categories.

Neutral (Earth, Air)	Charged (Water, Fire)
Left-brain	Right-brain
Objective	Subjective
Content	Process
Science	Art
Rational	Non-rational
Structure	Essence
Information	Meaning
Logos	Eros
Consensus Reality	Non-Consensus Reality

Content, information, and structure are the objective counterparts to our subjective participation (process, essence, art, etc.). "Charged" includes emotion, desire, opinions, and preferences, all of which may fluctuate wildly. Water and fire have levels of intensity and deal with quality, while earth and air function in terms of volume and quantity.

We can notice this contrast in numerous ways. Olympic judges score for precision with "technical merit," (neutral) and for "aesthetic presentation" (charged). You might go on a trip for business (neutral) or for pleasure (charged). We often see characters split up in this way to serve as foils for each other. In the classic Star Trek series, Spock was famously neutral in his Vulcan way, while Dr. "Bones" McCoy was frequently impassioned.

	Neutral	Charged
Yang	Air	Fire
Yin	Earth	Water

Element Organization

This fuller picture of the elements yields these results: Earth is receptive (yin) and neutral, and water is receptive (yin) and charged. Air is active (yang) and neutral, while fire is active

233

(yang) and charged. Earth and water are, respectively, the neutral and charged elements of the *physical* world. Air and fire are, respectively, the neutral and charged elements of the *nonphysical* world.

Consensus reality (neutral) is our common understanding of how the world is organized — including physical objects and their tangible qualities (earth). One object may be bumpy, while another is smooth. The internal *experience* among people may differ, but there is universal agreement about the relative feel of these objects — a consensus about our reality. The same is true with the air element, which structures the nonphysical world including language, mathematics, and logic. There is consensus that $1 + 1 = 2$, or that the sky is blue. The factual world has order just like the physical world — we just don't see it. Air also relates to how time, space, calendars, and musical notes are organized.

In contrast, the charged elements register in non-consensus reality. They're involved with unique subjective processes, which can never be fully experienced by another. The water element connects to our highly subjective relationship with the world. We process sensations and respond to them in our own unique ways. One person enjoys sand between the toes, and another finds it irritating.

Fire is the subjective element in the nonphysical realm and includes interpretations, opinions, theories, speculations, intentions, and our relationship to energy itself. Fire relates to the *quality* of energetic experience, how we might enjoy a particular form of music or agree with certain ideas. In contrast, air, in its objectivity, makes no such distinctions — music is just sounds, and ideas are just a collection of words. With fire, we have subjective preferences.

Earth provides structure. Air provides content. We can have a various number of possessions (earth) or sentences in a paragraph (air). The statement (air) "yellow and red make orange" is not a *better* statement than "France is a part of Europe." A statement can either be true or false, but qualitative judgments like better or worse are not applicable.

The charged elements carry degrees of intensity that can be rated on a scale from 1 to 10. Someone may rate the appeal of tuna fish at 6, and chocolate at 9. We also have subjective preferences for objective sounds (air). On paper, the musical scores for rap, pop, or classical music are not qualitatively different— they're just selections of notes in different arrangements. However, someone may rate choral music at 3, and rock music at 7.

The natural world illustrates the levels of intensity found with water and fire. There are placid lakes and raging seas, moderate climates and blazing hot deserts. The elements can be highly activated or relatively inactive. This variability is similar in people—note the difference between an angry (fire) or depressed (water) person and someone who isn't experiencing any charge at all. In contrast, earth and air (or space) provides the neutral setting, the physical and nonphysical structures to life.

Charged and Neutral in Astrology

Planets, signs, and houses can all be understood in terms of charge and neutrality, as they all have an elemental foundation. We can group them together in their common archetypal themes. When we interact with the neutral elements, we tend to have charged emotions or opinions *about* them, but this doesn't make them inherently charged.

The charge of Aries, Mars, and the 1st House shows up in our behavior choices, which are governed by instinct and impulse. We are motivated to satisfy our hungers and desires.

235

Taurus, Venus, and the 2nd House are neutral. We own tangible objects such as money and possessions. Although most of us have feelings about these things, the emotional charge is what we *add*. Remove this added emotion, and money is just paper; possessions are physical items.

Gemini, Mercury, and the 3rd House are also neutral, as they relate to information and communication. As we find in the dictionary or a phone book, facts can be organized. We may have favorite numbers, but that's our charge, not theirs.

Cancer, the Moon, and the 4th House are associated with internal feelings such as love and fear. The intensity of feelings may be mild or strong depending on the person and the situation.

Leo, the Sun, and 5th House involve personal expression, which is unique to every person. Every person's radiance carries a highly subjective charge, which is received completely differently by others based on their own preferences and personalities.

Virgo, Mercury, and the 6th House correlate with the functionality of the physical world. The round peg goes in the round hole, not the square one. There is no debate and no charge, unless we inject one.

Libra, Venus, and the 7th House relate to the neutral, social organization in consensus reality, which includes laws, customs, and norms. Although the ways in which social realms are organized may change, the organization itself remains neutral.

Scorpio, Pluto, and 8th House charges are unmistakable. From getting sexually turned on to saying difficult emotional truths, this theme is highly dramatic.

Sagittarius, Jupiter, and the 9th House also have a charged component. Opinions and declarations are not a description of objectivity; they stem from one's unique viewpoint. We also see the rising of a charge in what stimulates the expansion of experience. One person has a peak experience scuba-diving, while another prefers knitting.

Capricorn, Saturn, and the 10th House involve physical or structural organization. A transportation system or housing developments function as neutral frameworks for our use.

Aquarius, Uranus, and the 11th House illustrate an organization in the air—astrology, group dynamics, and the unwritten norms of how a community operates. We all connect within the interiors of a massive neutral matrix.

Pisces, Neptune and the 12th House include the subjectivity of dreams and spiritual experience, which cannot be understood in consensus reality.

Venus as Neutral

Venus is associated with the goddess Aphrodite and represents the *ideal* of beauty or perfection. The realities of life compromise how ideals can manifest—they are neutral because they are untouched by human distortion. The Moon is our humanness and, through its filter, Venus becomes emotion-alized. We tend to have strong feelings about our romantic ideals (Venus). We instantaneously charge Venus upon interaction with it, but in itself we can understand Venus as neutral. Its connection with Taurus can shed some light here.

Taurus, being associated with value, is not afraid to put a price tag on objects in the physical world. Venus can strip away sentimentality in favor of neutrality. Taurus might say a car is worth $20,000. The Moon could never say her child is worth any dollar figure. That is the essential difference between the charged Moon and the neutrality of Venus.

The neutrality of the airy expression of Venus is what we expect from our judges. They shouldn't be partial, but of course they have their biases like anyone else. However, we see the principle, *the ideal*, of fairness and justice through Libra. Upon the realization that our egoic charge has distorted Venus, we can then see and appreciate that it's a neutral energy. The neutrality of Libra and Taurus tends to be more easily understood than Venus. The folklore involving the planet of love and beauty really charges us up! When we take responsibility for our *reaction* to Venus, we see that it was a neutral mirror all along.

The egoic takeover is evident in our limited understanding of the elements. When we remove the injection of ourselves, we appreciate the dynamic between neutral and charged, instead of only seeing charged (the ego). The inclusion of this distinction can assist us in seeing life from a transpersonal perspective.

The Planets

There are six charged planets (Sun, Moon, Mars, Jupiter, Neptune, and Pluto) and four neutral (Mercury, Venus, Saturn, and Uranus). There actually is not an imbalance because Mercury and Venus both serve as the dispositor of two signs. The ways in which charge and neutrality play out is balanced.

	Neutral		Charged	
Yang	Mercury	Gemini	Mars	Aries
	Venus	Libra	Sun	Leo
	Uranus	Aquarius	Jupiter	Sagittarius
Yin	Venus	Taurus	Moon	Cancer
	Mercury	Virgo	Pluto	Scorpio
	Saturn	Capricorn	Neptune	Pisces

Planet and Sign Organization

Although there is this overall balance, the Sun and Moon—the two central energies in the system—are both charged. We live in a *participatory* universe full of meaningful relationships based on soul evolution. If our fundamental orientation were neutral there would be less dynamism of individuality. Instead, we are intimately involved with life to further our spiritual growth.

From the geocentric perspective, Mercury and Venus are always near the Sun. This arrangement illustrates how their neutral energies accompany and inform our being (Sun) as we connect with consensus reality. We instantaneously perceive the immediate environment and orient our mind (Mercury) and senses (Venus) to it. We approach the world as intelligent (Mercury) and social (Venus) beings. This orientation in consensus reality then becomes populated by our egoic (Moon) projections (Sun).

239

When we notice the interplay between charged and neutral within us, we can witness our emotional reactions and desires. We may choose to consciously move into charges to better manage them instead of being driven by them unconsciously. We might see the increasing intensity of a charge as an opportunity to channel it constructively—or to just be aware that we are in the grips of something less than rational.

Managing charges effectively can help resolve unprocessed material in the psyche. When we reach greater neutrality about an issue, we can understand that healing is underway. When we no longer get triggered (charge) by an issue, we are able to maintain our center. Then, we can *consciously* engage charges instead of unconsciously reacting— we can choose healthy ways to work with the energy. We can see how the separate self spends so much time and energy working out the charges of emotions or ego preferences.

The arousal of a charge points to a need for spiritual work—either for the resolution of the past, or by inspiring us to move forward. The point is not to maintain a state of neutrality, but to be mindful of why we are becoming activated. Ultimately we can view the personal story from a transpersonal perspective, while also participating in it fully. We can appreciate the subtleties and gifts of both charged and neutral.

With this neutral-charged understanding, we can see that the paradigm that initially informed astrology was not infallible. It was incomplete, missing something obvious to the modern mind and its understanding of the left and right brain. Astrology evolves just like we do and reflects our consciousness.

I have been writing and speaking about this method of categorizing the elements for ten years now. When I initially present this idea, listeners go through a brief period of letting it sink in, after which there is universal acceptance of it. *I have yet to find one single person who disagrees with it!* Having a horizontal division (left/right) to complement the usual vertical division (up/down) seems pretty obvious once it's considered.

Astrological Organization

We'll now look at how we can organize the facets of the system at this point. The following summaries of the 12 astrological phases include the neutral-charged distinction, as well as each phase's expression from the transpersonal and relative viewpoints. Each of the 12 phases is composed of a modality (cardinal, fixed, mutable) and an element (earth, water, air, fire). These combinations create broad, archetypal themes that lay out the cycle of evolutionary unfolding as it progresses through its 12 stages. Below is a brief summary—for more info, please see *Elements & Evolution*.

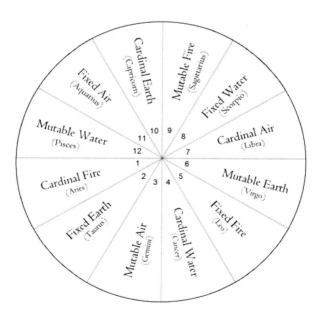

The Astrology Wheel

241

The Evolutionary Cycle

Stage 1: Cardinal Fire

Evolutionary Value: Establishment of behavior choices.
Related Planet, Sign, House: Mars, Aries, 1st House
Classification: Yang, Charged
Functioning Unconsciously: Unconscious behavior creates karma that will have to be addressed in the future.
Awakened Use: Behavior is the natural extension of putting awareness into action. The separate self acts in service of spiritual evolution.
Relative: This energy is often seen in masculine ways (war, competition, force, decisiveness); the power of the separate self.
Transpersonal: We are souls acting in bodies.

The first stage initiates the cycle, but it is informed by the visioning processes of the prior stage (12th). Cardinal and fire spark action and set the wheel in motion. Stage 1 is self-oriented, focused on meeting our personal needs and desires, venturing forth into the unknown. We learn the best way to *orient* to the surrounding world. If we are unconscious, this stage runs by instinct. By developing greater self-awareness, we learn to direct behavior consciously and achieve our goals. With the gift of autonomy, we are responsible for our actions and their subsequent impact. Cardinal fire is eager and driven. The journey has begun, and it's up to us to manage it well. Trusting that we can develop the awareness to align with soul intentions equips us with the *courage* to proceed.

Stage 2: Fixed Earth

Evolutionary Value: Establishment of resources.
Related Planet, Sign, House: Venus, Taurus, 2nd House

Classification: Yin, Neutral
Functioning Unconsciously: Hoarding of resources, identification with belongings, overly concerned with security, safety, money.
Awakened Use: The use of the body and the physical world to manifest spiritual creativity.
Relative: Beauty, serenity, and inner peace are often seen in feminine ways.
Transpersonal: We can learn to identify as a part of nature.

In Stage 2 we solidify (fixed) our resources and anchor (earth) into the self. By occupying the physical self, we get in touch with what is *worth* doing. Yin is receptive and restful, and soul intentions become more embodied. We take stock of our available resources and learn to manage issues of self-doubt and self-worth. We learn to spend money wisely and not to over-identify with our bodies and possessions. The evolutionary task of Stage 2 is to develop a solid commitment to the self. Poor navigation of this terrain results in an insecure base of operations for the rest of the evolutionary cycle. Fixed earth solidifies spiritual intent in the body, grounds us in this life, and compels us to show up. Resistance to this process creates insecurity, anxiety, and self-doubt.

Stage 3: Mutable Air

Evolutionary Value: Establishment of intellect, learning.
Related Planet, Sign, House: Mercury, Gemini, 3rd House
Classification: Yang, Neutral
Functioning Unconsciously: Over-identification with mental activity; heightened need for reason.
Awakened Use: The use of mind to send intention; the understanding of one's position in the world.
Relative: We tend to think there is an objective world that we can understand.

243

Transpersonal: We see how the personal mind is like a nerve ending of a larger mind.

In Stage 3 we develop the intellect. Mutable air is the combination most interested and open to new experiences. Here we learn to orient our minds to the immediate environment and develop our unique style of perception. We can then begin to approach the world from a place of conscious choice rather than merely strategizing for survival. The attempt to master nature through the mind can be a trap that binds us in the egoic prison of the separate self. In this stage we can become intellectually convinced that humans control nature instead of seeing that we are a part of it. Remaining open-minded allows us to discover what our souls intend for us to do in this life. Along the way we can enjoy our sense of wonder at everything there is to learn.

Stage 4: Cardinal Water

Evolutionary Value: Establishment of emotional center, self-love.
Related Planet, Sign, House: Moon, Cancer, 4th House
Classification: Yin, Charged
Functioning Unconsciously: Complete identification with egoic survival needs; over-attachment to defense mechanisms.
Awakened Use: Becoming aware of the unconscious, the gradual dissolution of egoic attachments.
Relative: Seen as feminine due to biological reality; involves nurturance, emotional needs, and bonding.
Transpersonal: The separate self is rooted to incarnate life, which enables the individual to bridge worlds for spiritual evolution.

In Stage 4, we become rooted to our soul condition, the *familiar* themes of our spiritual history, and these get played out in *family*. The spiritual curriculum stems from the ego's attachments and unfinished business in prior lives. In this stage we have the opportunity to touch in with our unprocessed emotional dynamics. If we do not cultivate awareness of who we are inside, we tend to repeat old dynamics that preclude further growth. The pull of past conditioning is very strong, so we must take the initiative (cardinal) to feel (water). Successful navigation of Stage 4 results in self-knowledge, a stable internal foundation. We can learn to release the attachment to what is most familiar and move into the soul intentions for the present life. Cardinal water initiates the flow towards wholeness.

Stage 5: Fixed Fire

Evolutionary Value: Displaying the radiance of Spirit.
Related Planet, Sign, House: Sun, Leo, 5th House
Classification: Yang, Charged
Functioning Unconsciously: The egoic takeover leads us to entitlement, over-identification with personality, and radiance of one's personal agenda.
Awakened Use: Soul realization, the connection of one's energy to all of life.
Relative: We may see this theme as masculine, in terms of personality, and relating to joy and recreation.
Transpersonal: The joy of selflessly illuminating Spirit.

In Stage 5 we're invited into the radiance of the present so that we can live with vitality, spontaneity, and trust in life. Ideally we become thrilled to be alive, which motivates us to deliver our unique gifts. Fixed fire suggests the eternal nature of Spirit. When we see that our radiance bridges the worlds of separation and unity, we accept our roles as powerful collaborators in the glorious unfolding of evolution. With this knowledge, we become aware that we are borrowing energy from Spirit, and we honor our role. The unconscious use is to claim ownership of energy and to maximize self-gain. Stage 5 can be hedonistic and indulgent—the more awake version is to exude grandeur, not grandiosity.

Stage 6: Mutable Earth

Evolutionary Value: The tangible distribution of creativity.
Related Planet, Sign, House: Mercury, Virgo, 6th House
Classification: Yin, Neutral
Functioning Unconsciously: Anxiety about development and competence; staying in unhealthy routines; disempowerment.
Awakened Use: Skill development to give a mature contribution; working with others to improve matters.
Relative: We compare the relative usefulness of things and have judgments of what is better or worse.
Transpersonal: We find the value and purpose in all things.

Stage 6 involves skill development and mastering a trade. We mature from youthful patterns and focus on our earthy contributions. We attend to our health, routines, and continual improvement with dedication. If we are unable to mature, we reinforce patterns of ineffectuality and underachievement. Managed unconsciously, we accept the role of the slave or servant. Mutable earth pertains to the variety of ways in which we can distribute Spirit. Selecting the proper craft, service, or skill to perfect helps distribute (mutable) creative impulses tangibly (earth).

Stage 7: Cardinal Air

Evolutionary Value: Socialization, artistry, diplomacy, under-standing the perspective of others.
Related Planet, Sign, House: Venus, Libra, 7th House
Classification: Yang, Neutral

Functioning Unconsciously: Lack of recognizing self in others leads to evaluating them in terms of self-gain.

Awakened Use: Social connecting to strengthen a more awakened civilization on this planet.

Relative: Other people are different than us.

Transpersonal: Others are us.

Cardinal air involves the initiation of equal relationships within realms of romance, business, or friendship. We broaden our involvement in the world through networking and social interdependence. We can approach the world as a reflection of ourselves, aware that we are spiritually connected to all that occurs. Without this perspective, we become prone to play out our dramas in separation consciousness. In this stage, we decide whether we approach others and the world as something to conquer or, rather, something to join with.

Stage 8: Fixed Water

Evolutionary Value: Integration with the shadow, intimate connection with others and life itself, right use of power.

Related Planet, Sign, House: Pluto, Scorpio, 8th House

Classification: Yin, Charged

Functioning Unconsciously: "Unacceptable" experiences are banished into the shadow only to be eventually met in the external world in need of integration.

Awakened Use: The interpenetration of souls.

Relative: Power is something to tame and control.

Transpersonal: Power is something to become.

Stage 8 is a relentless (fixed) confrontation with the psychology of the ego (water). We become conscious of our underlying psychological dynamics: our desires, motivations, and blind spots. Whereas Stage 7 mirrors (air) who we are, Stage 8 involves doing the emotional work to reach greater wholeness.

Through cultivating awareness, we address our shadow material and how it plays out with others. Associated with death, Stage 8 makes it clear that there are parts of us that need to transform in order for us to evolve. Poor management of this stage results in playing out our unaddressed wounding in public arenas. The evolution available is nothing less than ridding the forces of stagnation or regression that hold us back from our highest potential.

Stage 9: Mutable Fire

Evolutionary Value: Development of mission, perspective of life.
Related Planet, Sign, House: Jupiter, Sagittarius, 9th House
Classification: Yang, Charged
Functioning Unconsciously: Following a belief system without question; dogmatism.
Awakened Use: Living the life that is right for one's spiritual evolution.
Relative: We can discover a theory of everything and make sense of the world.
Transpersonal: We discover Spirit through engagement with life.

At Stage 9 we direct the separate self towards a mission for our collective evolution. We find a meaningful vision for life and expand into further reaches of discovery. We develop a guiding belief system and spiritual path to travel. Mutable fire has a variety of ways to discover the great reach of Spirit. Managed unconsciously we become overly identified with living life narrowly, and often suggest that others behave as we do. The promise of Stage 9 is a thrilling ride of awakening, which informs a profound understanding of this life.

Stage 10: Cardinal Earth

Evolutionary Value: The organization of society.
Related Planet, Sign, House: Saturn, Capricorn, 10th House
Classification: Yin, Neutral
Functioning Unconsciously: Vocation stems from advancing a self-serving agenda.
Awakened Use: One's contribution is in service to Oneness.
Relative: We create a consensus reality and rhythm to everyday life. It is expected that people take part and contribute to the system.
Transpersonal: How we organize society is the concretization of consciousness at a particular evolutionary level. The "center of gravity" of consciousness continuously evolves, so we must move the vise grip down the evolutionary line.

In this stage we act on what we understand to be a personal calling. We commit to its realization and do the earthly tasks necessary for it to blossom. Stage 10 is the pinnacle of achievement—the proverbial climb up the mountain or ladder of success in order to reach the summit. Ideally, we become an authority in our professional niche. Cardinal earth concerns the initiation of worldly authority. Handled unconsciously, we might see career solely as a way to make money or get ahead of others. Cardinal establishes, while earth is structural. This stage is about the tangible creation of social organization, the infrastructure and glue of society. We are inspired to use our stature and influence for the common good.

Stage 11: Fixed Air

Evolutionary Value: Understanding spiritual intelligence.
Related Planet, Sign, House: Uranus, Aquarius, 11th House
Classification: Yang, Neutral

Functioning Unconsciously: The ego distorts, and takes advantage of, innovations that would move us forward. The transpersonal is inaccessible and reduced to only relative understandings.

Awakened Use: The "center of gravity" of consciousness moves to incorporate the transpersonal and life becomes a reflection of our collective awakening.

Relative: We perceive the separate self within the functioning of broader systems. There is an evaluation of how one's inclusion in systems could be personally advantageous.

Transpersonal: We identify as part of nature and have the awareness of our interconnectedness.

At Stage 11 we identify with all of humanity and our collective evolution as we consciously connect the separate self with Oneness. We network, build community, and advocate progressive causes. Fixed air is the interconnected web of energy that has no beginning or end — the eternal intelligence of Spirit. If we are unable to transcend personal concerns, this stage can leave us feeling anonymous, marginal, or disoriented. There is the potential to succumb to group-think or become a cog in a system. If we attempt to hold on to the past (an outmoded paradigm, career position, or legacy), there is the potential for great upset and interpersonal challenge as the times continue to shift. This stage inspires us to claim the future. We all do our personal part (thinking globally, acting locally) to live in maximal accordance with nature. Fixed air relates to the eternal nature of evolution itself. The mind (air) that envelops us is everlasting (fixed).

Stage 12: Mutable Water

Evolutionary Value: The potential realization of Oneness.
Related Planet, Sign, House: Neptune, Pisces, 12th House
Classification: Yin, Charged

Functioning Unconsciously: Advanced levels of consciousness are misunderstood, seen as fantasy, devalued.

Awakened Use: Inspiration and visioning informs and nourishes life in every possible way.

Relative: Spirituality takes form within social organization.

Transpersonal: Spirituality invites us beyond conventional frameworks and paradigms and into direct experience.

Stage 12 completes the cycle and envisions the next. With mutable water, attachments are dissolved—we process our journey of incarnation, reflecting on everything that has occurred. We have compassion for ourselves and gratitude for the journey. If evolution has proceeded consciously, this stage brings the potential to realize heaven on earth. Most of the time there has been some degree of unconsciousness, so we experience the attendant karmic implications. This stage can be experienced like a holding cell or a "soul cage." We can't escape who we are or what we've done—it remains as work to eventually be addressed. Those who refuse to release attachments renew spiritual work for another cycle. The 12th Stage involves spiritual practices that assist us in loosening the ego. Mutable water suggests that Spirit's nourishment flows everywhere, without limitations, distinctions, or judgments.

Elemental Groupings

The most universal and fundamental components of astrology are the four elements. All planets, signs, and houses have associations with them. They operate in a multi-leveled way, a scope that is as broad as deep. Earth (physical), water (emotional), air (mental), and fire (soul) compose everything in the universe. We already commonly use the elements when we discuss signs and houses, but we can include the planets too.

The idea is to discuss the planets as *energetic frequencies* without projecting our relative values or preferences onto them. Like the spectrum of consciousness introduced earlier, there is a wide variety of ways we can connect with these planetary frequencies. When we are able to identify as an assemblage of spiritual energies, we might loosen our attachment to owning them. We can think, for example, of being composed of *Lunar*, *Mercurial*, or *Neptunian* frequencies, which not only exist throughout the human system but also connect us to the external world. A famous astrology adage says, "As above, so below." We could also say, "As outside, so inside."

We'll first look at how the elements are expressed in the external world, and then the in the internal—remember that they permeate both realms. We can categorize each of the frequencies along with the others of a similar element. We see that the planets join at the 4 levels of reality: physical (earth), emotional (water), mental (air), and soul (fire).

Earth: Externally, these planetary frequencies combine in the organization of the physical world. Saturn is responsible for overarching structure. Like gravity, it brings phenomena down to earth and enables objects to maintain form. Mercury inhabits the details. Within anything earthy is intelligence at the micro-level. Like Spirit's "paintbrush", Venus addresses sensual and aesthetic matters, including color and texture.

In the realm of the separate self, our *Saturnian* energy provides us with structural integrity and organizes our impact on the world. It takes the form of boundaries, such as the skin, and holds our energy together as a singular unit. As we age, we become more durable and learn to uphold our integrity as an elder.

Mercurial energy is found in the physical details such as in our DNA or cellular functioning. It relates to the operations that enable the system to run smoothly. With this energy, we are able to focus and prioritize our orientation to the physical realm.

Venusian energy provides us with a sensual attunement to the world. Our senses orient us to our bodies and how they reach out to the environment. We feel grounded to incarnate life, and learn to feel comfortable in our skin.

Water: The water planets also relate to the physical, and involve the flourishing of autonomous life. In the external world, we notice how *Lunar* energy impacts the tides of the ocean (*Neptunian*) and stirs up the processes of life. Within fluids is the genesis of life and creation (*Plutonian*)—the processes at the molecular level that catalyze growth. We see this with micro-organisms developing in a pond.

Inside the separate self, our *Lunar* energy is the well of the egoic unconsciousness that influences the navigation of the dream. Our *Lunar* energy is our basic humanness and relates to instinctual processes (eat, sleep, birth, etc.), as well as emotion and survival needs.

The *Neptunian* frequency is involved with the visioning process. As a transpersonal energy, it becomes active in dreams and other processes beyond our egoic control. This energy flows through us and connects us with the dream space that surrounds us. Ultimately, we can grow to manage this energy adeptly and consciously dream.

Plutonian energy is deeply buried beneath the unconscious (Moon) where it collects disowned dream material. This energy tends to be repressed, but when contacted, its power may be unleashed and used effectively. Whatever is not met with awareness becomes unconsciously projected into the world so we can integrate it and reach greater wholeness.

Air: The Air planets are grouped together for their intellectual, social, and nonphysical structure. In the external world, Uranus relates to the overarching matrix of psychic interconnectedness, and Venus concerns socialization within it. Mercury connects to the cognitive functioning of the lower mind, how each individual perceives the world.

Within the parameters of the separate self, the matrix of *Uranian* energy envelops us. We are psychically attuned with everything that surrounds us. There are endless channels of connectivity, which stimulate the awakening into Spirit.

Venusian energy operates at the personal level and involves the awareness of the nonphysical environment. This includes our connection with our surroundings and social energy in the milieu.

Mercurial energy relates to the personal mind, which is cognitive and reductionist in scope. We are familiar with the running commentary of mental chatter. We learn to understand ourselves and the world through hypothesis and learning.

Fire: The Fire planets deal with the spiritual purpose of energy. In the external world, *Solar* energy is the source of creativity, the awareness and presence of Spirit. This creativity has a multitude of meanings (*Jovial*) depending on the quality of consciousness which connects to it. *Jovial* energy is noticed in the tendency of the universe to expand outwards. *Martial* energy involves action and force. We see it active in the world through its properties of acceleration and movement.

In the separate self, our life energy is *Solar* and, like the Sun, we radiate it outwards. Solar energy is simultaneously an individual soul, while also part of the broader field of Oneness. It involves the process of spiritual realization.

Martial energy involves our action—the ways in which we behave from our impulses and instincts. It's the drive, the passion, the heat that motivates us.

Our *Jovial* energy compels us to expand our reach into the world, to connect our energy with greater purpose. We become *motivated* us to make a difference, to enlarge our capacity to act on our spiritual intentions.

Part of the reason why the planets are generally not associated with the elements is because of the ancient classification of "rulership." If Mars is associated with Aries and Scorpio, then it would be both a fire and a water planet. Jupiter would present a similar situation with Sagittarius (fire) and Pisces (water). Saturn would be paired with both earth (Capricorn) and air (Aquarius).

We can look back on the chapters on the planets and see that the planet Mars can be naturally paired with fire: Its red color, gaping battle scar, and dust storms, which get activated close to the Sun (fire). Unlike Mercury and Venus, the orbit of Mars breaks free from the Sun (from our Earthly perspective), so the planet establishes our free will (fire). Mars is clearly a fire planet.

Jupiter radiates more heat than it receives from the Sun. It has a magnificent, ongoing thunder and lightning show, as well as an enormous fiery red spot. Jupiter is a "gas giant" and has no physicality to its surface. Jupiter, too, is clearly a fire planet.

With its elaborate orchestration of particles, ice, and rocks (earth) which compose its rings, Saturn relates to physical structure. Its many moons also reflect a lot of mass that surrounds it. In contrast, Uranus is known for being cold, more distant (air) and bland. Its far fewer moons portray a diminishment of stature. It's appropriate to think of Saturn as an earth planet, and Uranus as an air.

Recall the charged-neutral dichotomy. We can think of fire as a positive charge (meaning yang, not "good") and water as a negative charge (meaning yin, not "bad"). The neutral elements lack a charge. We find a parallel with protons (positive), electrons (negative), and neutrons (neutral). The neutral planets Mercury and Venus can both have air and earth sides to their energy because there is no charge. This coexistence is not possible with the highly unstable and fluctuating qualities of the charged elements. Either a planet is fire or water, not both. The addition of the outer planets allows for Mars (fire), Jupiter (fire), and Saturn (earth) to be associated with just a single element. This framing allows the outer planets to fully have their accurate connections: Uranus (air), Neptune (water), and Pluto (water).

Grouping the planets in terms of their connection to the elements has some similarity with the idea of "higher octaves," which pairs an inner planet with an outer planet. In both cases, the suggestion is that the planets work together along similar lines. The difference is that the elemental groupings have an underlying link, whereas the higher octaves are more theoretical. The pairing of Mercury (the personal mind) with Uranus (the spiritual mind) does have a more obvious connection through the air element and is similar to the elemental grouping. The other two theoretical pairings are worth exploring further.

Venus involves togetherness, and Neptune is about global togetherness, so there is an obvious overlap. However, Venus generally includes the egoic distortion of injecting emotion (Moon) into the mirror (Venus) and onto the other. Neptune includes transcendent love, but Venus (earth, air) is not about emotion. Its air side (Libra) concerns romance, a glamorization of ideals, but love (emotion) tends to get messy: pregnancy, changing diapers, in-laws, security needs, sickness, etc. All of

256

these are linked to the Moon (Cancer/4th House), but since they are not the most idyllic facets of love, we tend to prefer the Venus idealization and have made it watery when in fact it's not. Seldom is there "happily ever after." Instead we tend to encounter an emotional reality check that pierces our romantic fantasies. The Moon and Neptune share a deeper connection (water) than the suggested one between Venus and Neptune. The dreamer (Moon) connects with the dream space (Neptune).

Mars and Pluto do share a connection with power. However, this pairing builds on the traditional association of Mars with Scorpio, which (as discussed earlier) has many issues of Patriarchal domination that underlie the connection. Mars power is fiery, while Pluto's is watery. Mars has to do with how spiritual intention is behaviorally carried out, so it has a fire link with the Sun. Pluto is involved with the reconciliation of the shadow, which is deep within the unconscious (Moon). Mars is not a planet of depth, while Pluto is unreservedly as deep as we go. Pluto and the Moon connect through the water element.

The underlying Patriarchal mindset of the two genders is found with these higher octave designations. We see its conventional view of women (Venus) as dreamy and impotent (Neptune), which we also find in the exaltation of Venus in Pisces. We also see the stereotype that men (Mars) are powerful (Pluto) in the ancient "rulership" of Scorpio by Mars. We can retract our egoic projections of outdated gender stereotypes on the planetary energy and learn to value them as threads that connect us in Oneness.

Classification Issues

So far we've reviewed the great evolutionary cycle of astrology with its 12 essential stages. We discussed each stage and its themes in terms of yin/yang, charged-neutral, element, modality, associated planet/sign/house, relative and trans-personal associations, as well as how it can be of service for ego or the soul. Then, grouping of planets together by element further illustrates how we are energetically connected to the universe. It's worth highlighting some issues at this point that arise in the absence of these novel perspectives.

When we look at the elements only in their conventional, vertical orientation, we see yin and yang alternate through the signs and houses. With the inclusion of the charged-neutral category, we have a more complete picture. The pattern of charged-neutral-neutral-charged (fire-earth-air-water) repeats three times around the cycle, in personal, social, and collective realms. Each realm (personal, social, collective) begins with the spark of fire (charged), becomes grounded as part of consensus reality in earth (neutral), expands into greater possibilities with air (neutral), and is subjectively processed with water (charged). Therefore, the evolutionary cycle unfolds along both of these lines, not just yin and yang.

Yin and yang are often used as synonyms for feminine and masculine. However, for the sake of discussion, one might argue that the two genders can be seen and understood in terms of charged and neutral as well. The masculine is *conventionally* categorized as more logical and left-brained (neutral), while the feminine is thought of as emotional, intuitive, and right-brained (charged). If we are to incorporate the neutral-charged axis in terms of gender, then air (neutral, yang), and water (charged, yin) are the two elements which are most purely male and female. Fire (charged, yang) and earth (neutral, yin) synthesize the *traditional* male and female value spheres.

However, the historical masculine has held the Sun (and the fire element) as part of its domain, while also making the earth realm the main focus of its agenda, mainly to control resources and preserve tradition. The Patriarchy has claimed

258

three of the four elements as its own (earth/physical, air/mental, and fire/spiritual), leaving only water (emotional) for women. It has operated in Saturnian ways, a power grab of the earth. As mentioned in chapter 9, the Cancer/Capricorn polarity is often discussed in terms of the traditional split of mothering (home) and fathering (world), despite Capricorn being an earth (feminine) sign. In Matriarchal times and cultures, earth was more in the domain of the feminine. My suggestion is to *not* rely on dualism (including gender) as our final authority in understanding astrology.

The absence of the charged-neutral distinction in astrological discourse has also confused the Sun and Moon, which tends to see the Sun as "head" (neutral) and the Moon as "heart" (charged). This framing is consistent with generalizations of the masculine and feminine, and the Sun and Moon are often seen as indicating father and mother. The issue, though, is that the Sun is not left-brain or neutral. Rather, it is energetically radiant and dynamically intense. Understanding that the Sun is charged brings us away from stereotypical male and towards the vitality of fire, the light and heat of the spiritual. The correct dichotomy of "head" and "heart" would be Mercury (neutral) and the Moon.

Another planetary pair that has been mixed up is Mars and Venus. As children develop (Mercury), they tend to split the world up into boy things and girl things. Trucks and blue are for boys, while dolls and pink are for girls. So we have Mars "things" (war, sports, competition) being paired with the masculine, and Venus "things" (relationships, beauty, peace) with the feminine. Mars is traditionally associated with Aries and the 1st House, and Venus goes with the 7th House. As astrology has largely been developed by men, the 1st House is seen in masculine ways because that is the orientation of

259

masculine consciousness. Women are associated with Venus and occupy the 7th House — they assume the role of "the other."

Considering that Libra (air) is a neutral yang sign, it would theoretically be the most masculine combination! So, seeing Mars/Venus in terms of gender doesn't work if yang is a synonym for masculine. Some might say that the use of the term "masculine" to describe Libra is only a *suggestion* of yang, not to be taken literally as in physical or social characteristics attributed to only men. I agree. We should not take these designations literally. However, the current practice tends to reinforce Mercurial polarizations and stereotyping; many people lack this linguistic nuance and do see these designations literally. As the dispositors of Aries and Libra, a more appropriate under-standing of the Mars-Venus pairing is in terms of *self and other*, not male and female. The air side to Venus (Libra) is a neutral mirror of how others reflect back who we are, regardless of our gender.

Gender is, of course, salient in the relative world. As babies, we tend to look alike, no matter if we're male or female. As we age, gender differences become obvious, and the sexes polarize. Elderly people then look somewhat like babies again. They are soft and saggy, sometimes in need of diapers. Gender differences become less relevant and obvious under the wrinkles and effects of aging. As we mature, we grow into a strong gender orientation, only to release it as we die. Interestingly, it is when we are closest to the doors of death (at either end) that it's less relevant.

Part of our growth involves seeing through the trickster quality of Mercury, learning how not to give our power away to dualisms by seeing them as absolutes. We can see that relative understandings have limited applicability and actually break down when the transpersonal is embraced. The neutral-charged distinction is from a non-egoic (transpersonal) frame of reference—only from a bird's eye view can we see that the ego charges everything. The transpersonal has been marginalized because it causes many problems with the ways Mercury likes to order life. It disrupts our attempts at seeing the world only in black and white ways. If we are to heal the mythic castration of Uranus, we must be able to complement the relative lens with the transpersonal. We must learn to embrace greater complexity.

Aspects

Aspects are based on angular distances between planets in the chart. These distances do not change or alter the nature of the planets that are in aspect, but rather facilitate a dialogue between them. As witnessed in nature, geometrical shapes facilitate the movement of energy in a variety of ways.

With an opposition, two poles can either come together or come apart. An equilateral triangle (trine) portrays a system of mutual support. A square is found at a traffic intersection and requires potential conflict management. A hexagon (sextile) shows up in a honeycomb, which is an efficient and supportive structure. None of these shapes are inherently positive or negative—they are ways in which nature interacts with itself.

Aspects are secondary to the planets that are in dialogue. Depending on the consciousness of the chart owner, they can be activated in countless ways. For every aspect, there are four issues to address. 1) What is the evolutionary purpose of the aspect? 2) What is the shadow possibility if the aspect is managed unconsciously? 3) What results if one side of the exchange dominates the other? 4) And when the other side has the upper hand? *Elements & Evolution* addresses these issues for all the major aspects, including the quincunx.

The classic Ptolemaic (or major) aspects are the conjunction, sextile, square, trine, and opposition. Each of the evolution-

261

ary phases has an evolutionary relationship with the ones that precede and follow it—the motion of the unfolding plot of the great evolutionary cycle. Through the major aspects, every phase is in aspect to all the remaining phases, except for when the stages are 150 degrees (or 5 signs) apart.

This 150 degree aspect is the quincunx. If we add it to our group, all the phases would have an evolutionary relationship with all of the others. This intuitively makes more sense than the current situation which leaves out two important connections. In the *Elements* book, I put forth the idea that the quincunx relates to advanced evolutionary lessons, which are only becoming understood and developed in recent times. For instance, Virgo quincunx Aquarius (*technology*), Cancer quincunx Sagittarius (*self-discovery*), Leo quincunx Pisces (*spiritual awakening*), or Capricorn quincunx Gemini (*media*) are sophisticated developmental programs that were less relevant hundreds of years ago. At this stage of evolution, they are fully relevant and needing our attention. Many spiritually-progressive astrologers agree that the quincunx should be upgraded to major aspect status.

Universal Principles

Here's we'll recap some of central ideas concerning the movement beyond the PVS. An awakened (Uranus) approach to astrology is based on several universal principles. Chief among them is the notion that *everything has evolutionary value and meaning.* The ego may have preferences for particular planets, signs, or aspects, but spiritual evolution concerns learning lessons, not necessarily having a good time. The willingness to engage our spiritual work ultimately allows is greater liberation.

The degree of free will we have is related to our degree of awakening. In the more unconscious stages of evolution, we tend to be in reactive mode, tethered to prior patterns. All of us are required to address the karma we've created. When we become more aware of the unconscious, we are better able to direct our life toward the resolution of our karma. The freedom that becomes available can then be used in service of the collective evolution. The guiding principle is that *free will is available for us to claim.*

The process of awakening is about expanding our identification beyond separation consciousness, but ultimately our task is to bridge worlds. Our membership in *the relative world is contained within the transpersonal*—Saturn orbits within Uranus. To respect this reality, we can change our approach, and even the language we use, to extend beyond the dualistic focus. This way, we are not kept *only* within the relative realm.

To respect both realms, we need to look at the astrology system through the relative and transpersonal lenses. This may seem cumbersome at first, but there is no way around it if we wish to add the transpersonal dimension. We are dealing with an entirely different perspective, with its own set of principles. In the 20th Century, the field of physics went through a radical adjustment in adding quantum mechanics (Uranus) to complement its classical roots (Saturn). As a result, the field grew enormously.

Mercury can be the "servant" of the intuitive mind, instead of the "master." The higher mind (Uranus) provides the overarching perspective on our development and awakening. The PVS tends to only promote what is obvious in the visible world and left-brain precision. A new value is to *fully acknowledge the relevance of both brain hemispheres and all levels of reality.* Whereas the PVS emphasizes an orientation on the physical (earth) and intellectual (air) realms, we can value the emotional (water) and the soul (fire) realms in equal measure. This shift promotes a balance of body-heart-mind-soul, which enables us to move forward in our spiritual evolution.

Instead of furthering the split between the relative and the transpersonal, we can strive to mend the mythological castration of Uranus and give the transpersonal a renewed potency. We can give full consideration to the outer planets and see them in transpersonal, rather than egoic, ways. Moving beyond Saturn's jurisdiction of separation consciousness, we may realize the universal principle that *everything is interconnected*. Whatever we do to the world, we are doing to ourselves. We may find spiritual value in everything.

Astrology can be guided by the universal principle of *evolutionary advancement*—the central reason why we participate in this meaningful exchange of energy we call life. One of the arguments I've heard against evolutionary astrology is that Spirit is perfection, and that there is no need for it to evolve. From an absolute view, we can agree wholeheartedly with this. However, at the relative level of separation, we're unresolved egos who are growing into reunion with this perfection.

Chapter 11
Towards the One

In this final chapter, we'll address movement towards the One. In order to bridge worlds, we respect and balance the transpersonal and relative views. Since most of us are more familiar with the relative view, we must continually strive to incorporate the wisdom of the transpersonal. We'll look at the resolution of dualities, which assists us in realizing Oneness, and also the soul as a guiding light which invites our awakening. Finally, I'll offer some ideas about Heliocentric astrology and some concluding thoughts.

Moving Forward

In the last chapter, I explained the idea of neutral and charged elements. I love the possibility that the full implementation of both the horizontal (charged-neutral) and vertical (yin-yang) axis is a pivot point of integration, the lesson of the Centaur and what Wilber describes as Level 6. At this point of our evolution, we are ready to move beyond Mercury's simplifications and expand into the transpersonal.

Every individual is ultimately a part of Oneness and therefore has *full access* to everything in the astrology system. We all have the same planets, signs, and houses, which are all based on the four elements, the building blocks of life. From the transpersonal view, we can see all of this in terms of being *energy*. There are no stories, attachments, or preferences for this energy—it just is. As we are souls that incarnate into the human experience, energy takes on personal relevance in the relative world. We *take on roles*, and gender is a part of this journey.

We can rightfully locate gender in terms of yin and yang, but our identification is not *limited* to one side of the polarization. We can maintain the identity of souls having temporary human experiences. In the state of separation, we are able to recognize the self in the other and thereby arrive at greater unity. The inability to connect in such a way reinforces polarization and keeps identity on only one side of the pairing. Astrology is currently organized around the role self (Wilber's Level 4), which makes awakening from polarities a challenge.

A more awakened astrology is able to see duality as a necessary part of incarnation, but to also see it as relative instead of absolute. This view is the key for a paradigm shift—we realize that there is no objective world, and our categorizations are limited to our frame of reference.

As discussed in previous chapters, each of the planets can be used to bolster the ego or in service of spiritual realization. As our essential energy is transpersonal, we can refrain from seeing the planets themselves as good or bad, masculine or feminine. Instead, we understand that *within the context of the ego*, our experience of the planets can be positive or negative or in terms of the two genders. For instance, we all have a Moon, but lunar energy connects with a mature female body with the potential to incubate a child. A very young or older woman is not able to become a mother, and therefore this potential facet of lunar energy is not as relevant for them, as it wouldn't be for men either. Only certain people take on that role.

All the planets take on roles in the unique circumstances of the separate self. Venus's role is different for men and women, as well as varying over time. There was no plastic surgery 2,000

266

years ago as there is now. In 2,000 years from now there will be new Venusian developments we can't conceive of. All energy must be seen within the *context* of the consciousness relating to it. We shift our focus from the car to the driver and see that it is we who determine how the planets function.

The key for a new epoch of astrological understanding is that we are in a co-creative relationship with the universe. The many types of astrology reflect the many qualities and stages of consciousness. The universe is an enormous canvas for our projections. Any type of astrology reflects the consciousness of the dominant paradigm occurring at the time of its formation. As we move away from Patriarchy, we are positioned to refashion astrology in accord with universal principles that are more relevant to this time.

Resolving Dualities

One of the specific places to work at the bridging process that I've referenced throughout this book is by looking at the opposition aspect. The lesson here is about coming together instead of coming apart. The spiritual lessons of the six oppositions invite us to the transpersonal when we successfully master the programs. We'll look at each of the oppositions now—including the planets that disposit the signs—to find clues as to how we can attain greater wholeness.

Aries/Libra: The Sacred Mirror

Most of us, most of the time, operate as if the boundary between self and other is irrefutable. I'm different and separate from you. I can honor and even love you, but at the end of the day we are distinct beings. All of this is true at the relative level.

At the transpersonal level, though, others *are* us. Unfinished in our soul work, we can be sure that the external world continually catalyzes awareness for us to integrate. Other people provide the incredible gift of mirroring to us our disowned parts, offering us more awareness and the opportunity to love what we had been pushing away. Whenever we feel an emotional charge in reaction to the actions or energy of others, we can know that something is asking to be seen and integrated in the self. Carl Jung said, "Everything that irritates us about others can lead us to an understanding of ourselves."

Of course, since we disowned it in the first place, we're usually not thrilled about owning it when it appears in the guise of another. Instead, most argue with it in some way and reinforce the relative, separate identity. Aries-Libra can manifest as endless conflict, divisiveness, and, ultimately, estrangement.

With the opposition, the eternal question is: Are we going to come together, or come apart? How we manage the associated planets of Aries (Mars) and Libra (Venus) determine this outcome. To move towards the transpersonal possibility, we must courageously (Mars) find ways to connect (Venus) with others. We must take a long and unflinching look into the sacred mirror and fiercely accept all that we find. Ultimately, we can approach the meaning of the Sanskrit greeting *Namaste*, which is about honoring the divinity in the other.

Taurus/Scorpio: The Comfort of Death

Taurus wants personal security and comfort, while Scorpio invites us beyond our safety zone into gripping drama and transformative experiences. Connected to the transpersonal planet Pluto, Scorpio brings us beyond the immediacy of ego and everything lurking in the shadow: our fears, death, the taboo, etc.

268

Part of the movement from the personal to the transpersonal involves honoring the great cycle of life, which includes death. Like a tree that willingly sheds its leaves in autumn, our souls do not resist the ways of nature. The soul is timeless and boundless, an energetic extension of Oneness. It's impervious to decay or death because it is not made from the impermanence of the physical world (Taurus). A lesson of this opposition is to bring soul wisdom (Scorpio) into the body (Taurus).

Death includes the "death" of the ego, which is not a literal death, but a conscious decision to withdraw the complete identification with ego. We can accept and make inner peace (Taurus) with our own death. Resolving this opposition provides us with authentic power, the regeneration (Pluto) into greater security (Venus). If we can accept—and even *love* our death—what could we possibly be afraid of? Not only would everything become welcome, we might actually see anything calamitous (Scorpio) as a further opportunity to deepen into relaxation and calm (Taurus).

We must be willing to connect with any and all experiences that life offers: the realities of abuse, genocide, the intense pain and suffering on this planet, everything that resides in the dark (Pluto). Spirit does not shelter its eyes from anything, and we don't have to either. When we are willing to embrace it all, we are empowered with fierce stamina (Scorpio), and we can find tranquility and peace (Taurus) in it. The alternative is the eternal pain of resistance—needless suffering and wailing in the dark.

Gemini/Sagittarius: Questioning Beliefs

It may seem at first glance that there is nothing leading to the transpersonal in this polarity. Both Mercury (Gemini) and

269

Jupiter (Sagittarius) orbit within Saturn, which structures the relative world. However, the resolution of this duality brings us a fascinating, and quite perplexing, outcome. Hermann Hesse said, "Our mind is capable of passing beyond the dividing line we have drawn for it. Beyond the pairs of opposites of which the world consists, other, new insights begin."

Gemini is the great questioner, while Sagittarius puts information together to arrive at conclusions. Most of us eventually relax the need to continue questioning everything and arrive at a particular world view. However, if we continue to question, something very interesting happens. We can perpetually ask, "Can I completely, irrefutably, know that this is true?" We can never *really* know anything for sure because the mind is within the relative world and therefore limited about absolute knowledge. The mind becomes deconstructed through endless inquiry.

We can use Mercury to question Jupiter, and Jupiter eventually understands the limitations of the whole endeavor of the intellect. If this inquiry is not taken to its conclusion, then the ego thinks it will find the right information (Mercury) or the long sought-after theory of everything (Jupiter) to find absolute truth. Ultimately, we can't unlock Spirit's secrets through analysis—we must become Spirit to *experience* it. A key in becoming Spirit is to deconstruct the thinking patterns that remove us from the experience of it.

Cancer/Capricorn: Emotional Maturation

This polarity deals with the acceptance of the past, a necessity for being present in the now. Most of us carry a load of unresolved issues and emotional pain. This material is sustained inside of us through the ego's resistance to them. The Moon reveals the ego's attachments amidst the spiritual journey.

270

Capricorn involves maturation—taking a sober look at the state of things and complying with reality. Since the past is the past, it is unrealistic to attempt to go back and change what happened. Therefore, the most logical and strategic plan (Capricorn) is to completely accept reality. Then, we can legitimately become the master (Capricorn) of our emotions (Cancer) instead of being unconsciously and reactively driven by them.

Many people operate with the assumption that we must simply "grow up" and leave the past behind. The attitude of being tough is prized; some even ridicule emotional displays as signs of weakness. Boys and men, especially, receive this conditioning, though women and girls are also encouraged to "get over it," and are prone to many forms of subtle emotional conditioning (Saturn). As a result, we perpetually stay immature (Moon). The common strategy of repression only delays addressing the emotional material, which never goes away. William Faulkner said, "The past is not dead. In fact, it's not even past."

We are our experiences, and eventually we must own it. This polarity is resolved when we *choose the past*: the good, bad, ugly, and everything else. Through choice, we gain the emotional (Moon) strength (Saturn) needed to leave the egoic trap that attachments ultimately bring. When non-attached, we are able to connect with what life brings us.

Leo/Aquarius: Awakening

I find it fascinating that Uranus's axis points at the Sun. Known as "The Awakener," it fittingly points towards what we awaken into, soul realization. These two bodies are inexorably linked through their opposing dispositors, Leo and Aquarius.

Identified with ego, we mistakenly take ownership of the energy we have access to. We may swell with pride and think of

271

the self as some form of star or celebrity (Leo) who is revered and applauded by the collective (Aquarius). Once we move beyond this folly, we can breakthrough (Uranus) and selflessly claim spiritual realization (Sun).

The resolution of this polarity occurs when we are present and aware (Sun)—in connection with the fantastic nervous system of the cosmos (Uranus), which connects everything. Through developing the Sun, we increase our access to Spirit's intelligence. This polarity invites us to expand the energy body and identify with the matrix.

Virgo/Pisces: Distributing Spirit

What motivates you to perform charitable, altruistic, or selfless acts? Is there some need for gain, or is it motivated solely from unconditional love? The ego can be sneaky. Many times we think we're acting in non-egoic ways, but the ego is mostly unconscious!

The ego likes recognition or some form of credit for what it does. Whether this desire takes the form of a paycheck, enhanced reputation, or some form of social reward, it tends to keep score. The ego might believe that acting responsibly (Virgo) entitles us to live in a carefree manner (Pisces)—you've earned it. Have a beer! Service is given with expectations.

When the ego is not involved, we are able to distribute Spirit without this interference. What we do (Virgo) is less and less for the self and more and more about helping to heal the world (Pisces). Inspiration and intuition (Neptune) can fill the mind and inform our decisions (Mercury). We sculpt a tangible contribution or work with others (Virgo) with of a deep grati-tude for life (Pisces). The mind (Mercury) is cleansed (Neptune) and is able to appreciate and have compassion for the various

272

troubles of the world. With humility, we play a role in bringing the pieces of Spirit together.

The Nodes and Duality

Another area where we reconcile polarity is with the Nodes of the Moon. As mentioned earlier, we can conceptualize the Moon as the roots, the Nodes as the process of gardening, and the Sun as the flower. In order for us to awaken (Sun), we must resolve our karma (Nodes), and be conscious of who we are (Moon).

We all navigate with some degree of unconsciousness as we mature. The South Node is a snapshot into the inner workings of ego. The astrology chart allows us to see our modus operandi objectively, from a bird's eye view. The ego's mechanisms become exposed, but this knowledge does nothing in itself. We must take action towards the resolution of the dynamics we set into motion. Karma deals with the consequences of prior action. Picture a wader in a pool. The motion into the water creates a wide variety of affects. How we personally affect life has been elaborately saved and imprinted into the world. This is the work of Uranus, which in good measure tells us about it through astrology.

The North Node and its attendant factors point the way towards greater wholeness. When we complement patterns with their opposite, we resolve the polarity. Therefore, we must take action in the world to balance the tides. As the North Node is directly opposite the South, we have to become the very thing most estranged from us. What better way to be completely open and engaged with everything!

We must integrate the entire Nodal axis, which also involves doing the South Node more consciously. This can be joyful if we are truly doing our work. We gladly serve Spirit and all of its earthly expression with highly developed skills, talents, or wisdom. We "give back" our karmic debts through selfless service. The North Node learning informs the South Node with a fresh perspective and complementary skills. We balance the karmic books, the ultimate test of resolving polarity. With successful "gardening," we can flower into the light of soul realization.

On "Wounded" Souls

Much of the way the soul is described, both in astrology and in many broader spiritual contexts, is in the language of woundedness. There is a widespread belief that we incarnate to heal, grow, and resolve our soul wounds. However, an important question to ask is this: Is it our souls which are wounded, or is it the ego?

The soul is transpersonal, inhabiting a realm *beyond* the immediacy of the bump and grind of incarnated life. The ego (Moon) is involved with autonomy, physicality, survival, the pursuit of happiness, and everything else natural to the human condition.

All of us are impacted by life, and we have the necessity to smooth out our wounds, heal our karma, and strive to live a more awakened life. The soul initiates the incarnation into a specific physical set of circumstances to address the egoic wounding that has been absorbed. However, the soul is *guiding the process*, akin to a "higher self" which holds wisdom and guidance, connected with Source.

Wounding results when the ego (Moon) takes measures to defend itself by going unconscious. The soul (fire) is actually trying to catalyze greater awakening into our higher selves. From this view, the soul is a lot healthier than we've construed. It is the ego which is wounded. Many people develop a right-

274

eous (and self-defeating) story that their souls are just so irrevocably wounded that growth is improbable. Perhaps this view allows a certain distancing from responsibility, for it may be our personal attachments to our stories, our identification with our pain, and habitual reactions to life (Moon) that sustains our wounds. Maybe our souls serve as our greatest allies along our journey. When we remove the projection that our souls are wounded, we are better able to intuit and partner with them.

The ego has projected its inherent woundedness on everything else. First and foremost, the Moon is traditionally associated with women. They have carried the brunt of handling egoic wounding—as mothers, wives, nurses, and in other caretaking roles. As a corrective measure, we all must take responsibility for the condition of our Moons, not see it only in feminine terms. Next, we must retract the idea that our souls are wounded. Finally, we must refrain from projecting woundedness externally on to others and society at large. They are only mirrors.

Heliocentric Astrology

When we secure our lunar foundation with love and acceptance, the world opens up. As the awakening process unfolds, we expand into new ways of being and learn to navigate in connection with soul realization. Geocentric astrology is most appropriate for us as we address our egoic condition, but Heliocentric astrology becomes increasingly relevant the more the awakening process progresses.

The shift from Geocentric to Heliocentric parallels the movement from the relative to also engage with the transpersonal. Geocentric astrology is Earth-centered—we live on a beautiful planet which supports autonomous life. Orbiting around the Earth is the Moon, the great basin of unconsciousness

275

that fills up with experience and therefore has a memory of the past. Heliocentric astrology relates to the creativity of the present and the Sun at the center of the action. It pertains to what the soul is activating within the matrix. The Sun is a great ball of spiritual creativity, and the rest of the planets orbit around it in an elaborate orchestration of energetic possibility.

Heliocentric astrology is about soul manifestation, not the resolution of egoic wounding. There is no Moon on a Heliocentric chart—it's in the same place as the Earth from the Sun's perspective. When we look at the Earth, we can think of it as the Earth/Moon system representing separation consciousness and manifestation in physical form.

From the transpersonal perspective, the separate self is an illusion, the journey of the dreamer. When we see that the egoic stories and machinations were all made up, we begin to transcend them and learn to abide in the clarity of awareness. The Moon's disappearance from this chart means that the Nodes are also absent. *The human drama and its karma is not the province of the Heliocentric chart.* The soul is guiding the journey *into* incarnation—it assists the ego, but doesn't actually resolve karma, for that is our job here "on the ground."

Our Earthly position makes it difficult to even have this discussion. Heliocentric astrology is a portrayal of our awakened self, how we might approach the world as realized beings. Since most of us are not awakened, it can be a foolish exercise to go down this road. We're going anyway, but let's remember that we continually project our unconsciousness onto *everything*. We must guard against the egoic takeover and resist the impulse of turning Heliocentric astrology into Geocentric. It's literally night (Geocentric, Moon focused, emerging from the dark) and day (Heliocentric, Sun focused, coming from the light).

Heliocentric astrology portrays the soul motion through the manifesting channel described earlier. Whereas the ego

276

wants to liberate from the chains that bind us and ascend to new heights, the soul is interested in crystallizing its intentions on the earth plane. The soul wants to matter, in both meanings of the term. Matter is earthy substance, and when something "matters" there is meaning attached—it increases in significance or potency.

Souls descend from the fire level to the air, where a plan is developed, then into the waters of the womb. A child is born in the relative world on the Earth in a state of unconsciousness. The reference point is the separate self, enveloped in the symbiotic connection between the Earth and Moon. The liberating channel and the Geocentric chart is immediately engaged. The transpersonal (including the Heliocentric chart) tends to be forgotten in unconsciousness.

The Geocentric chart is like the energetic magnet pulling the separate self upwards through the liberating channel. That is the pull of spiritual growth—heat (soul) wants to rise. The Sun becomes our life energy, continually inviting expansion and awakening. The weight of the ego (Moon) is necessary for us to be grounded and to define ourselves. However, when we over-identify with this definition, we claim ownership of the *borrowed* energy and so remain unconscious. Upon awakening, we return the energy to Source.

There is no Sun represented on the Heliocentric chart, just as there is no Earth on a Geocentric chart. The Sun is in the center of the chart, just as it's the center of the Solar System. All of the planets move in the same direction so there are no retrogrades. Retrogrades involve *process*, which has relevance to humans who need to absorb experiences. Mercury and Venus are not tied within a certain range to the Earth as they are to the Sun with Geocentric astrology. The planets are *free* to move about as they wish.

The Heliocentric Earth always appears exactly opposite the Geocentric Sun. If you're used to being a Sagittarius, you have your Heliocentric Earth in Gemini. Geocentric Cancer Sun corresponds to a Heliocentric Capricorn Earth. Always in opposition, the Geocentric Sun and the Heliocentric Earth illustrate another reconciliation of polarity on the way to Oneness. We see the great dance between the ego and the soul going in opposite directions, meeting in the middle as you. In the separate self we identify with matter (earth) and grow to realize soul/Spirit (fire). We inhabit the life force (the Sun in geocentric chart) of the very thing we're *becoming*. We have already arrived, but we have to catch the past up with the present. In the opposite direction, Spirit/soul is emerging *through* us. The Heliocentric chart portrays how it descends through increasingly denser levels of energy to wind up as us. We are in the middle of the sacred marriage.

We don't fully inhabit our Heliocentric Earth until we *dissolve* everything on the water level for the energy to move down and fully manifest. We have to empty our cups to allow the fire of Spirit/soul to move through us. Most of us have not loosened our attachments, so the water level hardens, and souls are unable to root in the Earth. In order to embrace the Heliocentric reality, we have to loosen our attachment to everything we think we know about astrology, including our identification with our Geocentric charts. Most of all, we must not bring the egoic takeover to Heliocentric astrology. Ego finds a natural home with Geocentric astrology and has projected itself all over it. I plan on making Heliocentric Astrology a centerpiece to *The Astrology of Awakening* series, and I'm well aware of the central challenge, but Uranus in Aries is inviting us to take the next steps into a new world.

It's no wonder that only a very small percentage of all astrology is Heliocentric at this point. Big respect to the authors

278

who have begun the dialogue! As we awaken, Heliocentric astrology is bound to attract its appropriate audience. We are discussing this because we are ready; perhaps it has something to do with 2012 and a shift in consciousness. We can locate the Heliocentric revolution Copernicus initiated as the time when we first realized that we are not the center of the universe. Almost 500 years later astrology may catch up with it.

I believe we are ready to address the next step, to welcome Helocentric astrology right alongside Geocentric—to embrace both soul and body, the transpersonal and the relative. Comprehending a chart that portrays soul realization is quite different from actually inhabiting it. For those ready to look through the transpersonal lens, an entire new world is available to explore. What is Spirit contributing to the planet *through* you? Can you identify as a soul having a human experience? Can you live with complete non-attachment? Are you ready to turn everything upside down?

Spirit, Benevolence, and Laughter

Shakespeare famously wrote in Hamlet, "There is nothing either good or bad, but thinking makes it so." Perhaps the most astounding part of the transpersonal level, as I mentioned before, is the notion that nothing "bad" could happen—in fact, nothing "bad" has ever happened! From the transpersonal view, it's all been a gigantic exchange of energy. Shifting beyond the personal level and its nearly continual stream of reactions and resistances leaves us increasingly empty of interpretations, preferences, or stories. Contrary to what some would like to believe, Spirit is not rooting for one sports team to defeat another, or holding one particular country or religion in a special light. This kind of thinking is a projection from a state of separation.

Spirit is just fine having periods of millions of years where there isn't any life on Earth. A Golden Age, when humans awaken and realize Spirit, is not *better* than the Jurassic period or The Dark Ages. From the transpersonal perspective, it makes no difference whatsoever what we do on this planet because energy recycles.

Oneness divides into separateness then gradually realizes Oneness, a motion like breathing in and out. It's been compared to a colossal game of "hide and seek." Why this game is happening in the first place is wide open for speculation. Ultimately, who could ever say? It doesn't matter anyway. The point is that the present is a benevolent gift for us to awaken into. When we arrive, we can identify as energy and are liberated from the imprisonment and isolation of our apparent separateness.

The "cosmic joke" is a phrase that refers to the hilarity that tends to arise when we arrive in the present. When all the strategies, anxieties, and defenses are seen for what they are, lightness and laughter can take root. We may laugh and wonder, "This is it? Certainly there must be more?"

We may come to see that we made it all so much more difficult than it had to be. We were convinced of a reality that turns out to be just an elaborate series of projections of ourselves. As we awaken, the imagination we have of ourselves dissolves. As William Blake famously said, "If the doors of perception were cleansed, everything would appear to man as it is, infinite." There were never any problems, just the thought that there were problems. There was never any you, just the thought that there was a you. *A Course in Miracles* says that at the end of the world, there is laughter—that is, at the end of *your* world as an ego.

Now

The Sun illuminates the Now, inviting us to renew our life energy in the exact circumstances we find ourselves in. In order to arrive in the present, we must be willing to let go of the past. We learn from it and retain the preciousness of those lessons to create a brighter tomorrow. We can honor the past with love and gratitude for playing such an important evolutionary role.

It is difficult to conceive of life many centuries ago. Many of us can fly around the globe, checking our fancy laptop computers through hi-tech security systems as we go. The life span in the Western World keeps growing longer, and we have dozens of modern conveniences that make our lives more comfortable. Earlier in history, there were more uncertainties. As a result, there was an impulse to conquer, to make sense of the world, and arrive at greater security. This is epitomized by monarchs who adorn themselves in regality and splendor.

Democracy was founded on universal principles that aim to level the playing field. It is now the dominant paradigm that governs the modern world, and it rightfully should be the mindset which informs our astrology. We must decide if it's more important to preserve tradition or to create the brighter tomorrow. On the great evolutionary line, the Saturnian vise grip has been set just a few inches forward after the development of egoic functioning. Ahead is infinity. When we find ways to move it along, the world has opened up. In just the last 100 years, the car and plane became commonplace, women got the right to vote in the United States, the evolution of consciousness became understood, and Einstein pointed out the relative nature of human reality.

The world is adjusting to these and many other advances. It takes courage to change, and there is usually resistance to it.

281

Uranus is now in Aries, inviting us all to summon the courage to confront (square) outdated paradigms and structures of Patriarchal and plutocratic control (Pluto in Capricorn). Some arenas where this is found include tyrannical political regimes, the greed on Wall Street, and yes, even astrology. When we arrive in the now, we are able to see history more clearly. Lets heed the wisdom of Plato, "We can easily forgive a child who is afraid of the dark; the real tragedy of life is when men are afraid of the light." In order for us to connect with light, we must renounce any attempt to own or control it. We are all learning to surrender to its spiritual majesty.

Extras

The following essays are all relevant to the themes of this book, though they didn't fit directly within its structure. The first one is a version of an essay that was initially published in the NCGR Research Journal. It discusses the significance of the 15.5-year cycle of Uranus/North Node conjunctions. I first learned of this cycle from Robert Blaschke, and the article is dedicated to him. Next, I present the astrology of the upcoming winter solstice, 12/21/12, in light of the increasing collective chatter about its possible significance. Then I have a little fun with Pink Floyd's *Dark Side of the Moon* and the movie *Moon*, interpreting them through the lens of awakening that I've presented in this book. Finally, I touch on our experiential connection with the Sun with mindfulness practice and intentional invocations.

Uranus, The North Node, and The Future of Astrology

At *The Blast* astrology conference in Sedona, Arizona in 2007, Robert Blaschke thrilled the audience with his lecture on the Uranus/Nodes cycle. As synchronicity would have it, the conjunction between Uranus and the North Node was nearly exact as he was talking. As a tribute to this brilliant and compassionate man who has passed on at this point, this essay reviews the basic idea of the Uranus/Nodes cycle, takes a look at a few recent examples of the cycle, and offers some additional commentary on future trends.

Uranus forms a conjunction with the North Node roughly every 15.5 years. According to Blaschke, these conjunctions signal that a new chapter in the history of astrology is being born. The North Node is an invitation towards developing new skills and attributes, to gain new mastery with the themes of the sign it resides in. As Uranian terrain includes astrology itself, these conjunctions of Uranus with the North Node illustrate new astrological developments according to the sign of the conjunction. The South Node and the planets that have a connection with the Nodal axis all play roles consistent with their placements.

Prior Chapters

Before we look at the current cycle, let's explore the last few. The previous conjunction of Uranus with the North Node occurred at 11Capricorn 02 on November 12, 1991. Blaschke mentioned that at this time, interest in traditional, medieval, and Hellenistic systems of astrology were attracting increased interest. Project Hindsight and ARAHAT were founded to rediscover ancient texts and bring their wisdom to the field. Also, astrology made inroads with accreditation and inclusion in educational institutions. During this phase, Kepler College began to graduate students with advanced degrees in astrology. Astrology based on methodology and tradition was in vogue; the field got more serious.

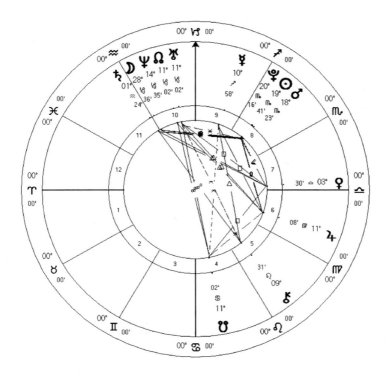

The Moon was at 28 Capricorn 36 at the time of the exact conjunction. Serving as the dispositor of the Cancer South Node, it strongly suggests a return to the past. Saturn, dispositor of the Capricorn North Node, was in a conjunction with the Moon from 1 Aquarius 24. This configuration illustrates how the retrieval from the past (Capricorn Moon) can ideally be brought to astrological institutions (Saturn) in a modernized (Aquarius) way. This shift could also draw on the Uranus/Neptune conjunction, which points to potential breakthroughs (Uranus) in incorporating right-brain pathways of knowledge (Neptune) into the historical canon (Capricorn). Uranus trine Jupiter in Virgo signals a philosophical revolution to inform our methodologies. The Sun conjunct Mars and Pluto in Scorpio depicts an enormous power struggle in realizing the transpersonal intentions, though operating under the surface (Scorpio).

Going back, we find the previous conjunction on September 8, 1976 at 4 Scorpio 29. Fittingly, it heralded the proliferation of psychological astrology. Major works from Liz Greene, Stephen Arroyo, Donna Cunningham, and many others helped make astrology a powerful tool for understanding the unconscious. Many books on Pluto were also released at this time, including the seminal works from Jeffrey Wolf Green. There was an emphasis on soul evolution, confronting the shadow, even a curiosity about occult possibilities of astrology. Saturn at 11 Leo 36 square the Nodes presents the challenge of bringing astrology to the mainstream (Saturn) in such a profound way—in contrast to the superficiality of prior uses. In order to support the Scorpio intention, Leo must mature (Saturn).

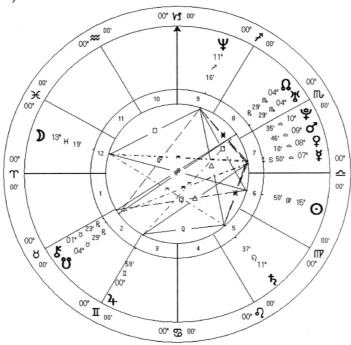

Rewinding once more, we find the prior conjunction on September 4, 1961 at 27 Leo 10, which marked the emergence of popular versions of astrology. Linda Goodman's *Sun Signs* led the way. People came to see astrology in simplistic terms—as entertainment, or as a way of categorizing the personality. "What's your sign?" became a popular pick-up line, and simplified astrology columns filled magazines and newspapers.

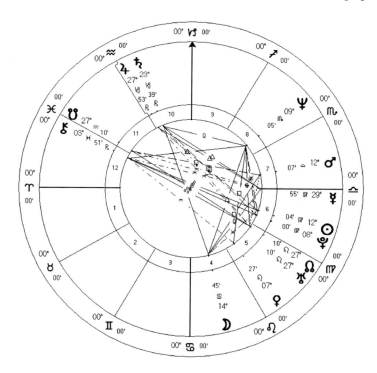

Some astrologers lament the legacy of this Leo chapter, feeling that it led the public astray with its focus on Sun signs. I share their sentiment, but also feel that perhaps this is a necessary cost of astrology having become popular and wide-spread quite quickly. It's as if astrology roared again, emerging from its prior versions into a new articulation. We can see this in the Uranus/North Node in Leo chart, which has an Aquarius

South Node. As the dispositor of the South Node, Uranus, from this analysis, does have a connection with astrology's prior uses. The conjunction of Uranus with the Leo North Node illustrates that astrology is now becoming vibrant (Leo) once again. However, there is tension (opposition) between Uranus in Leo (with its newfound vibrancy) and the Aquarius South Node, which is indicative of the astrology's past.

The Current Phase

These prior astrological chapters have cemented into the collective consciousness. The last three phases saw astrology roar into society (Leo) and then add greater depth (Scorpio) and seriousness (Capricorn). The current phase (begun 3/31/07) has Uranus conjunct the North Node at 16 Pisces 07, inviting us to the transpersonal. Mercury at 14 Pisces 11 is with this conjunction, while the Moon at 13 Virgo 26 is in conjunction with the South Node. Jupiter at 19 Sagittarius 43 squares the Nodes.

Astrology may be incorporating a more experiential component, how it connects us with our divine nature (not just an exercise for the mind). With Mercury closely conjoined Uranus, our intellectual notions about astrology may become more innovative (Uranus) to incorporate a broader spirituality. The lower mind can team with the higher, connecting the "servant" with the "master." Blaschke noted that Mercury's inclusion with Uranus points to contributions from younger people, which *The Blast* conference was designed to showcase.

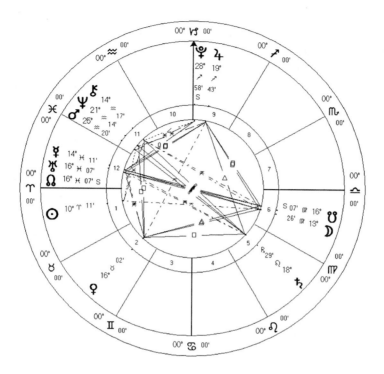

Though Uranus/Mercury suggests a potential intellectual revolution, it's in opposition with the attachment (Moon) to the tried and true methods (Virgo) that have been in place (South Node). Underlying these methods is an emotional (Moon) need for order (Virgo), and the entrenchment (Virgo) in ego (Moon). Uranus in Pisces is a great leap into the unknown. The liberation (Uranus) from attachments (opposite Moon) allows a new paradigm (Uranus square Jupiter in Sagittarius) to be born.

The focus can be on understanding the breadth of astrology and joining together in collective purpose. Astrology can further inform our place in the cosmos and provide perspective and meaning (Jupiter in Sagittarius). Additionally, Uranus/Jupiter is interested in greater cross-fertilization of global understandings. Perhaps advances from other fields (from wisdom traditions to science) can find inlets into the field. This phase promises revitalized spiritual uplift and direction, a plethora of new ideas, and the potential for emotional freedom. Already we are seeing a marked increase in the spiritual dimensions of astrology, including ways to integrate different approaches.

Future Trends

After the Pisces period, Uranus will form a conjunction with the North Node at 18 Taurus 41 and Mars at 17 Taurus 56, on July 31, 2022. Saturn at 22 Aquarius 55 and Mercury at 23 Leo 58 square the Nodal axis from either side. This conjunction in Taurus may signal a "grounding" chapter, bringing astrology to the "everyday" after the transpersonal phase. The inclusion of Mars could indicate the potential for astrology to have greater impact, perhaps serving a leadership role in some way. Areas to look for this leadership are within the realms of Taurus: the environment and natural resources, the economy and wealth, the arts, issues pertaining to the body, agriculture, and security. Astrology may inform a wider variety of people how to live in consort with nature. However, living in new, more progressive ways, requires the desire (Mars) for reinvention.

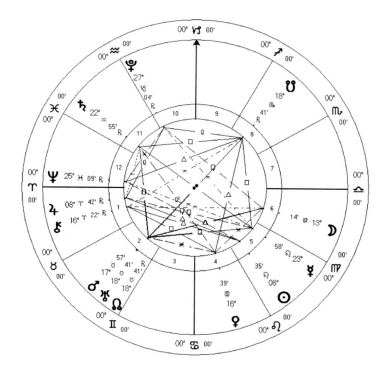

Saturn in Aquarius suggests that our institutions will be modernizing. The square to the Nodes illustrates the inevitable resistance (Saturn) to change (Aquarius), which tends to accompany the implementation of any new paradigm or framework. In fact, with a Scorpio South Node, there might be pronounced conflict on the road towards realizing the peacefulness and connection with nature the Taurus North Node offers. Mercury in Leo suggests that communication areas (media, areas of learning) particularly in realms of entertainment or geared towards youth (Leo) might have another renaissance. As Mercury is in aspect to both Saturn (seasoned, learned) and Uranus (transpersonal), astrology could be poised to enter mass communications in a more informed way (in contrast to the 1960s chapter). The global changes of this period are substantial.

293

The extent to which these innovations become realized will be contingent on our collective courage (Uranus/Mars).

The final conjunction that I'll touch on will take place on October 20, 2037 at 24 Cancer 09, conjunct Jupiter at 28 Cancer 42. Neptune squares the Nodes from 27 Aries 41 from one side, and the Sun at 28 Libra 06 squares them from the other. Uranus/Jupiter in Cancer seeks to create a world family. Astrology may inform the philosophy which guides the realization of our shared roots, our collective identity in (what Robert Blaschke calls) this "Earthwalk." This vision of togetherness is initially at odds with the hierarchical or separation tendencies of the Capricorn South Node, which can be rigid or orthodox.

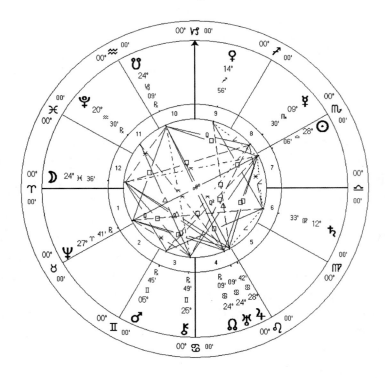

Neptune in Aries asks for some dissolution of the "me first" attitude, as displays of ego would weaken the promise of

294

togetherness. Each individual (Aries) is being invited to also serve the collective consciousness (Neptune), to "be the change you wish to see in the world," as Gandhi is famously quoted. The Libra Sun calls for an awareness of our interdependence, a call toward greater civility and concern for others. In order to do this, we must collectively learn how to follow our hearts (Cancer), and astrology may play a role in providing this life direction (Jupiter).

Summation

Robert Blaschke put forth the hypothesis that a conjunction between Uranus and the North Node of the Moon suggests the future direction of astrology for a period of approximately 15.5 years. A review of the last three of these conjunctions does show merit to this claim. Though there are many types of astrology (and many possible avenues to explore), it appears that the chart for these conjunctions clarify the new astrological advances or movements that enter the collective imagination. The current phase is clarifying the relationship between astrology and spirituality, while the next two phases have much to do with how astrology further enters society. The details of the future are unknown. However, it does appear that we have a guide to know the general evolutionary themes of the coming decades and astrology's potential role in this great unfolding of the human project.

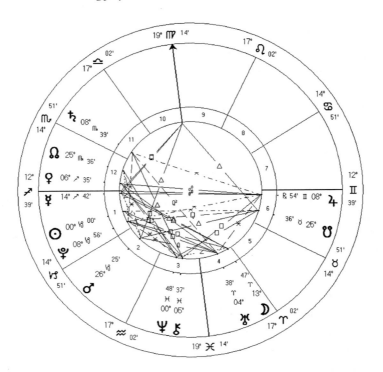

The chart above is cast for Chichen Itza, a hub of focus for the Mayans and also located centrally in the Yucatan Peninsula. The time is 5:13am, the moment when the Sun moves into Capricorn for the 2012 winter solstice. (Though I'm uncertain as to where the best location would be to cast the chart, any spot in the region would yield similar results.)

The Moon conveys great unease and restlessness, the desire to revolutionize (conjunct Uranus) our emotional need for power (Aries), and our attachment to individuality and separation consciousness. The Moon is also square Pluto in Capricorn, portraying the underlying anger at Patriarchal control. Residing in the 4th House, the Moon is unresolved (quite bothered!) about how the homeland (4th House) is being taken care of. Aries involves new beginnings, and the Moon wants that badly. The Moon is also trine Mercury in Sagittarius on the Ascendant, signaling the need to communicate a new (1st House) philosophy of greater unity (Sagittarius) that can bring us together (Mercury conjunct Venus) in a shared spiritual vision (Venus located in Sagittarius in the 12th).

The Sun is conjunct Pluto in Capricorn in the 1st House, a statement about awakening into a new (1st House) day (Sun) in our dominant organization of society (Capricorn). We must completely transform (Pluto) our institutions, traditions, and attachment to the past. The 1st House emphasizes this impera-tive. If we don't manifest it, we unconsciously (Pluto) create our destruction. The Sun is not only conjunct Pluto, the dispositor of the North Node (new attributes), it's square Uranus (new paradigms) in the first house (new beginnings), and we can also see the Sun itself as what we're in the process of becoming. Therefore, it points toward transforming and awakening from traditional Capricorn, though the egoic takeover is always available. Those entrenched in plutocratic control may lead us (1st House) to our demise (Pluto).

The South Node in Taurus indicates the resistance to change, particularly in how we make use (6th House) of our planetary resources (Taurus). It points to our tendency to pick apart, dissect, and exploit the earth element for financial reasons. We do know that the "tipping point" of oil depletion is evident, and Neptune (often associated with oil) is square the Nodes (in the water sign Pisces). Neptune in the 3rd House is learning to change perceptions, to be able to see nature with intuition and right brain (Pisces) faculties. Instead of dualistic separation, we can now perceive the luminosity of Spirit and thereby cleanse and heal our minds (Chiron in Pisces). Neptune/Chiron is square Jupiter, indicating the challenge and necessity to forge philoso-phies of greater spiritual nourishment.

297

Venus in Sagittarius is the dispositor of the South Node, suggesting that the philosophy (Sagittarius) that has bound us together (Venus) has been misguided (12th), stemming from a materialistic (Venus), righteous (Sagittarius) ideal we've given our power away to (12th). The rigidity of belief systems and religions (Sagittarius) provides a social (Venus) justification to our resource depletion. There are regional, political, and national alliances, the sharing of culture, customs, and languages that have connected us as a world civilization.

The residence of the North Node in the 12th House suggests a transformed (Scorpio) connection with divinity, one of greater depth, bonding, and transpersonal consciousness. We are learning to surrender to Spirit, instead of working tirelessly (6th House) for self-gain (Taurus). The North Node wants accountability (Scorpio) and process, to work through our dark ways in order to release them (12th House). The flavor of the North Node is visionary, some might call it "shamanic" — it's certainly a powerful and dramatic embrace of mysticism and endless probing of the unknown. Pluto serves as the dispositor of the North Node and reinforces the necessity for all individuals (1st House) to awaken (Pluto conjunct Sun) into a transformed way of being, and thereby changing everyday life on this planet (Capricorn).

Pluto is sextile (and in mutual reception with) Saturn in Scorpio in the 11th House, further connecting the intention for catalytic transformation with how we organize (Saturn) our collective milieu (11th), as well as for greater solidification of our interconnectedness. A new way of structuring (Saturn) power (Scorpio) that is in accordance with progressive humanistic ideals (11th) is suggested. If we don't mature around power, we renew intransigence (Saturn) and control (Scorpio), which limit the realization of our hopes for humanity (11th).

The sextile between Saturn/Pluto forms a yod (with Jupiter) of remarkable tightness. All planets are at 8 degrees, and the greatest separation of any 2 planets in this configuration is only 15 minutes. Jupiter in Gemini signals a philosophy of openness, new ideas and greater communication. Jupiter is retrograde, suggesting the rethinking of our philosophical assumptions—the various ideas (Gemini) that have been applied in our daily routines (6th House). Now we can transform (Pluto quincunx Jupiter) educational systems (Capricorn-Gemini), and bring expansiveness (Jupiter) into more a more progressive and interconnected (11th House) social organization (Saturn).

Jupiter is opposed (and in mutual reception with) the Mercury in Sagittarius, as well as Venus. The placement of both the inner planets is on the (sometimes-called) "yod release point," which is thought to channel the energy of the yod beyond the configuration. We may join together (Venus) in a mission (Sagittarius) of shared learning (Mercury). This does sound idealistic and reminiscent of a dawning of a new age (note the emphasis on the Ascendant). With the inclusion of the Venus/Mercury (at the release point), the yod configuration resembles a peace sign (on its side). The spirit of bringing people together is further accentuated by the trine of Venus with Uranus, an aspect of bridging differences and creating a new social contract. Furthermore, Jupiter is sextile Uranus, which calls for a philosophical revolution.

Mars in Capricorn in the 2nd House is trine the Taurus North Node. This shows the harmony (trine) between the powerful machinery (Mars in Capricorn) that digs into the earth for financial gain (2nd House), with the spiritual lessons of the South Node situation. Instead of valuing corporate gain, Mars can be connected (sextile) with the Scorpio North Node intention of transformed spiritual interconnectedness. Then, we become spiritual warriors asserting (Mars) transpersonal consciousness (sextile Scorpio North Node in the 12th) on the earth plane (Capricorn 2nd House).

This chart is a radical wake-up call for us to learn how to coexist for our collective survival and evolution. The dominant configuration of the current times is the Uranus/Pluto square and both the Sun and Moon form conjunctions with its parts! We are invited to completely renovate our guiding paradigms. We are resolving our attachment to domination and separation, flowering into a more awakened organization of society. The astrology of this fabled day is every bit as transformational as the hoopla and hype surrounding it!

Awakening in Culture

"The white light streams down to be broken up by those human prisms into all the colors of the rainbow." ~Charles R. Brown

It's been said that the role of art is to reflect life. Oftentimes, art captures the collective imagination in such a way that it attains iconographic status. Da Vinci's *Mona Lisa*, Baum's *The Wizard of Oz*, or Tolkein's *The Lord of the Rings* are a few examples. These works transcend their mediums and resonate deeply with the broader human condition. In the 2nd half of the 20th Century, music played such a role for many. From Elvis to the Beatles to Madonna, musicians captured the spirit of their times and gave voice to our shared experience.

The Dark Side of the Moon

For our purposes, let's explore the album that stayed on the charts for an astonishing 15 years following its release (1973-1988), the longest run in all of music history: Pink Floyd's *The*

Dark Side of the Moon. (This album was released on the 500th Solar return of Copernicus (10 Pisces), with many interesting contacts).

Lyricist Roger Waters is not known to be interested in astrology — and certainly not the paradigm that is written about in this book. It seems reasonable to conclude that he and his band were tapping into something greater than they could rationally conceive of, which is the hallmark of inspired art. I was born in 1971 and, like many others, I got a copy of this album (yes, a *real* record album) in my teens. I listened to it hundreds of times and had absolutely no idea as to the significance of what I was hearing. I later discovered that this work was a perfect reflection of the egoic takeover, including the direct referencing of the Sun being eclipsed by the Moon!

The working title was actually *Dark Side of the Moon: A Piece for Assorted Lunatics*. The album opens with the sound of a heartbeat, indicative of the pulse of human life. The opening of the first song, *Breathe*, "don't be afraid to care," illustrates the existential dilemma: we must invest and care about life, even though it's likely to hurt and bewilder us; the alternative is certain madness. Along the journey, there are many things we must face. The songs discuss different stages and settings of the human condition, particularly how life is filled with dramas we must cope with and make sense of: conflict, fear, time, death, money, war, health, sexuality, relationships, family, home, and fame. In short, much of what it means to be human.

Eclipse is the finale. Here we find a more literal listing of the various day-to-day sensations and activities that compose a human life: what we see, feel, buy, say, the people we meet, etc. Then there's a mention about "all that is now," (the eternal present), followed by "all that is gone," and "all that's to come," which illustrates the passage of time in the relative world. Next we hear that, "everything under the Sun is in tune." To me, this is a statement about there being no problems — nature is actually in a state of harmony. Then...the clincher: "but the Sun is eclipsed by the Moon." It is of course our humanness, which in its unconsciousness gets caught by the various trappings that the album outlines, obscuring the radiance of the Sun. Finally, what sounds like an old man tells us that, "there is no dark side of the Moon really, matter of fact, it's all dark." The Moon is not a luminary. The curriculum of our human condition is about awakening from the dark—we can only *borrow* the light of our source energy. The album ends with the same beating pulse we heard at the beginning, inviting us to continue pondering the human condition.

Moon

The theme of awakening has been a part of several recent movies. The big-budget *Avatar*, *Inception*, and *The Adjustment Bureau* were widely viewed. However, a lesser known film called *Moon* is the focus here. (Spoiler alert: You may want to rent it before reading this!)

With incredible synchronistic precision, this movie portrays the essence of the Moon and the process of awakening from it. The main character Sam is doing a temporary solo stint working for a company (which we later learn is indifferent to the vulnerabilities and humanness of its employees in order to maximize profit). Sam works on the actual Moon, mining its resources for human usage. Similarly, we are each alone in our ego dream learning to use our physicality to ideally contribute to the world. Sam works at the "Sarang" base, which means "love" in Korean. From a base of love, we are able to attend to our spiritual work. Sam began his stint on the Moon while his wife was pregnant (Moon), and he anticipates being able to someday have a connection with his child. Sam's last name is "Bell," and bells often alert us to being in the present or to wake up. At the start of the movie, Sam is wearing a t-shirt which reads, "Wake me up when it's quitting time."

Sam's only companion is GERTY, an artificially intelligent assistant. On a screen GERTY flashes a smiley face when there is positive news or a frown when there is something challenging. Sam too draws smiley faces and tends to give himself pep talks to assure himself that he's ok. The music from Sam's alarm clock that wakes him in a morning scene blares, "I am the one and only." This is suggestive of the aloneness of his situation, but also that the nature of reality is Oneness.

Sam eventually finds out that he is not alone. Due to some developments unknown to him, GERTY is instructed to keep Sam contained in the base. Sam arranges a way to break out of the base (Saturn), and realizes a whole new reality to his situation (Uranus). Sam learns that he is one of many clones (of the original Sam Bell) who are programmed to work at the lunar base. At first, he is understandably disturbed and full of disbelief but eventually learns to accept the realities of his situation. In one interaction with another clone he yells, "Wake up!" We, too, are awakening from the stories we have of ourselves, coming to realize that we're actually interacting with ourselves *through* others. Upon discovering that the company he's working for has intentionally blocked communications to Earth and is thereby imprisoning Sam on the Moon, he vomits. Here is a literal portrayal of purging or releasing the false self that holds on to misguided egoic assumptions.

Clones believe that after three years of service they will be able to get into a "hibernation pod" and return to Earth. It turns out that the pod is actually an incinerator. The film here mirrors how our expectations of ongoing existence are futile — we end up being burned up (fire) and returning to Spirit.

As clones only live for three years, part of Sam's process, now that he knows what's going on, is about managing his own

303

undoing. His body is deteriorating— the separate self is literally decomposing. Plot developments bring the possibility of leaving the Moon. Though it would be Sam's right to go, he allows another clone to take a trip. Sam shows compassion for this clone as he *recognizes himself* in him. They share a touching scene of mutual identification. Though the movie is bleak, there is redemption. Sam dies at peace with himself and in acceptance of reality...with a smile on his face.

Invoking the Energy Body

At an experiential level we engage with solar energy just by being alive. When we empty the proverbial cup of self, we may intentionally enhance our connection with the Sun's sustaining energy. Part of this process involves getting the machinations of the separate self out of the way. It turns out that this is not so much a matter of will, but rather an allowance to rest in our inherent nature. We can be aware of the separate self but refrain from attaching to it. Mindfulness practice is helpful in gaining perspective on how the separate self operates.

We can notice how our sensations, emotions, and thoughts all just do what they do. They all arise within awareness and presence, which we can connect with consciously and learn to identify as. Whereas some people think that all meditation involves many years of practice and great discipline, there are forms which are very simple. The key for this basic mindfulness approach is to increasingly become aware of the life energy that supports us.

With the knowledge that we're enveloped within a magnificently intelligent universe, we can be open to whatever might pour into our consciousness. As we become increasingly attuned to our surroundings, we open the door for inspiration and connection. We strengthen our relationship with the universe and our "wattage" can increase.

We can also intentionally enhance our connection with the solar life force. Shamanic astrologer Benjamin Bernstein has developed several invocations designed to connect with the energy body. As Benjamin sees it, we may consciously invoke the light (or energy) body for our "highest need." There is respect and gratitude for Spirit for creating the connection. Benjamin suggests that these invocations are best to be spoken aloud while the mind just focuses on the breath. This practice may help to release egoic control, which allows us to connect with what is beyond. The more we are connected with our heartfelt sincerity in doing this process, the more we strengthen our connection with Spirit. Below are some invocations to try:

"Spirit, please grant me, the maximum awareness, of my light body, that serves my highest need, right now, thank you."

"Spirit, please expand my light body, to the hugest size, that serves my highest need, right now, thank you."

"Spirit, please make me one, with my higher self, to the greatest extent, that serves my highest need, right now, thank you."

"Spirit, please integrate, my light body, and my physical body, to the greatest extent, that serves my highest need, right now, thank you."

"Spirit, please place my primary consciousness, in my light body, to the greatest extent, that serves my highest need, right now, and throughout this incarnation, thank you."

"Spirit, please grant me, full physical coordination, as I drive this physical body around, to the greatest extent, that serves my highest need, right now, and throughout this incarnation, thank you."

Glossary

Awareness: An all-enveloping field, which is the context that holds all the content of the manifest world, including every aspect of our experience.

Charged: The elemental energy that aligns with the right brain, primarily involves various degrees of quality.

Consciousness: The result of the mixture of awareness with the unconscious of the separate self.

Dreambody: The connection between soul and body, (Sun and Moon), which bridges the transpersonal with the relative.

Duality: Oneness as it appears in multiple forms in the relative, manifest world.

Ego: The apparent separate self that is pre-occupied with its survival and personal preferences. It correlates to the astrological Moon.

Ego dream: The experience of being caught in relative reality, unaware that the external world is a projection of the psyche. What most people simply call "my life."

Egoic takeover: The individual claiming ownership of transpersonal phenomena for personal reasons.

Enlightenment: The abiding state of complete awakening into Spirit.

Evolution: A process of incremental growth towards a more advanced stage of being. Human evolution includes healing as well as growth.

Evolutionary Astrology: A branch of astrology that asserts reincarnation and the growth of the soul as the overarching human story.

Integration: The result of having processed necessary lessons sufficiently such that noticeable and consistent changes occur in perceptions, belief, and behavior.

Karma: The law of cause and effect; the natural consequences of our actions; the collection of prior behavioral tendencies that will eventually need to be addressed and integrated.

Left brain: The left hemisphere of the brain, which pertains to content, order, rationality, precision, reason, logic, temporal distinctions.

Liberation: The evolutionary channel from the physical and personal to the nonphysical and transpersonal in the sequence of earth, water, air, fire. This channel involves the evolution of consciousness in the direction of spiritual awakening.

Manifestation: The evolutionary channel that moves in the reverse direction from the liberation channel. It's most dramatic event occurs when a soul incarnates into an individual human.

Neutral: The elemental energy that aligns with the left brain, involving various degrees of quantity but not quality.

Nondual: The foundational level of reality. The Oneness that exists outside of time and space and yet also gives rise to both of them.

Patriarchal Value System: The dominant paradigm on the planet for the last several millennia. Found in many facets of culture and society across the globe, this value system is based on aggression, accumulation of material resources, traditional values, and obedience to authority.

Personal story: The narrative each of us carries about our separate self. It is usually rife with interpretations and preferences which derive from the ego.

Presence: The capacity for focusing consciousness on whatever is unfolding in the moment.

Progressive evolution: The development of consciousness through elemental levels in the process of spiritual growth.

Relative reality: The common, everyday world filled with separation, value judgments, and egoic attachments.

Right brain: The right hemisphere of the brain, which relates to process, creativity, intuition, emotion, inspiration.

Samsara: The cycle of birth, death, and rebirth.

Shadow: Any part of ourself that we'd prefer not to see and that we typically repress, deny, and project onto others.

Soul: A part of Spirit which separates to fulfill evolutionary work.

Soul cage: Staying limited in separation consciousness and orbiting around ego. The inability to move beyond creates confinement in the relative realm.

Spirit: One of many words used to describe the all-encompassing context of Existence. Other names include God, Goddess, Allah, the Creator, Brahman, the Tao, Oneness, or the Absolute.

Spiritual awakening: The experience of loosening the identification with ego and connecting with *and identifying as* the broader field of awareness. Also referred to as "awakening."

Spiritual giveback: The reverse of the egoic takeover. The individual releases the claim of the transpersonal back to Spirit.

Transpersonal: Pertaining to phenomena beyond the personal, including soul and Spirit.

Unconscious: The deep well of accumulated experiences absorbed by the separate self.

Vise grip: A metaphor for the appropriate contraction of evolutionary possibilities in order to create an operable society. For evolution to proceed, we must judiciously move the vise grip down the evolutionary line by releasing our attachment to our past ways.

Wholeness: The state of accepting and connecting with all of who we are, not just what meets ego preferences.

Bibliography & Further Reading

Adyashanti. *The End of Your World*. Sounds True. Boulder, CO. 2008.

-----. *True Meditation*. Sounds True. Boulder, CO. 2006.

Alli, Antero. *Astrologik: The Oracular Art of Astrology*. Vertical Pool. Berkeley, CA. 1990.

Arroyo, Stephen. *Astrology Karma & Transformation*, 2nd Edition. CRCS Publications. Sebastopol, CA. 1992.

-----. *Astrology, Psychology and the Four Elements*. CRCS Publications. Sebastopol, CA. 1975.

Bogart, Gregory. *Astrology and Spiritual Awakening*. Dawn Mountain Press. Berkeley, CA. 1994.

Diaz, Armand. *Integral Astrology: Understanding the Ancient Discipline in the Contemporary World*. Integral Transformation, LLC. New York, NY. 2012.

Fernandez, Maurice. *Astrology and the Evolution of Consciousness: Volume 1*. Evolutionary Astrology, Inc. Land O' Lakes, FL. 2009.

Forrest, Steven. *Yesterday's Sky*. Seven Paws Press. Borrego Springs, CA, 2008.

-----. *The Book of Pluto*. ACS Publications. San Diego, CA. 1994.

Foundation for Inner Peace. *A Course in Miracles*. Mill Valley, CA. 1976.

George, Demetra. *Asteroid Goddesses*. ACS Publications. San Diego, CA. 1986.

Godman, David, ed. *Be As You Are: The Teachings of Sri Ramana Maharshi*. Penguin. 1992.

Grasse, Ray. *The Waking Dream*. Quest Books. Wheaton, IL. 1996

Green, Jeffrey Wolf. *Pluto: The Evolutionary Journey of the Soul, Volume 1*. Llewellyn Publications. St. Paul, MN. 1985.

Greene, Liz. *Relating*. Weiser. York Beach, ME. 1977

Greene, Liz & Howard Sasportas. *The Luminaries*. Weiser. York Beach, ME. 1992.

Guttman, Arielle. *Venus Star Rising*. Sophia Venus Productions. Santa Fe, NM. 2010.

Hand, Robert. *Horoscope Symbols*. Schiffer Publishing. Atglen, PA. 1981.

Huxley, Aldous. *The Perennial Philosophy*. Harper & Row. New York, NY. 1945.

Katie, Byron. *A Thousand Names for Joy*. Harmony Books. New York, NY. 2007.

-----. *Loving What Is*. Harmony Books. New York, NY. 2002.

Katz, Jerry. *One, Essential Writings on Nonduality*. Sentient Publications. Boulder, CO. 2007.

Le Grice, Keiron. *The Archetypal Cosmos*. Floris Books. Great Britain. 2010.

Levine, Rick. *Quantum Astrology*. Levine & Associates. Redmond, WA. 1994.

Marks, Tracey. *The Astrology of Self-Discovery*. CRCS Publications. Sebastopol, CA. 1985.

McDermott, Robert, ed. *The Essential Aurobindo: Writings of Sri Aurobindo*, 2nd Edition. Lindisfarne Books. Great Barrington, MA. 2001.

McKenna, Jed. *Spiritual Enlightenment: The Damnedst Thing*. Wisefool Press. Fairfield, IA. 2002.

Merriman, Ray. *Evolutionary Astrology: The Journey of the Soul Through States of Consciousness*. Seek-It Publications. W. Bloomfield, MI. 1991.

Meyers, Eric. *Elements & Evolution: The Spiritual Landscape of Astrology*. Astrology Sight. Asheville, NC. 2010.

-----. *Uranus: The Constant of Change*. Astrology Sight. Longmont, CO. 2008.

-----. *Between Past & Presence: A Spiritual View of the Moon & Sun*. Astrology Sight. Longmont, CO. 2006.

Mindell, Arnold. *Quantum Mind*. Lao Tse Press. Portland, OR. 2000.

Rudhyar, Dane. *The Astrology of Personality*. Aurora Press. Santa Fe, NM. 1991.

-----. *The Planetary and Lunar Nodes*. CSA Press. Lakemont, GA. 1971.

Sedgwick, Philip. *The Sun at the Center*. Llewellyn Publications. St. Paul, MN. 1990.

Tarnas, Richard. *Cosmos & Psyche*. Penguin. New York, NY. 2006.

Tolle, Eckhart. *The Power of Now*. New World Library. Lovato, CA. 1999.

Wilber, Ken. *Integral Psychology*. Shambhala. Boston, MA. 2000

-----. *The Marriage of Sense and Soul*. Random House. New York, NY. 1998.

-----. *A Brief History of Everything*. Shambhala. Boston, MA. 1996.

Zukav, Gary. *The Seat of the Soul*. Simon and Schuster. New York, NY. 1989.

-----. *The Dancing Wu Li Masters*. Morrow Quill. New York, NY. 1979.

End Notes

[i] Eckhart Tolle, *The Power of Now*, p.29

[ii] From *Zeitgeist: Moving Forward* (2011) by Peter Joseph

[iii] Dr. Gabor Mate quote from *Zeitgeist: Moving Forward*

[iv] *A Course in Miracles*, p.338

[v] Don Jose Ruiz from www.healyourlife.com

[vi] Rainer Maria Rilke from a written letter called *The Dragon Princess*

[vii] Eckhart Tolle, *The Power of Now*, p.189

[viii] From Deepak Chopra's Earth Day message in 2009

[ix] Ramana Maharshi, *Be As You Are*, p.189

[x] Eckhart Tolle, *The Power of Now*, p.12

[xi] Philip Sedgwick, *The Sun at the Center*, p.47

[xii] Eckhart Tolle, *The Power of Now*, p.29

[xiii] Ibid., p.38

[xiv] Ramana Maharshi, *Be As You Are*, p.14

[xv] Dane Rudhyar, *The Planetary and Lunar Nodes*, p.45

[xvi] Eckhart Tolle, The Power of Now, p.72

[xvii] Ibid., p. 101

[xviii] Jed McKenna, *Spiritual Enlightenment: The Damnedst Thing*, p.115

[xix] Eckhart Tolle, *The Power of Now*, p.50

[xx] Maharshi, *Be As You Are*, p.131

[xxi] Byron Katie, *A Thousand Names for Joy*, p.230

[xxii] Ken Wilber, *A Brief History of Everything*, p.191

[xxiii] Eckhart Tolle, *The Power of Now*, p.72

[xxiv] Wilber, *A Brief History of Everything*, p.14

[xxv] Ibid.,p.211

[xxvi] Ibid.,p.199

[xxvii] Ibid.,p.217

[xxviii] Ibid.,p.232

[xxix] Ibid.,p.235

[xxx] Holotropic Breathwork is a technique developed by Dr. Stan Grof designed to access transpersonal consciousness through group process, intensified breathing , evocative music and expressive drawing.

[xxxi] Wilber, *A Brief History of Everything*, p.13

[xxxii] Neil Young from "Cortez the Killer" on *Zuma*, 1975

Acknowledgments

Deep appreciation to Josh Levin for being an excellent editor and friend. Your wisdom and ability improved this book enormously. Thanks for helping me become a better writer and also a more conscious person. Sajit Greene has been my partner in love, work, and awakening—so much gratitude to you, my companion in realizing our soul vision. Bill Streett's impeccable artistic precision flows through the graphic design and figures—thanks so much for your enduring support and friendship. Appreciation to my son Drew for taking the back cover picture (and for being so wonderful), and to Dana Schneider for support with the title (you're an amazing ally)! Thanks to my clients, students, and readers—you bring joy and meaning to my life.

Much gratitude also goes to Andrew Smith and Kate Sholly who provided helpful input on the content and such generous endorsements for the cover. Armand Diaz and Steven Forrest—thank you so much for your gracious words too. To all astrology friends, allies, and colleagues, thank you for sharing the journey. It's an honor to be a part of the tribe!

I cannot overstate the importance of all the teachers and authors who have taught and influenced me—many of whom are quoted in these pages. The wisdom from the awakened minds, the brilliance from the innovators, the perspectives from the philosophers, and the tools of the trade from the astrologers—it has been an incredible joy to endeavor to synthesize your work and articulate it in this way.

What interesting times these are! I send out a heartfelt appreciation to anyone involved in the work and play of supporting greater awakening on this precious planet. May we truly learn to put the sword down and pick each other up. Finally, I have utmost gratitude for our miraculously intelligent and loving universe.

CPSIA information can be obtained at www.ICGtesting.com
Printed in the USA
LVOW070538171012

303188LV00001B/3/P